Modern Power and
Free Speech

Modern Power and Free Speech

Contemporary Culture and Issues of Equality

Chris Demaske

LEXINGTON BOOKS

A division of
ROWMAN & LITTLEFIELD PUBLISHERS, INC.
Lanham • Boulder • New York • Toronto • Plymouth, UK

LEXINGTON BOOKS

A division of Rowman & Littlefield Publishers, Inc.
A wholly owned subsidiary of The Rowman & Littlefield Publishing Group, Inc.
4501 Forbes Boulevard, Suite 200
Lanham, MD 20706

Estover Road
Plymouth PL6 7PY
United Kingdom

British Library Cataloguing in Publication Information Available

Library of Congress Cataloging-in-Publication Data

The hardback edition of this book was previously cataloged by the Library of Congress
as follows:

Demaske, Chris, 1969–
  Modern power and free speech : contemporary culture and issues of equality /
Chris Demaske.
      p. cm.
  Includes bibliographical references and index.
  1. Freedom of expression—United States. I. Title.
  KF4770.D48 2009
  342.7308'53—dc22   2008029285

ISBN: 978-0-7391-2783-4 (cloth : alk. paper)
ISBN: 978-0-7391-2784-1 (pbk. : alk. paper)
ISBN: 978-0-7391-3160-2 (electronic)

Printed in the United States of America

♾™ The paper used in this publication meets the minimum requirements of American
National Standard for Information Sciences—Permanence of Paper for Printed Library
Materials, ANSI/NISO Z39.48–1992.

Contents

Acknowledgments

This book has been made possible through the support of an eclectic array of institutions and individuals. I will begin with institutional support and then move onto the individuals. For the initial intellectual development of this work, I'd like to thank the University of Oregon for awarding me a doctoral fellowship. That financial assistance offered me the opportunity to focus an entire year on what became the foundation for this book. I also would like to thank the University of Washington, Tacoma, for the quarter release that allowed the time for me to complete the book proposal. Some versions of the text have previously appeared in *Communication Law & Policy*, 9:3 (2004) and *Democratic Communiqué*, 22:1 (2008) and in papers presented at the International Communication Association annual conference, the National Communication Association annual conference, and the Union for Democratic Communication conference. The feedback I received from colleagues through those activities was of utmost value when working through ideas. Much appreciation to the editors at Lexington Books for assisting with the final stages of revising and production that led to the book you now hold in your hands.

The individuals, both professional and personal, who have assisted in the completion of this book, are numerous, and, at the risk of inadvertently failing to mention someone important, I would like to thank some of them. My overall appreciation to the faculty, staff, and students at the University of Washington, Tacoma, who assisted me in a myriad of ways. Special thanks to Michael Forman and Bill Kunz for the boundless professional and emotional support they offered that enabled me to take the book manuscript to the next level. At the University of Oregon, several colleagues assisted in the early development stages, including Leslie Steeves, Janet Wasko, and Caroline

Forell. Most notably, I'd like to thank Tim Gleason, dean of the University of Oregon School of Journalism and Communication, and Julie Novkov at the University of Albany, SUNY, for suffering through endless early drafts, and Randy Nichols at Niagara University for tolerating many late night conversations about every tedious step of my thought process.

Many others have played an important role in the completion of this book, not as directly, but just as significantly. I owe my initial curiosity in the area of First Amendment law to Bill Bennett at California University of Pennsylvania, who sparked my interest in the news media, and to Jeanni Atkins at the University of Mississippi, who introduced me to the intricacies of free speech and free press. Without the long-term support of a few instrumental people, I may never have pursued my doctoral degree. So, thank you to Brenda Fetsko, one of my oldest and dearest friends, who throughout the decades has continued to encourage me to follow my dreams no matter how unlikely they seemed at the time; to Toni L'hommedieu, who has impacted my life in so many positive ways I can't even begin to list them here; and to my grandparents John and Mary Hutzel, who always accepted me for exactly who I am.

The bulk of the writing of this book took place during my years in Tacoma, Washington, and many, many, many people in the community helped me maintain my sanity and sense of humor throughout this process. While I cannot thank everyone who played a role in this, I would like to offer special thanks to Susan Dyer, Lisa Dupuy, Glenn Leonard, and Sally Stewart. In particular, I am indebted to my best friend Jerry Crow, who has always made himself available to listen, to support, and, most importantly, to make sure that I remember not to take life so seriously.

Finally, I owe the highest gratitude to Hannah Arnoske and Adrienne Ione. Hannah, your companionship and unconditional love throughout the writing of this book were immeasurable. Adrienne, the intensity of your love, encouragement, and patience are more than I ever expected—you are awesome.

Introduction

A Critical Approach to Free Speech

No one can doubt that we are at a critical juncture in U.S. history in terms of individual civil rights. From the unprecedented invasion of privacy of American citizens to the ever-tightening restrictions on access to government information to the accusations of abuse of terror suspects, there is now growing concern that we are trading our concrete, well-established freedoms for an illusive, unsupported sense of safety. The Bush administration has, in short, far exceeded any other historical period in the United States in infringing on constitutional rights.

Scholars, as well as political and social commentators, are now focusing on the role of the Bush administration in its overt attempts to restrict constitutional rights in the name of the "war on terrorism." But these overt attempts are not the only consequences. One of the major side effects of this focus on terrorism is the creation of a climate of fear in which those who are different from the majority are targeted, hunted, and punished. Since September 11, 2001, hate crimes against Muslims and those who appear to be Muslim have increased greatly. Hate crimes against historically disempowered groups in the United States—African Americans, women, and gays and lesbians—have continued in large numbers across all sections of the country. These crimes, which other legal scholars have argued, in essence, silence the voices of members of the targeted groups, are even more likely to silence the victims in today's culture of fear.

The stakes also are higher right now. If we are indeed at a critical junction in U.S. history in terms of civil rights and liberties, then we need, now more than ever, to hear the voices of those who are most likely to be adversely affected by the current changes in our democratic political system. This book, *Modern Power and Free Speech: Contemporary Culture and Issues of Equality*, argues that the First Amendment should function as a safeguard of our other civil liberties. Currently, the First Amendment operates almost exclusively as a negative liberty. This approach, however, does not take into account the ways in which power operates in contemporary culture and, as a result, hinders the First Amendment from functioning at its fullest capacity.

APPROACHING THE PROBLEM

Civil rights and liberties—the struggle to obtain and maintain them—is always an important area of study in the United States. Today, however, research into these areas is even more timely and significant. Many of our civil liberties are being eroded in the name of national security, further illustrating the problem with only relying on them as negative liberties. This book focuses on one particular right—freedom of speech—and does so in a way that allows for the study of more recent developments, such as the propagation of Internet pornography and the persecution of political dissidents, while also reminding readers of the continuing disparate situations of several minority groups. This book includes historical explanations of First Amendment doctrine, a review of various theoretical and philosophical thoughts on freedom of speech, and the development of a new theoretical conception of how the First Amendment can best facilitate free speech in contemporary U.S. society. In addition, this book adds to the existing substantial body of feminist legal scholarship by moving the debate into the free speech realm.

In this book, I use case analysis to support the position that the liberal paradigm in general, and the U.S. courts more specifically, have failed to adequately protect the speech of disempowered groups. I argue that this failure has led to a system of free speech law in which groups that already have been disempowered or marginalized continue to find themselves with less *freedom* of speech because they lack *equality* in a larger social context. Starting with the premise that social equality is a predeterminate for free speech, I argue that we need a new interpretation of the First Amendment, a reformulation that will begin by problematizing the autonomous agent in liberal theory.

What is being proposed in *Modern Power and Free Speech* is at once both simple and radical. It is simple in that it builds on already-existing critical legal theory. Instead of creating an entirely new area of theoretical inquiry, this book uses proven approaches, modifying them to the particularly thorny issue of freedom of speech. It is this modification to First Amendment law that is new and radical because it pushes the boundaries of heavily entrenched assumptions of the way in which freedom of speech operates and how the First

Amendment application must change in accordance with that operation. While critical legal approaches in general, such as feminist legal studies and critical race theory, have made significant inroads in other areas of constitutional law, First Amendment theory and application have remained stubbornly resistant, relying on empty platitudes about the importance of free speech to support a rigid adherence to traditional First Amendment principles. For example, critical theory has already offered critiques of the conception of neutrality and the construction of the autonomous, rational individual in legal doctrine, and as a result effected change in substantive areas such as equality in hiring and the treatment of sexual harassment. However, unlike unfair hiring practices or sexual harassment, the First Amendment has offered some level of benefit to members of disempowered groups. As a result, pinpointing the inequality in application requires a much more narrowly focused critique of the underlying principles supporting inequality in levels of freedom of speech.

In terms of First Amendment application, critical scholars have attempted at various times to question the protection of hate speech or pornography, but to date to no avail. Those scholars have attempted to develop constitutionally sound frameworks to remedy speech inequities in specified areas. For example, critical races theorists Richard Delgado and Mari Matsuda both attempted to fashion arguments for the restriction of hate speech. Catharine MacKinnon, most associated with dominance feminism, and Andrea Dworkin drafted an ordinance aimed at offering redress for victims of pornography. However, both attempts to restrict hate speech and pornography failed under First Amendment scrutiny.[1] My attempt here is not to suggest a remedy for merely one problematic area of speech. Instead, I have created a formula applicable in free speech cases dealing with any member of a disempowered group, hopefully circumventing the counterarguments supplied by the Court when only attempting to distinguish one disempowered group.

This book then offers a much-needed, long overdue approach to analyzing tough speech cases and facilitates a radical shift in the fundamental assumptions of free speech case analysis. It accomplishes both of these goals while offering a concrete, constitutionally workable test for case analysis. Specifically, I use current feminist and poststructuralist theories of societal power and individual agency to create a new conception of freedom of speech and a formula the courts could apply when analyzing speech cases involving disempowered groups. Framing my study in this light allows me to formulate and apply an approach to free speech analysis that will be both theoretically sound and applicable by the courts as well. This framework both deconstructs liberal conceptions of autonomy in case law and dispels the discourse in those free speech areas that sidestep or ignore issues of power and agency.

LEGAL THEORY AND THE FIRST AMENDMENT

Both First Amendment doctrine and traditional First Amendment theory are grounded in the same fundamental philosophical ideas of liberal democracy and its relationship to free speech. Traditional theoretical approaches to the First Amendment have their basis in the liberal paradigm, which is heavily influenced by Enlightenment thinking. When considered in direct relationship to the First Amendment, this reliance on Enlightenment philosophy translates into certain First Amendment values, most notably the need to protect almost all speech to ensure that the search for truth, self-fulfillment, and self-government can occur.[2]

In the traditional liberal conception of free speech, the individual is both autonomous and sovereign, and the protection of speech is viewed with an assumption of intrinsic societal value that leaves little or no room for discussions of possible harm. I argue, however, that the legal system's current conceptualization of free speech is inadequate to deal with many of today's important speech issues. In effect, I question the very foundation of liberalism that drives First Amendment application and call for a shift in the way that the courts view the relationship between freedom of speech and other issues such as liberty, equality, and the individual's role in U.S. society. I study the First Amendment not as a self-contained, isolated unit, but as a part of a larger constitutional debate about the most effective way to ensure civil rights and liberties. By placing my analysis inside of this larger debate, I avoid favoring the liberty of free speech at the expense of other liberties, thus emphasizing equality. In addition to reviewing First Amendment and constitutional theoretical inadequacies, I also problematize the way in which First Amendment doctrine focuses on objectivity and neutrality. In constitutional law, both the theory and the method are driven by the outdated concepts of liberty discussed earlier. It is not that traditional liberal philosophy leaves no room for discussions of equality. Rather, the construction of the autonomous individual has not allowed for a complex discussion of power and thus of speech and its relation to equality.

Critiques of the legal system's handling of speech issues are not new. For the past twenty years, other critical scholars—such as critical race theorists, feminist legal scholars, and critical legal scholars—have made similar critiques of the First Amendment's ability to protect the speech of disempowered groups.[3] For example, critical race theorists such as Richard Delgado and Mari Matsuda have argued that the First Amendment perpetuates racial inequality through its protection of hate speech.[4] Of particular interest to this study are those feminist legal scholars who have begun to theorize social construction, agency, and the public/private divide in power in terms of constitutional law. Critical feminist scholars are trying to find a way to combine this earlier work on equality and dominance with new perspectives on "difference, particularly, context and identity."[5] During the past two decades, feminists, primarily located in the postmodern and poststructural arenas, have been searching for a way to move feminist legal scholarship away from the essentialism of the sameness/difference debate and the limitations of dominance analysis into a more complex discussion of the way in which power operates in society.

WHY FEMINIST LEGAL THEORY?

Doing any substantial critique of the First Amendment requires a strong weapon—the legacy of our free speech doctrine is steeped in deep-rooted inequities and protected by two hundred years of liberal discourse concerning the First Amendment's role as protector of everyone's individual rights. In other words, one cannot merely address the issue of poorly ruled cases or misinterpreted doctrine and expect to reach a more equitable free speech system. In order to facilitate the changes in First Amendment discourse and doctrine that I am suggesting here, the entire underlying liberal legal system must be both investigated and reimagined. Feminist legal theory is distinctive in its ability to frame a project as monumental as the deconstruction of the sacred First Amendment. As legal scholar Martha Chamallas notes, feminist legal theory allows a more complex analysis of the law because it "goes beyond rules and procedures to explore the deeper structures of law."[6] In other words, it allows for an interrogation of underlying legal principals—in my case, those of objectivity, neutrality, and autonomy. In addition, feminist legal theory is both self-reflexive and solution-motivated, meaning that it constantly reassesses theoretical strategies available and then constructs viable legal solutions based on the application of that theory.

Of the various feminist legal theories available, this study relies on the works of those scholars who question both the development of the individual self and the role of the state and other institutional power on that development. Specifically, much of the theoretical framework developed in chapter 3 is influenced by postmodern and poststructural theory. Feminist scholar Deborah Rhode explains that both postmodernism and poststructuralism in general rely on the premise of knowledge being socially constructed. As a result, feminists operating within those frameworks face the challenge of "maintaining that gender oppression exists while challenging our capacity to document it."[7] Postmodern and poststructural feminists rely on discourse analysis to study the interpretation of reality rather than on preconceived universals. This

shift in focus replaces "the binary pairs of modern theories" with "an interpretation grounded in partiality and perspectivity."[8]

Of the various feminist approaches available, those emphasizing social
construction, agency, and diversity are the most promising ways to begin an
examination of First Amendment issues from a feminist standpoint. The social constructivist approach allows us to move past the assumptions about autonomy and neutrality, acknowledging instead that the legal system is riddled
with value-based decisions that have developed inside a patriarchal ideology
that does not permit all people to operate autonomously. Theorizing power in
this socially constructed universe as being diffuse and diverse will allow the
richness needed to deal with the complexity of a new First Amendment critique. In other words, when dealing with constitutional analysis, particularly
of an amendment like the First Amendment that seems only to serve for the
betterment of diverse communities and ideas, the movement away from the
modern binary system of analysis can problematize seemingly positive characteristics of the law. Moving, for example, past the content-neutral versus
content-based distinction in free speech analysis allows a consideration of
other elements such as historical context and individual agency. Combining
this critique of First Amendment doctrine with a theory of incomplete agency
takes us a step further, allowing us to argue that while the system is constructed to eliminate women's agency, it actually only has the power to reduce
that agency, thereby still leaving women with some agency.

Feminist legal theorists from various camps have made great legal strides
for women and other disempowered groups throughout the past century.
However, contemporary feminist scholars have dealt primarily with the legal
questions involving the female body, such as sexual harassment, abortion, or
domestic abuse, leaving areas such as the First Amendment speech clause relatively untouched. These theorists are trying to find the most accurate balance
between difference and equality. In doing so, feminists from varying backgrounds, including liberal, dominance, poststructural, and postmodern feminists, have grappled with various constitutional issues but have focused little
on First Amendment application as an area needing improvement (with the
exception of certain theorists' attempts to restrict pornography).[9]

To meet this end, I build on and expand feminist discussions of agency in
general and then more specifically apply this refined theory to First Amendment legal issues, resulting in contributions to both areas of study. Relying
primarily on critical feminist scholarship, but also incorporating critical race
theory and critical legal studies, I argue that the Court's current conceptualization of liberty is inadequate to deal with many of today's speech issues and
that redefining liberty will lead to a new framework for analyzing free speech
cases.[10]

POWER AND AGENCY

I also focus on power and agency in order to critique the Court's application of freedom as merely a negative liberty in regard to speech and expression. For example, using a feminist critique of freedom as a negative liberty, I interrogate other societal power structures ignored in that definition of freedom. Under liberal interpretations of constitutional law, it is only the government whose power we must fear—constitutionally, there are no safeguards against private institutional power. The First Amendment can neither stop censorship of speech by private institutions, nor can it promote speech based on group identity. As a result, the U.S. Supreme Court has repeatedly contended that it is not the government's role to ensure and/or enforce equality in speech under the First Amendment. The traditional argument is that the First Amendment only deals with restricting the government from suppressing speech, not with the possibility of the government acting as a promoter of speech. In this system, members of society are protected from governmental restrictions on their right to speak. However, what cannot be considered in those traditional arguments is how nongovernmental agencies also have the power to restrict speech. If the bottom line of free speech protection is to foster a more democratic society, then social or economic institutions should be considered just as suspect as the government in abridging speech rights.

Focusing on the relational nature of modern power complicates—and ultimately invalidates—traditional notions of the First Amendment, particularly traditional liberal notions of autonomy. Departing from the traditional liberal notion of the autonomous individual, the contemporary feminist conception of partial agency seeks to balance women's subordinate position in society with their ability to facilitate some change.[11] There is no absolute autonomy, only varying levels of agency. Therefore, by reconceptualizing agency as partial and group-based, I elaborate and restructure a framework for theorizing incomplete agency within constitutional law. By using the framework based on incomplete agency to focus on various problematic areas in First Amendment law, I deconstruct not only the liberal paradigm supporting the case law, but also the discourse in those free speech areas that sidestep or ignore issues of power and agency. This framework offers a much-needed approach to analyzing tough speech cases, such as those pertaining to hate speech and the Internet. This new framework facilitates a radical shift in the fundamental assumptions of free speech case analysis, while still offering a concrete legal test. For example, this new approach may facilitate a way in which the courts could allow for some restrictions on hate speech without infringing on First Amendment liberties. Recognizing the incomplete agency of individuals, this framework calls for a much more complex application of such First Amendment tests and principles as public forum doctrine and content neutrality. These concepts remain components in free speech analysis but are expanded to include historical context and individual power relationships.

In this book, I describe the historical development of First Amendment jurisprudence. I use a review of traditional interpretations to establish what I see as the major problems in First Amendment analysis. Then, focusing on three areas of free speech law—hate speech, Internet pornography, and political dissident speech—I elaborate on the ways in which those problems manifest themselves in actual case law development. For example, in reviewing hate speech cases, I critique the Court's reliance on content/viewpoint neutrality. I demonstrate that a framework grounded in a feminist conception of incomplete agency provides a better means of addressing this issue when applying First Amendment analysis.

BUILDING A NEW APPROACH

This book is organized into two parts. The first three chapters offer an introduction into First Amendment discourse and doctrine, summarize the major theoretical foundations of legal theory, and formulate a new approach to the analysis of First Amendment cases dealing with the speech rights of members of socially, economically, and/or politically disempowered groups. The second half, chapters 4–7, is application-based, applying the framework developed in the first three chapters to various contentious areas of case law.

Chapter 1, "Theories of the First Amendment," lays out the traditional perspectives on the meaning of the First Amendment, focusing specifically on the relationship between liberty and equality. This chapter examines various theoretical approaches to the U.S. Constitution in general and to the First Amendment specifically. While this chapter outlines various approaches (including traditional liberal theory, critical race theory, and critical legal studies), the main focus is on feminist theory. In addition to exploring the various debates/points of contention among the scholars from different theoretical approaches to the study and application of the First Amendment, this chapter outlines the approach developed and tested in this book.

In chapter 2, "Liberalism and the Legal History of Free Speech," I trace the historical development of the concept of the liberty of freedom of speech through First Amendment case law. While the ways in which we understand speech and its relationship to society have changed during the past one hundred years (particularly the past fifty years), those changes have been impeded by broader conceptions of liberal philosophy. These broader themes in liberalism, such as the existence of an autonomous individual and the construction of the government as the main adversary to freedom, only allowed for a certain amount of change in the development of freedom of speech in U.S. society. This chapter explores the problematic relationship between liberty and equality. In this chapter, I first discuss the philosophical political origins of liberalism. I then review liberalism and its construction of liberty in regard to the historical development of First Amendment case law.

Chapter 3, "Agency and the Evolution of First Amendment Analysis," argues that the current concept of liberty needs to change, but in order to do that we must first reconceptualize the individual in contemporary society. The role of the autonomous individual in free speech specifically, and constitutional law in general, fails to take into account the social nature of humans. We are socialized into this culture, not raised in a vacuum. As a result, individual autonomy is virtually impossible. Depending on one's socialization—economic class, gender, race, etc.—how much "autonomy" one has is questionable. In chapter 3, I argue that the focus needs to shift from autonomy to agency. This shift to agency allows us to explore configurations of partial or limited agency. I argue that partial agency needs to be reconstructed to specifically encompass power relationships in terms of the First Amendment's free speech clause. This reconfiguration of the individual and power leads to an alternative framework for case analysis.

In chapter 4, "Rethinking Hate Speech: *Skokie* and *R.A.V.*," I argue that the reasoning applied in *Village of Skokie v. the National Socialist Party of America* and *R.A.V. v. City of St. Paul, Minnesota*, failed to consider important contextual elements including historical evidence of long-term societal power imbalances and individual power relationships between the speaker and the spoken to. I conclude that both of those elements need to be considered when determining whether or not a particular type of hate speech should receive protection under the First Amendment.

In chapter 5, "*Virginia v. Black*: An Evolution in First Amendment Doctrine?" I review the 2002 Supreme Court ruling in which the Court found that a Virginia statute that restricted cross burnings was constitutional. My initial development of the alternative framework developed in this book focused on hate speech. At that time, the only Supreme Court ruling was *R.A.V. v. City of St. Paul, Minnesota*. I presented my initial research on that case at several communication conferences. The response from First Amendment traditionalists was always the same: the Court had already ruled on *R.A.V.* and conclusively decided that under First Amendment analysis, hate speech could not be restricted. A decade following the *R.A.V.* ruling, *Virginia v. Black* would offer the first opening to restrict hate speech and prove my contentious colleagues incorrect. Because of the seemingly incongruous nature of the *Black* ruling with previous hate speech cases, I address this case in its own chapter, analyzing the ruling using the framework developed in chapter 3. Through application of the framework, I illustrate that while the result was promising, the legal reasoning applied in *Black* is still problematic.

In chapter 6, "The Internet: (Re)Assessing the Pornography Question," I review several Supreme Court cases dealing with hate speech and pornography on the Internet. I focus specifically on the cases arising from the Communications Decency Act and conclude that (1) the Court needs to develop a coherent method of dealing with Internet speech cases, and (2) in many circumstances, the framework developed in this book would assist in Internet speech cases dealing with pornography and hate speech. In order to address the issue of Internet pornography, I examine previous theoretical and legal attempts to restrict pornography in general and conclude that a minor reworking of Catharine MacKinnon's anti-pornography ordinance combined with my framework can establish a constitutionally viable approach to restricting the most egregious forms of pornography.

Chapter 7, "Terrorism and the Culture of Fear," reviews current pertinent political and legal issues surrounding the war on terrorism and its effect on issues of free expression in the United States, which have abounded since September 11, 2001. This chapter will review those instances when the government has attempted to stifle political speech through the true threats doctrine. By applying the framework developed here to the incitement standard in *Brandenburg v. Ohio*, a more concrete standard can be developed to protect political speech while also considering the more complicated landscape of threatening speech when placed against a backdrop of perceived terrorism.

NOTES

1. For more thorough discussion of hate speech and pornography, *see* chapters 4 and 6.

2. For a more in-depth discussion of these First Amendment values, *see* chapter 2.

3. Research focusing on critical legal studies, critical race theory, and feminist legal theory will be expanded on in detail in chapters 1, 3, 4, and 6.

4. For example, *see* Richard Delgado, *Words that Wound: A Tort Action for Racial Insults, Epithets, and Name-Calling,* 17 HARV. CR-CL L. REV. 133 (1982) and Mari Matsuda, *Public Reponses to Racist Speech: Considering the Victim's Story*, 87 MICH. L. REV. 2320 (1989).

5. Nancy Hirschmann, *Difference as an Occasion for Rights: A Feminist Rethinking of Rights, Liberalism, and Difference*, in FEMINISM, IDENTITY AND DIFFERENCE 29 (Susan Heckman, 1999).

6. MARTHA CHAMALLAS, INTRODUCTION TO FEMINIST LEGAL THEORY xix (2003).

7. Deborah Rhode, *Feminist Critical Theories*, in FEMINIST LEGAL THEORY: READINGS IN LAW AND GENDER 333 (Katharine T. Bartlett and Rosanne Kennedy eds., 1991).

8. MARY JOE FRUG, POSTMODERN LEGAL FEMINISM xix (1992).

9. For a more in-depth discussion of these theoretical positions, *see* chapters 1 and 3.

10. The reconceptualization of liberty is developed in chapters 1, 2, and 3.

11. CHAMALLAS, *supra* note 6.

Chapter One

Theories of the First Amendment

The First Amendment was ratified in 1791 following months of discussion and rewriting by the Congressional Committee that had been organized to develop a Bill of Rights.[1] Despite the meetings held to construct the language of the First Amendment, there are relatively few records of what the founders exactly intended the First Amendment to mean. Many authorities agree that the First Amendment was intended to, in the least, protect Americans from prior restraint.[2] Specifically, the greatest concern was prior restraint of speech critical of the government—seditious libel.[3] Prior to the 1950s, free speech was defined almost exclusively in terms of prior restraint and seditious libel.[4] The era of the Warren Court ushered in a change in the way the courts thought about life, liberty, and property.[5] The Warren Court moved away from the focus of property ownership as the key to liberty toward a more civil-rights-based approach. The Warren Court opinions in First Amendment cases set the foundation for contemporary free speech doctrine.[6]

The Warren Court broadened the array of speech issues included under the First Amendment umbrella and developed an intricate balancing system that gave preference to speech over conflicting rights in almost all circumstances. In developing this area of case law, the Court built on traditional theories of freedom of speech and expression that heralded those freedoms as essential to the democratic process, the search for truth, and the individual's sense of fulfillment and self-realization.[7] All of these principles spring from and reinforce liberal democracy with its roots in Enlightenment philosophy and its emphasis on the autonomous individual.[8]

From the groundbreaking libel case *New York Times v. Sullivan*[9] to the issue of dissident speech in *Brandenburg v. Ohio*,[10] there is no doubt of the First Amendment's power and importance in our democratic society. There is no doubt about the significance of the contribution by the Warren Court and its legacy to current application in free speech law.[11] However, as I will illustrate later in this chapter, in recent years, many legal scholars have begun questioning both the traditional principles inherent in First Amendment doctrine in general and the contemporary Court's reliance on what arguably is an outdated idea of liberty. This chapter begins by explaining what I mean by liberty. As will become apparent, the term liberty is often used but seldom defined in any concrete manner and frequently contradictory. The approach to identifying liberty that I find most satisfying, both because it offers a more extensive historical explanation and because it is most significant to my concerns of equality in speech rights, is one expounded by historian Michael Kammen. Kammen suggests that liberty can best be defined in relation to other qualities and I concur, focusing specifically on the pairing of liberty and equality in relation to freedom of speech.

Once I have clarified the relationship between liberty, equality, and freedom of speech, I map out the various theoretical positions in constitutional law in general, in traditional First Amendment analysis, and in critical legal approaches. Because of the centrality of feminist legal theory to development of my analytical framework, I focus extensively on its progression throughout the past four decades, highlighting the ways in which feminist legal theory might be important to the study of the First Amendment.

LIBERTY, FREEDOM, AND EQUALITY

The concept of liberty is difficult to define in absolute terms.[12] As Abraham Lincoln said in 1864, "The world has never had a good definition of the word liberty. . . . We all declare for liberty; but in using the same word we do not mean the same thing."[13] In *On Liberty*, John Stuart Mill discussed liberty in terms of "limits to the power which the ruler should be suffered to exercise over the community."[14] In the book *Spheres of Liberty*, historian Michael Kammen developed in detail the relationship between the definition of liberty and the social, political, and historical context in which the term is used.[15] Kammen starts with the assumption that when it comes to certain terms such as liberty, "it is the justices who make the meaning."[16] He then analyzes court rulings in an historical framework to uncover what he sees as three separate but overlapping spheres of liberty in U.S. history—liberty and authority, liberty and property, and liberty and justice. These pairings, according to Kammen, are meant to show that liberty is consistently defined in relation to other qualities. He explains the historical development of these spheres as follows:

[D]uring the colonial period, liberty and authority—[were] followed yet over-lapped by liberty and property; throughout the nineteenth century, primarily lib-erty and order, although liberty and property was revived for a half a century (1884–1934) in the guise of "liberty of contract"; and finally, in the twentieth century, liberty and justice.[17]

Two elements from Kammen's study are most important: (1) he describes liberty as both fluid and historically determined; and (2) liberty is best de-fined in relation to other qualities. Defined as historically situated, the con-cept of liberty becomes less abstract. Conceptualizing the importance of lib-erty to the socio-political environment from an historical perspective allows it to be examined and defined in terms of a continuum that shifts and changes over time. Because liberty is historically defined, its definition can and will constantly evolve, allowing for new formations to alter or replace older ones. Kammen not only positions liberty in an historical context, but also further defines it through relational comparisons. He argues that liberty becomes de-fined, in part, by other qualities important during specific historical periods.[18] In order to comprehend liberty in contemporary First Amendment jurispru-dence, one must define it within the parameters of specific qualities of free-dom and equality.

Qualities of freedom become key in First Amendment analysis because so much of the discourse is concerned with freedom of speech and expression. Liberty in regard to the First Amendment cannot be examined without con-sidering freedom. With few exceptions, when dealing with First Amendment cases the U.S. Supreme Court has embraced what Isaiah Berlin calls the neg-ative conception of freedom. Berlin describes negative liberty in this way: "You lack political liberty or freedom only if you are prevented from attain-ing a goal by human beings. Mere incapacity to attain a goal is not lack of po-litical freedom."[19] This perspective of freedom leaves complex issues of non-governmental power out of the free-speech equation, allowing socially marginalized groups to be further silenced:

Freedom is lacking, and remains an empty promise, if the agent (or agents) in question lacks powers of self-determination. It is misleading to say that some-one is *free* to do something when she lacks effective power to do it, even if she has legal rights or liberties that permit her (or leave her "at liberty") to do it.[20]

Seen in this way, the liberal conception of negative freedom found in First Amendment discourse and doctrine does not, in and of itself, guarantee lib-erty for all. In actuality, it may reinforce the loss of liberty for some in favor of extending liberty for others.

Examples of this loss of liberty are seen in the federal courts' repeated protection of hate speech (see cases such as *Village of Skokie v. the National Socialist Party of America*, *Doe v. University of Michigan*, *R.A.V. v. City of St. Paul, Minnesota*).[21] The traditional liberal perspective argues that speech should be *valued* as a major element in the functioning of a democratic society. Thus, the remedy for troublesome speech—such as hate speech—is more speech, not more government regulation. However, this formulation does not give appropriate weight to the *harm* inflicted upon members of already oppressed or silenced groups. The assertion that some may lose their liberty in favor of others is simply not a point to be contended.

Freedom of speech as defined by both the traditional Enlightenment underpinnings of liberalism and the more recent Warren Court and its legacy fail to fulfill the contract of "liberty and justice for all." One possible solution to this inequity in liberty would be to shift the focus from freedom to equality. The concept of equality, unlike those of liberty and freedom, is relatively new, historically speaking, in U.S. legal discourse. According to Kammen, "the concept of equality did not even appear in American Constitutional law until adoption of the Fourteenth Amendment by the states in 1868 and . . . Americans showed scant interest in enforcing the spirit of liberty and equality until well after World War II."[22] He notes that until the past few decades, equality was most often seen as not only incompatible with the idea of liberty, but actually counter to it. Kammen further argues that in the first half of the twentieth century, "Americans of very different ideological dispositions were far more concerned about the inevitability of friction than persuaded of the possible compatibility between liberty and equality."[23]

Despite these early, and to some degree continuing, concerns about the compatibility of liberty and equality, various American political theorists, particularly since the 1950s, have returned to the concept of equality as essential to liberty. Included in this group are scholars from various ideological backgrounds who have tried to reconcile possible conflicts between liberty and equality.[24] However, those scholars were not successful in altering the conception of liberty to make equality a primary component.[25] The racial and gender equity supported by the Warren Court has been eroded by the Burger, Rehnquist, and Roberts Courts. The Warren Court, in its attempt to establish substantive equality, developed a formula where equality was secondary to freedom and based on a citizenry who already had the individual autonomy to gain equal political and social opportunities. As a result, subsequent conservative courts have been able to use the same guiding conception of liberty to repeal or significantly alter much of the Warren Court's work toward equality.[26]

SITUATING THE FIRST AMENDMENT

As Kammen suggests, "historical sequences rarely are [precise and tidy] and when discussing historical moments there is frequently 'a lot of chronological overlap and intermingling.'"[27] Throughout the more than two hundred years of case law and constitutional interpretations by various courts, "theories of constitutional interpretation have competed for favor within our Supreme Court."[28] Constitutional scholar Bruce Ackerman points out that while Americans have borrowed much from thinkers such as Hume, Locke, Kant, and Weber, they have also built "a genuinely distinctive pattern of constitutional thought and practice."[29] The constitutional debates, while most definitely informed by early liberal philosophers, have developed in a uniquely U.S. context.

In this section, I outline the "distinctive pattern of constitutional thought and practice." The First Amendment must be situated in this larger constitutional framework because, when studying one constitutional element specifically (here the First Amendment), the implications for broader constitutional concerns cannot be ignored. This section is intended to offer a contextualization of the major constitutional debates and a brief history of traditional First Amendment theory. "Traditional" scholars are those who adhere to the main tenets of liberal philosophy discussed as interpreted by the Supreme Court. This section also introduces the ideas and assumptions brought into constitutional and First Amendment debates by critical scholars. "Critical" scholars may or may not adhere to these same tenets in liberal philosophy, but in either case offer a substantive or more complicated analysis of power. Because my analytical framework draws primarily from feminist perspectives on law and speech, I focus most extensively on the development of feminist legal scholarship.

THE CONSTITUTION

The landscape of constitutional theory can be difficult to navigate. There are virtually almost as many ways of grouping the approaches as there are approaches themselves. For example, one can study different strands of constitutional thought by tracing the rulings in significant Supreme Court cases such as *Marbury v. Madison*,[30] *Dred Scott v. Sandford*,[31] *Lochner v. New York*,[32] *Brown v. Board of Education*,[33] and *Griswold v. Connecticut*.[34] Philip Bobbitt applies a categorical approach in which he identifies "six modalities of Constitutional argument."[35] Still, others search for an organizational structure by examining the philosophical basis behind different theoretical approaches.[36]

For my purposes, I will focus on a few of the most influential, or at least longest lasting, methods proposed for interpreting the Constitution. Broadly, these areas are textualism, legal realism, natural law, structuralism, critical legal studies, critical race theory, and critical feminist studies. What these approaches agree on is the importance of the Constitution (and by proxy the judiciary) in our democratic society. How to measure to what extent and in what ways the Constitution should be applied is the main point of contestation.

Textualism is a theory of constitutional interpretation that dictates, in the broadest sense, that "the constitutional text, history, structure, and precedent are valid sources for constitutional advocacy and judicial decision making."[37] In other words, texualists hold that primary weight in Constitutional analysis should be given to the text itself, specifically to the way in which the average person would understand the text. Through this type of legal interpretation, textualists purport to uphold the objective meaning of the law. Textualists then are concerned with the ordinary meaning of the law and believe that meaning can be found in the words themselves. This reliance on the text is driven by their skepticism of the ability of judges to determine the intent of the lawmakers. Justice Antonin Scalia, probably the most noted contemporary textualist, explained:

> The meaning of terms on the statute books ought to be determined, not on the basis of which meaning can be shown to have been understood by a larger handful of the Members of Congress; but rather on the basis of which meaning is (1) most in accord with context and ordinary usage, and thus most likely to have been understood by the whole Congress which voted on the words of the statute (not to mention the citizens subject to it), and (2) most compatible with the surrounding body of law into which the provision must be integrated—a compatibility which, by a benign fiction, we assume Congress always has in mind.[38]

Scalia's statement touches upon the key concerns of textualists. First, it is not the role of judges to make law, only to make sure the law is being applied in accordance with the Constitution. Second, it is impossible for the Court to assess the overall intent of the legislature without relying on the guidelines in a particular law's text. Finally, the law needs to be interpreted based on its most obvious meaning because this is the way the ordinary citizen could be expected to understand it.

Textualism has been a constant method for interpretation throughout U.S. history; however, debate continues among those subscribing to textualism concerning when and if it is appropriate to step outside of the text itself. For example, in terms of the First Amendment, Scalia explains that while the free speech and free press provisions do not list every type of communication, one can assume that handwritten letters are included under this protection.[39] For Scalia, some reasonable amount of interpretation existing outside of the text itself is necessary to understand the full context of the law. On the other hand, strict constructivists, such as Justice Hugo Black, argued for a pure reading of the text. Black, who served on the Court from 1937 to 1971, rigidly read the text "Congress shall make no law respecting . . . freedom of speech, or of the press" as meaning exactly that—no law whatsoever. While there can be significant disagreement about the extent to which different doctrinal texts— for example, the Constitution, case law, etc.—should be relied upon, practitioners of this approach look to the documents as a way to ensure objective legal decision making.

Also playing a role in early constitutional development were the natural law theorists. While this approach to constitutional interpretation did not directly address free speech issues, I discuss it here briefly due its impact in other areas of constitutional analysis, including the legal positivism and neoconservative approaches. Mark Murphey explains: "Natural law theorists claim that, necessarily, law is a rational standard for conduct: it is a standard that agents have strong, even decisive, reasons to comply with."[40] In other words, the standards by which we choose to govern ourselves are inherently based on the moral standards that as a society we feel should govern us. As a result, most, if not all, of our legal standards are derived from those moral standards. In essence, the natural law theorists considered there to be certain rights that naturally are or should be protected under the Constitution. These theorists believed that there was a higher law of nature that the law of man should try to preserve. Obviously, the natural law form of interpretation ran counter to the textualist approach. While the textualists advise against discussing legislators' motivation, the natural law theorists focus almost exclusively on that motivation.

In the early 1920s, a group formed that would take to task both the textualists and the natural law theorists. The legal realism movement, reacting against the laissez-faire attitude toward political economic principles during that period, argued that the law was inherently biased. These scholars critiqued the existing system of legal method, complaining that "[C]ommon law rules were legal rules, with predictable coercive and distributive effects. . . . Common law rules did not merely describe a preexisting set of categories; they were human devices that created the very categories through which judges perceived legal and social realities."[41] In the most basic sense, they argued that because human beings create law, it is therefore subject to the same fallibility that human beings are.

Legal realism did not start in a vacuum; it was heavily influenced by, among others, Oliver Wendell Holmes Jr., Roscoe Pound, and Benjamin Cardozo. Those jurists adhered to the idea that the law should be used as an instrument toward increasing social welfare. Both those earlier progressive jurists and the proponents of legal realism held the following: (1) the law was indeterminate and left to the discretion of judicial whim; (2) multidisciplinary approaches were important in the study of law, particularly sociology and anthropology; and (3) that law should be used for improving social conditions. While legal realists began to raise questions previously not possible under the formalist approach, their critiques did not include any methodological or analytical solutions, an issue that would be raised later with their successor— critical legal studies.

The structuralist movement, which emerged during the late 1960s, offered a significantly different approach than legal realism. Structuralism proposed a return to the answer-driven analysis of doctrinalism, without the usual politically conservative spin that the doctrinalists brought with their textual interpretations. Two leading structuralists were Charles Black Jr., who wrote *Structure and Relationship in Constitutional Law*,[42] and John Hart Ely, who wrote *Democracy and Distrust: A Theory of Judicial Review*.[43] Structuralism espouses that judicial review should not be based strictly on the text of the Constitution, as early doctrinalists and later textualists would have it, but instead should be derived more from the overall structure and purpose of the Constitution.

Although structuralists tended to be more politically "liberal" than their textualist counterparts, their analyses still relied on finding the essence of the ideas that the founding fathers had built into the structure of the Constitution. For example, contemporary textualist Antonin Scalia's main critique of current legal interpretation is that it relies too much on the common law approach of case analysis and not enough on a textual reading of legislation and the Constitution.[44] He wrote:

> My point in all of this is not that common law should be scraped away as a barnacle on the hull of democracy. . . . But though I have no quarrel with the common law and its process, I do question whether the attitude of the common-law judge . . . is appropriate for most of the work that I do. . . . Every issue of law resolved by a federal judge involves interpretation of text—the text of a regulation, or of a statute, or of the Constitution.[45]

Scalia demanded that the text be the guide to the interpretation in an effort to keep bias out of the justices' rulings and to stay true to the foundational principles of the Constitution. It can be argued that this is, in a sense, exactly what the structuralists were calling for. Both Black, who focused on "structures and relationships created by the Constitution,"[46] and Ely's own brand of "interpretavism"[47] still developed theoretical frames focused on the judiciary's role and not necessarily on the law itself. Critiquing both of these approaches, legal scholars Kimberlé Crenshaw and Gary Peller fashioned what they termed process theory. Process theorists, who include both textualists and structuralists, "concentrate on developing constitutional theories concerned with the interrelation between the judiciary and the legislature rather than the content of just laws."[48] Crenshaw and Peller argue for a move away from proceduralism toward a different sort of discourse analysis in law that would lead to substantive changes in the lives of those who are oppressed or otherwise disempowered. Their work can be viewed as part of the more recent critical legal interpretations.

In the past two decades, several schools of critical theorists have developed. These include critical legal studies, critical race theory, and critical feminist theory. Although I will discuss these theories in more detail in relation to First Amendment critiques, the key that connects them is their potential for the critique of power relations—a movement away from the government power model toward a more dispersed model in which power is found and executed in various aspects of society.

THE TRADITIONAL FIRST AMENDMENT

The preceding review of constitutional approaches is not intended to be all-inclusive, but rather to set up an historical context so as to further understand the development of major discursive themes in First Amendment theory and application.[49] The following review will offer an overview of these themes that will be investigated further in chapters 2 and 3.

In the 1700s and 1800s, the First Amendment was, for the most part, ignored.[50] When First Amendment cases arose, they tended to focus predominantly on seditious libel and prior restraint, and the opinions from those cases were hardly inspired explorations into the meaning of free speech in society.[51] In the early 1900s, the first major discursive theme in free speech discourse emerged—using the First Amendment as a means of promoting speech in the "marketplace of ideas."[52] In *Abrams v. United States*,[53] Justice Holmes became one of the first justices to begin shaping what the First Amendment would mean in later decades. In *Abrams*, Holmes wrote:

> But when men have realized that time has upset many fighting faiths, they may come to believe even more than they believe the very foundations of their own conduct that the ultimate good desired is better reached by free trade in ideas—that the best test of truth is the power of the thought to get itself accepted in the competition of the market, and that truth is the only ground upon which their wishes safely can be carried out. That at any rate is the theory of our Constitution.[54]

The "rhetorical power [of that] single paragraph"[55] ensured that the "marketplace of ideas" conceptualization of free speech would continue to resurface again and again in First Amendment discourse, despite the critiques of the market that would enter into legal discourse through the legal realism movement. Holmes's conception of the relationship between free speech and "truth" is informed by political philosopher John Stuart Mill's work *On Liberty*.[56] In this nineteenth-century essay on political and social liberties, Mill called for an almost absolutist approach to free speech and certainly for a complete protection of political speech. Key to Mill's views on speech was that only through open discussion would the truth be discovered. Mill argued that allowing the government to restrict speech based on the falsity of an idea was impractical for three reasons: (1) the suppressed opinion might be true, (2) all false ideas contain some element of truth, and (3) false opinions are needed to keep the truth from becoming dead dogma. This interpretation of Mill by Holmes concerning the protection of speech would continue through the next several decades when the focus of First Amendment discourse would move from the search for truth to the importance of speech as part of the political process.

A second major discursive theme in First Amendment doctrine came nearly fifty years later in the landmark case *New York Times v. Sullivan*.[57] Occurring in the midst of the Warren Court's civil rights cases, *Sullivan* gave voice to the new First Amendment. In his opinion, Justice Brennan wrote:

> [We] consider this case against the background of a profound national commitment to the principle that debate on public issues should be uninhibited, robust, and wide-open, and that it may well include vehement, caustic, and sometimes unpleasantly sharp attacks on government and public officials.[58]

In *New York Times v. Sullivan*, the emphasis on the importance of free speech dictated by Holmes and Brandeis in the early part of the century finally receives both discursive and doctrinal support. The Court's language about "free and robust debate" became a mantra for later Supreme Court justices in cases supporting free speech.

This conceptual development by the courts was predated by the work in the 1920s through the 1940s by Zechariah Chafee and in the late 1940s through the early 1960s by political theorist Alexander Meiklejohn. Chafee's work is considered the "seminal legal scholarship"[59] on the First Amendment during the early part of the twentieth century.[60] Chafee's writings focused specifically on sedition and the cases concerning the Espionage Act of 1917. More generally, Chafee focused on the protection of speech as a means to spread truth. He wrote: "The true meaning of freedom of speech seems to be this. One of the most important purposes of society and government is the discovery and spread of truth on subjects of general concern. This is possible only through absolutely unlimited discussion."[61] Meiklejohn pinpointed a more specific value in freedom of speech—its necessity for ensuring self-government. His reasoning, however, would still incorporate the ideas about truth found in Holmes's interpretation of Mill. He wrote: "To be afraid of ideas, any ideas, is to be unfit for self-government. Any such repression of ideas about the common good, the First Amendment condemns with its absolute disapproval."[62] Under Meiklejohn's theory, only speech that served the democratic or political function deserved protection.[63]

Other theorists, although not adhering to the absolutism of Meiklejohn, have focused on the importance of the First Amendment to the protection of political speech to foster and maintain participation in our democratic system of government.[64] Harry Kalven Jr., for example, argued that a primary purpose of the First Amendment is to protect seditious libel, a very specific type of political discourse.[65] Vincent Blasi took a similar approach, although instead of focusing entirely on seditious libel, he expanded the conception of free speech, arguing that a major reason we protect speech is because of the checking balance it offers against government control.[66]

Perhaps the most influential First Amendment theorist in the past fifty years is Thomas Emerson. Emerson added breadth to earlier free speech theory by arguing that in addition to the importance of speech in politics, speech also carries with it some intrinsic "human" value. Emerson, in his groundbreaking work *Toward A General Theory of the First Amendment*, began a movement in First Amendment scholarship in which speech was seen as somehow responsible for creating fully realized individuals, not just to enable them to participate in a democratic form of government, but also to enjoy complete social lives.[67]

Emerson posited that the value of free speech rights in U.S. democratic society could be grouped into four categories: (1) a means of assuring individual self-fulfillment; (2) a means of attaining the truth; (3) a method for securing citizens' participation in the political and social process; and (4) a means of maintaining the balance between stability and change in society.[68] Emerson felt so strongly about the need for complete freedom of speech that he believed the "suppression of belief, opinion and expression" was "an affront to the dignity of man, a negation of man's essential nature."[69] Building on Emerson's frame of analysis, other constitutional scholars, such as C. Edwin Baker and Martin Redish, have restructured discussions of speech to include its importance to self-fulfillment[70] and self-realization.[71] Baker, arguing that the First Amendment protects "not a marketplace but rather an arena of individual liberty," collapsed Emerson's four categories into two—protection of speech as means of assuring individual self-fulfillment and as a means of maintaining the balance between stability and change in society. Redish went so far as to contend that the First Amendment protection of speech serves only one purpose—"individual self-realization."

Other contemporary legal scholars, such as Lee Bollinger,[72] Kent Greenawalt,[73] and Steven Shiffrin,[74] ask different questions about the value of speech and what the First Amendment should and does mean. However, because they are still operating within the liberal paradigm, they come to the same conclusions as earlier theorists. For example, while Bollinger spends a great deal of time deconstructing earlier approaches to free speech theory, his own theory of protecting speech to ensure tolerance in society is still embedded in the U.S. Supreme Court's conception of the autonomous individual and Mill's principle of truth.[75] Shiffrin's theoretical development led him to define the purpose of protecting speech to be that of protecting the political dissenter. Again, however, this approach relies on the autonomous individual as the model for the political dissenter.[76] In each of these critiques of First Amendment jurisprudence, power is assumed to be governmental, and individual autonomy remains unquestioned.

CRITICAL APPROACHES

It is in some ways disingenuous to talk about "critical approaches" as one cohesive category. Critical theorists come from various perspectives, including feminism, race theory, Marxist theory, etc. However, critical theorists do have one major point of agreement—they question the basic assumptions of the liberal paradigm, including ideas of the autonomous individual, the possibility of actually searching for a "truth," and the ability for anyone or any institution to be objective or neutral. Because critical theorists begin with a different set of assumptions than their liberal counterparts, their perspectives raise questions not possible inside the liberal paradigm. For example, one major tenet of the liberal paradigm is that people are autonomous. Building on this idea of autonomy, liberal theorists argue that everyone has the freedom to speak. This assumption makes it difficult to question the inequities in access to speaking forums or to subscribe to the possibility that the speech of those with power (economic or otherwise) often silences the speech of those in less powerful positions. The issue then is not that theorists and judges are not aware of the disconnect between the "ideal" of protecting everyone's right to free speech and the inability of applying the First Amendment to ensure it; the issue is that by continuing to study these contradictions while operating inside the liberal democratic paradigm, the answer will always revert to the autonomous individual's role in correcting society's injustices and inequalities.[77]

Critical theorists, rather, question the basic tenets of the liberal paradigm and lay their own foundation of assumptions about how government and society should work, about the nature of the individual, and about questionable definitions of justice, liberty, and social responsibility. Among these assumptions are the idea that the First Amendment does not contribute to "healthy, robust debate," but instead perpetuates the status quo; that instead of being purely autonomous, rational human beings, we are also products of a socially constructed system in which some groups have been historically empowered and others systematically disempowered; that not all speech has value—some only causes harm; and that there is no "equality" in "freedom" of speech.

In First Amendment analysis, critics from differing scholarly and epistemological backgrounds have tackled issues such as hate speech, pornography, media access, campaign finance reform, and government funding of the arts. The theoretical camps most notably associated with offering recent substantive and epistemological criticism of First Amendment theory and application are critical legal studies,[78] critical race theory,[79] and feminist legal studies.[80] All three of these approaches involve questioning who makes up the power structures in our society and how those structures affect different groups. In law, more specifically, these theorists view the legal system as a power structure developed and operated predominantly by and for the benefit of those in control. However, despite the similar philosophical base, there are significant theoretical and methodological differences among these approaches.

The critical legal studies (CLS) movement gained recognition in the legal community in the 1980s with scholarly works critiquing various aspects of the U.S. legal system.[81] Strongly influenced by Marxism, particularly as espoused by the Frankfurt School, the CLS movement sought to "explore the manner in which legal doctrine and legal education and the practices of legal institutions work to buttress and support a pervasive system of oppressive, inegalitarian relations."[82] CLS scholars critique liberalism's focus on the individual and on the idea that there was somehow a separation between law and politics. To them, this intertwining of the two (law with politics) creates a legal system in which law is used "as a means through which powerful elements in society legitimated their control."[83]

Using methodological and theoretical approaches associated with Marxism, legal realism, poststructuralism, postmodernism, and deconstructionism, CLS scholars set out to unmask the power behind power, to in effect show how capitalism (the market) distorted and controlled democratic politics. CLS, while contributing a substantial amount of scholarship to the critical legal field, began to come under fire in the mid-1980s from both feminist scholars (who critiqued the movement's lack of discussion of gender) and a newly growing group of critical race theorists.

Although it has its underpinnings in the philosophical writings of Derrick Bell in the 1970s and early 1980s,[84] critical race theory (CRT) by most accounts started as a reaction to CLS and did not become a unified theoretical approach until 1989 at the first annual Workshop on Critical Race Theory. Although CRT primarily focuses on issues of race, it is by no means only a critique of racial injustice.[85] Some of the basic tenets of critical race theory include the belief that racism is a "fundamental part of American society, not an aberration that can be readily remedied by law"; that "culture constructs its own social reality in its own self-interest" (minorities are not part of the legal system's self-interest); and that "white elites will tolerate or encourage racial progress for minorities only if doing so also promotes white self-interest."[86]

Because CRT scholars are "skeptical of dominant legal theories supporting hierarchy, neutrality, objectivity, color blindness, meritocracy, ahistoricism, and single axis analysis," CRT draws from several different theoretical foundations such as feminism, law and society, Marxism, postmodernism, pragmatism, and cultural nationalism.[87] Critical race theorist and feminist scholar Angela Harris elaborates on the meshing of various theoretical approaches:

> Race-crits clearly have much to gain from a dialogue with feminist legal theorists, who have been able to develop a broad and sophisticated literature not only in law but in social theory more generally. . . . In addition, as "queer theory" emerges as an area of legal scholarship, race-crits should gain a better understanding of "race" by approaching it in the context of sexual identity formation. Together, these various strands of "outsider jurisprudence" can contribute to a general theory of the legal subject for a reconstructed modernism.[88]

As will be discussed in more detail in chapter 4, this redefining of the legal subject had ramifications for critical race theories about hate speech and the First Amendment.

THE DEVELOPMENT OF FEMINIST LEGAL THEORY

Although my work is informed by all three groups of critical approaches, my alternative three-prong framework will be most informed by feminist legal theory. This area of scholarship has undergone substantial changes in the past several decades. From initial questions raised in the 1970s concerning issues of formal equality between men and women, feminist legal scholarship now encompasses issues of identity politics, multiculturalism, and subjective (or substantive) equality. Before entering into a discussion of what constitutes feminist legal studies, I must, as many other feminist scholars have before me, acknowledge the difficulty in defining and categorizing the various stages and components in the development of feminist legal scholarship. From just the brief discussion above, it becomes apparent that there is not one definition of feminist legal theory. Feminist scholars disagree on which problems should be addressed, what theory should be used to address those problems, and what exact policy or legal changes need to take place in order to achieve a solution. Because of the differences, a categorization system must be employed, regardless of the fact that any system utilized will necessarily be non-exhaustive and contain overlapping membership.[89]

Various feminist legal theorists have organized the development of feminist legal theory in different ways. For example, Martha Chamallas divides her discussion by time periods—the equality stage of the 1970s, the difference stage of the 1980s, and the diversity stage of the 1990s and beyond.[90] Nancy Levit identifies four categories based on theoretical commonality— liberal feminism and equal treatment theory; cultural feminism, or difference theory; radical feminism, or dominance theory; and postmodern feminism.[91] Patricia Smith focuses on difference, dominance, domesticity, and denial[92] and Nicola Lacey explores what she calls four main theoretical points of distinction in feminist legal theory—methodology and written style; underlying theories of sexual differences; substantive or methodological continuities with other legal and social theories; and political orientation.[93]

Each of those theorists offers a distinctive way of categorizing the history and current climate of feminist legal studies. Here, I rely roughly on Chamallas's timeline of the 1970s, the 1980s, and the 1990s and beyond. Her breakdown of the development of feminist legal theory, I think, is the clearest way to approach what encompasses an amorphous and intricately connected field of study. What will be distinctive in my discussion is where the emphasis is placed. While offering an overview of the field, I will privilege those feminist theories that are most connected to the study of free speech rights and First Amendment application. Specifically, I will address the sameness/difference debate, dominance theory, and, most currently, postmodern/poststructural theories dealing with social construction, agency, and diversity.

The 1970s: Equality and Liberal Feminism

Although there is no doubt that feminist thinking was a key component leading to the passage of the Nineteenth Amendment, most scholars attribute the late 1960s through the 1970s as the grounding upon which contemporary feminist legal theory is built. This approach to legal theory developed alongside and amid the tumultuous civil rights era.

The equality movement of the 1970s began as a backlash to the separate spheres ideology that had come before it. According to separate spheres, women's place before the law was distinct from men's place, with women existing in the private sphere and men in the public sphere. While this approach did give women a sense of legal identity separate from their husbands' identities, it placed women in a secondary position to men. In the 1970s, the separate spheres ideology began to be repudiated, particularly through the rulings in several U.S. Supreme Court cases that acknowledged the application of a more rigorous standard of review in sex discrimination cases.[94]

Equality advocates such as Ruth Bader Ginsburg brought about these changes in the legal system's treatment of women. Such equality advocates argued that "for all legally relevant purposes men and women are equal and should be treated so in the law."[95] Through various court cases, as well as the push for ratification of the Equal Rights Amendment, equality advocates made strides in the law in areas including equal pay, employment, and education. During this time of change in women's legal rights, those most associated with the changes did not classify themselves as feminist legal scholars. However, those equality advocates are most often associated with the school of thought better known as liberal feminism.

Liberal feminism, also known as sameness feminism, got its name because of its reliance on the traditional liberal approach to law. As Nancy Levit explains: "The hallowed building block of liberalism, that all men are created equal, was recast to include women. The goals of liberal feminism were assimilationist in nature: making legal claims that would ensure women received the same rights, opportunities and treatment as men."[96] This adherence to liberalism included acceptance of the legal system's reliance on the concept of neutrality and on the construction of the autonomous individual. In other words, liberal feminists sought to be treated equally under the law, not to fundamentally change it.

Liberal feminism during the 1970s, mostly because of its push for formal equality, did not address First Amendment application in any way. Freedom of speech was assumed to already be applied fairly and did not fit in with the more substantive issues of equal pay and equal access to education and employment. It would be the 1980s before liberal feminism would focus on the First Amendment at all, and then only to defend the First Amendment against dominance feminists' critiques of it. Most notably, liberal feminist Nadine Strossen posited that "all censorship measures throughout history have been used disproportionately to silence those who are relatively disempowered."[97] She warned that even if the system were flawed, trying to correct it through speech restriction ultimately would make matters worse for women.

The 1980s: Difference and Dominance

Chamallas states that "Feminist legal theory came of age in the 1980s."[98] I agree. In the 1980s, two new types of feminism arose in reaction to the liberal, equality-based feminism of the 1970s. Feminists of the 1980s shifted focus from issues of formal equality and set the foundation for the future of feminist legal theory. It also would be during this period that feminist scholars would begin questioning First Amendment doctrine and application. The feminist theories of the 1980s fall into two camps: difference feminism and dominance feminism.

Difference feminism can be traced on the one hand to the ruling in *Geduldig v. Aiello*[99] and on the other hand to Carol Gilligan, a developmental psychologist who produced a groundbreaking study based on her work with children.[100] *Geduldig* was an equal protection case in which the Supreme Court ruled that denial of insurance benefits for work loss time resulting from a normal pregnancy did not violate the Fourteenth Amendment. *Geduldig* used the equal treatment argument to deny the rights of pregnant women. This ruling led to a movement in feminist legal theory where scholars would begin critiquing various legal structures instead of blindly supporting them as liberal feminists did. The difference theorists can be seen as diametrically opposed to liberal feminism. They argue that there are fundamental differences between men and women and that these differences need to be accounted for in the law. They were particularly interested in areas such as pregnancy, rape, and sexual harassment.

In terms of theoretical development, many refer to Carol Gilligan's *In a Different Voice: Psychological Theory and Women's Development* as the defining study from a difference perspective. Gilligan's study set out to investigate how men and women make moral choices and solve moral dilemmas. Her study of the responses of two respondents—known as Jake and Amy—can be considered one the most significant aspects of her overall study in terms of its effects on feminist theory. Jake and Amy were asked to solve the "Heinz" dilemma in which a man, Heinz, cannot afford to buy the drugs he needs for his dying wife and the pharmacist refuses to lower the price. The question posed to the eleven-year-olds in Gilligan's study was: Should Heinz steal the drugs?[101] What Gilligan found was that while Jake immediately offered the answer of yes supported by a logical argument, Amy responded with a series of other solutions, grounded not in logic but in human relations. Gilligan's study ultimately established that men and women's approaches to life's questions are fundamentally different. Although this study was performed from a physiological perspective, it was quickly picked up by feminist legal scholars because, as Chamallas noted, "The resemblance between Jake's hierarchical orientation and dominant legal discourse made Gilligan's methodology a useful tool to critique the law and to suggest alternative analysis and solutions."[102]

The advent of difference theory led to one of the earliest debates in feminist legal scholarship—the sameness/difference debate. In this debate, women and men are either essentially the same (and so should be treated as such under the law) or are essentially different (and as such should receive different treatment). While this debate has been found to lack the nuances necessary for in-depth, critical analysis of gender and power in the law, it is nonetheless the building block for later feminist debates and as such can offer the general background necessary to understanding contemporary feminist legal theory.

Although the sameness/difference dichotomy is an enticing theoretical proposition to consider, it tends to trivialize women's issues. The question of whether men or women are different or the same is for most areas of constitutional law a question that is not quite on point. Even if men and women are fundamentally the same, socially they hold different positions of power and so equalizing the law would do little more than maintain that power imbalance. On the other hand, if they are fundamentally different, then that difference can either be a positive or a negative for women.[103] In a system constructed by men, however, this question leads to a dead end, where women's difference and how that difference should be treated will be decided by a male-centered legal system. Neither of these views takes into account how the differences might have occurred and how those differences are maintained through current social systems. In addition, the sameness/difference debate has been critiqued for ignoring the problem of essentializing gender. Black feminist scholars and lesbian feminist scholars, in particular, have argued that the sameness/difference debate does not account for difference based on race or sexuality.

Also developing during the 1980s was dominance feminism.[104] These feminists placed themselves in opposition to both traditional legal doctrine and to liberal feminists. In general, they argued that women face gender oppression due to inequalities of power fostered and maintained through men's sexual coercion. Dominance theory posits that women are socially constructed in a society that is predominately patriarchal, leading to inequities in the legal system that could not be rectified through equal treatment because men and women had different levels of societal power. As a result, women are subordinate to men in most organized institutions, including (and, for some feminist scholars, especially) the legal system. Dominance theory pushes for re-evaluating laws that may contribute to women's subordination by focusing on power rather than sameness or difference.

Catharine MacKinnon is perhaps the most widely recognized dominance feminist. Throughout the 1980s, MacKinnon would push for extensive changes in the legal system, particularly in the areas of sexual harassment, rape, and pornography. MacKinnon, applying a more complicated theory of gender, sexuality, and power, developed dominance theory in a way that stood in opposition to liberal feminism's "sameness" standard, locating the source of oppression in gender hierarchy instead of individual discrimination.[105] MacKinnon deconstructs the epistemological underpinnings of the legal system and finds it to be a patriarchal institution that subordinates women by perpetuating the status quo, which is inherently filled with inequity. She explains: "The perspective from the male standpoint enforces woman's definition, encircles her body, circumlocutes her speech, and describes her life. The male perspective is systematic and hegemonic. . . . Each sex has its role, but their stakes and power are not equal.[106] This male perspective is historically supported and pervasive."[107]

She argues that what the legal system says is neutral is actually the male stance or the male point of view. This male point of view in the legal system ensures that woman's point of view is not heard, or, if it is heard, it is dismissed as somehow invalid. Combining a legal system weighted against women with the view that this imbalance is socially constructed and thus reinforced through the institutions that perpetuate it, MacKinnon develops dominance theory to demonstrate that women as a group will continue to be dominated by men unless a complete overhaul of the legal system takes place. In effect, the substantive changes sought by liberal feminists not only are incapable of facilitating any real change, but also are exacerbating the problem by reinforcing the male standpoint.

MacKinnon's work greatly impacted the legal treatment of sexual harassment. She is attributed with development of the concepts of quid pro quo (sexual harassment where sexual compliance is exchanged for employment opportunities) and hostile work environment (where sexual harassment is a persistent situation).[108] MacKinnon has also been instrumental and prolific in terms of critiquing the speech issue of pornography. Her work in this area will be discussed in greater detail in chapter 6.

Scholars in the late 1980s and early 1990s have critiqued MacKinnon's work for supporting gender essentialism, for ignoring the different situations of women of color, and for failing to acknowledge that lesbians have a different relationship with male sexuality than do heterosexual women. Despite these critiques, dominance theory remains a viable and important base when examining the social construction of women in society in general and in the legal system in particular.

The 1990s and Beyond: Postmodernism and Poststructuralism

Current critical feminist scholarship is trying to find a way to combine this earlier work on equality and dominance with new perspectives on "difference, particularity, context, and identity."[109] During the past decade, feminists, primarily located in the postmodern and poststructuralist arena, have been searching for a way to move feminist legal scholarship away from the essentialism of the sameness/difference debate and the limitations of dominance analysis.[110] These scholars question both the development of the individual self and the role of the state and other institutional power on that development.[111] Feminist legal scholar Deborah Rhode explains that because postmodern and poststructuralist traditions "presuppose the social construction of knowledge," feminists in these areas find themselves in the paradox of "maintaining that gender oppression exists while challenging our capacity to document it."[112] Critical or postmodern feminists rely on discourse analysis to study the interpretation of reality rather than on preconceived universals. This focus on positionality moves us past "the binary pairs of modern theories" to look instead at "the partiality and perspectivity of interpretation."[113] For example, feminist scholars have focused on the discourse in legal education to point out the gendered, racist, and heterosexist nature of the legal academy.[114]

Once feminist theory began to move away from the binary concept of gender equality feminism, scholars began to problematize the concept of agency, particularly as MacKinnon vocalized it. If we acknowledge positionality as being inclusive of multiple categories of diversity and begin to look at power not as structural per se but as more diffuse, then agency must be more carefully defined than MacKinnon's conception of the all-powerful male institution over the generic female. This idea of the "standard" or generic female experience, a necessary component of being able to define the limits of women's agency, has come under attack, primarily by black feminist scholars and lesbian feminist scholars. These "other" groups, according to MacKinnon's conception of agency, have no way of identifying themselves in the woman experience. For example, Patricia Cain has argued that MacKinnon's discussion of the sexualization of women is based on heterosexual women and thus completely ignores lesbian agency.[115] In Cain's version, women are not always the victims of male power, as MacKinnon's version of agency suggests.

To try to overcome the victim mentality and also to bring into the discussion the "difference dilemma," several scholars have recently moved toward trying to theorize agency in a more complex manner. For example, Kathryn Abrams is working on a concept of "partial agency" in which women are neither totally "unencumbered" nor are they completely victimized.[116] Similarly, constitutional law scholar Tracy Higgins has developed her own conception of incomplete agency.[117] She proposes that dominance theory, while claiming to radically alter the legal system's structure that enforces women's subordinate position, really suffers from continuing to frame discussions of gender inside an outdated, patriarchal definition of democracy. In chapter 3, I will expand on the works by Higgins and Abrams, using their conceptions of incomplete agency to redefine the role of the First Amendment in contemporary society.

CONCLUSION

Conceptions of liberty have changed throughout U.S. constitutional history. Scholars have been able to point to periods of change by focusing on a socio-legal critique of history. Coinciding with changing legal conceptions of liberty have been the addition of new perspectives on the Constitution in general and the First Amendment in particular. This complex history of constitutional debates, as outlined in the previous section, demonstrates the evolving nature of constitutional theory and law. It also, however, shows that while there have been many constitutional theories posited throughout the past one hundred years, these theories, up until recently, have clung to certain tenets of the Enlightenment age, most notable of which is the ubiquitous acceptance of the autonomous individual.

Currently, the U.S. political and social systems, in part as a result of constitutional theory, are experiencing another moment of change. However, because of the addition of new types of scholarship, such as race theory and poststructuralism, that critique the core of liberal philosophy's conception of the individual, this moment offers a greater possibility for long-term social change. Applying a critical feminist framework to First Amendment doctrine, I urge a shift in the conception of liberty, a shift from freedom as a means to equality to equality as a precondition for true freedom.

Of the various feminist approaches available, those emphasizing social construction, agency, and diversity may be the most promising way to begin an examination of First Amendment issues from a feminist standpoint. The social constructivist approach allows us to move past the assumptions about autonomy and neutrality, acknowledging instead that the legal system is riddled with value-based decisions that have developed inside a patriarchal ideology that does not permit all people to operate autonomously. Theorizing power in this socially constructed universe as being diffuse and diverse will allow for the richness needed to deal with the complexity of a First Amendment critique. In other words, when dealing with constitutional analysis, particularly of an amendment like the First Amendment that seems only to serve

for the betterment of diverse communities and ideas, the movement away
from the modern binary system of analysis can problematize seemingly positive characteristics of the law. For example, bypassing the content-neutral/
content-based distinction in free speech case analysis[118] allows a consideration of other elements, including historical context and individual agency.
Combining that alteration with a theory of incomplete agency further complicates the analysis, allowing us to argue that while the system is constructed
to eliminate women's agency, it actually only has the power to reduce that
agency.

Contemporary feminist scholars have dealt primarily with legal questions
involving the female body, such as sexual harassment, abortion, or domestic
abuse, leaving areas like the First Amendment speech clause relatively untouched. In chapter 3, I add to the already substantial body of feminist legal
scholarship by moving the debate into the free speech realm. Prior to refram-
ing power and agency in the context of First Amendment doctrine, it is first
important to define the basic liberal ideology informing contemporary speech
cases. In the following chapter, I address the liberal underpinnings of First
Amendment discourse and doctrine, identifying three broad themes that drive
the Court's interpretation of the First Amendment.

NOTES

1. The original version of the First Amendment drafted by James Madison read: "The
people shall not be deprived or abridged of their right to speak, to write or to publish their
sentiments and freedom of the press, as one of the greatest bulwarks of liberty, shall be
inviolable." After several revisions, the First Amendment was ratified to read: "Congress
shall make no law respecting an establishment of religion, or prohibiting the free exercise thereof; or abridging the freedom of speech, or of the press; or the right of the people to peaceably assemble, and to petition the Government for a redress of grievance."

2. Prior restraint refers to the practice of stopping publication before it occurs. The
colonists were extremely sensitive to prior restraint because the practice was common
in England prior to and during the American Revolution. For discussion of prior restraint and original intent, *see* ZECHARIAH CHAFEE, FREE SPEECH IN THE
UNITED STATES (fourth prtg. 1941); MARTIN H. REDISH, FREEDOM OF
EXPRESSION: A CRITICAL ANALYSIS (1984); RODNEY A. SMOLLA, FREE
SPEECH IN AN OPEN SOCIETY (1992).

3. *See*, for example, ZECHARIAH CHAFEE, FREE SPEECH IN THE UNITED
STATES, 18–22 (fourth prtg. 1941).

4. For an extended discussion of the history of the development of the First
Amendment during that time period, *see* chapter 2.

5. The Warren Court, under the direction of Chief Justice Earl Warren, existed
from 1953 to 1969. The impact of the Warren Court, however, did not end in 1969.

Several cases heard in the early 1970s, including *Roe v. Wade*, 410 U.S. 113 (1973) (legalizing abortion) and *Reed v. Reed*, 404 U.S. 71 (1971) (dealing with gender discrimination), built on work started by the Warren Court. For further discussion of the Warren Court era, *see* MORTON HORWITZ, THE WARREN COURT AND THE PURSUIT OF JUSTICE: A CRITICAL ISSUE (1998).

6. Many of the free speech issues tackled by the Warren Court continue to be significant First Amendment issues today, including pornography, libel, and seditious speech. More importantly, several types of analysis applied to First Amendment cases can be traced to Justice William Brennan, who joined the Court in 1956. Brennan forged new First Amendment doctrines, including vagueness and overbreadth.

7. For further discussion of these particular theories of freedom of speech and expression, *see* THOMAS EMERSON, TOWARD A GENERAL THEORY OF THE FIRST AMENDMENT (1963).

8. For early discussion of the individual, *see* JOHN STUART MILL, ON LIBERTY (Emery Neff, Intro., 1926) (1859) and JOHN MILTON, AREOPAGITICA (Richard C. Jebb ed., Folcroft, Pa.: Folcroft Press, 1969) (1644). For more contemporary discussions of individual autonomy, *see* GERALD DWORKIN, THE THEORY AND PRACTICE OF AUTONOMY (1988) and ROBERT YOUNG, PERSONAL AUTONOMY: BEYOND NEGATIVE AND POSITIVE LIBERTY (1986).

9. 376 U.S. 254 (1964).

10. 395 U.S. 444 (1969).

11. The Warren Court's legacy has been chipped away in recent years by a more conservative Supreme Court. For a further discussion of this trend in free speech cases, *see* Margaret Blanchard, *The Twilight of the First Amendment Age?* 1 COMM. L. & POL'Y 329 (1996). Blanchard wrote: "As the twenty-first century approaches, support for freedom of speech is on the decline in many venues in the United States. . . . Some of this suppression of expressive rights is occurring through the court system, where judges and justices, using tests developed to protect government interest and private property, have found ways to eliminate free speech from the marketplace."

12. For the purposes of this book, the term liberty will refer to the set of important qualities for a high-quality political and social existence. Freedom and equality will be considered qualities under the concept of liberty.

13. THE COLLECTED WORKS OF ABRAHAM LINCOLN 301 (Roy P. Basler ed., 1953).

14. JOHN STUART MILL, ON LIBERTY (Emery Neff, Intro., 1926) (1859).

15. MICHAEL KAMMEN, SPHERES OF LIBERTY: CHANGING PERCEPTIONS OF LIBERTY IN AMERICAN CULTURE (1986). It should be noted here that while Mill was dealing primarily with a philosophical conception of liberty, Kammen is situating his analysis of liberty within a legal framework. In so doing, he grounds his analysis by focusing mainly on case law and Supreme Court discourse. His conception of liberty, as a result, is not only Western, but also specifically U.S.-based.

16. *Id.* at 10.

17. *Id.* at 5.

18. *Id.*

19. ISAIAH BERLIN, FOUR ESSAYS ON LIBERTY 122 (1969).

20. BRUCE BAUM, REREADING POWER AND FREEDOM IN J. S. MILL 6 (2000).

21. *See Village of Skokie v. the National Socialist Party of America*, 373 N.E.2d 21 (Ill. 1978), *Doe v. University of Michigan*, 721 F. Supp. 852 (E. D. Mich. 1989), *R.A.V. v. City of St. Paul, Minnesota*, 505 U.S. 377 (1992).

22. KAMMEN, *supra* note 15, at 162.

23. *Id*. at 164.

24. *Id*.

25. *Id*.

26. For discussions of this erosion of civil rights post-Warren Court, *see* Christopher Smith, *The Malleability of Constitutional Doctrine and Its Ironic Impact on Prisoners' Rights*, 11 B.U. PUB. INT. L.J. 73 (2001) (examining how Justice Scalia appropriated Justice Marshall's "deliberate indifference" test), Thomas R. Hensley and Christopher Smith, *Membership Change and Voting Change: An Analysis of the Rehnquist Court's 1986–1991 Terms*, 48 POL. RES. Q. 837 (1995) (analyzing individual justice's voting behavior in civil rights and liberties cases), and Eric K. Yamamoto, *Symposium—Civil Rights in the New Decade: Dismantling Civil Rights: Multiracial Resistance and Reconstruction*, 31 COLUM. L. REV. 523 (2000) (examining Court rulings interpreting Title VI reveals an erosion of civil rights enforcement).

27. KAMMEN, *supra* note 15, at 6.

28. WILLIAM VAN ALSTYNE, INTERPRETATIONS OF THE FIRST AMENDMENT 5 (1984).

29. BRUCE ACKERMAN, WE THE PEOPLE: FOUNDATIONS 3 (1991).

30. 5 U.S. 137 (1803) (Court explicitly claimed the power of judicial review).

31. 60 U.S. 393 (1857) (ruled that people of African descent could never be citizens of the United States).

32. 198 U.S. 45 (1905) (ruled that the right to free contract was implicitly protected through the due process clause of the Fourteenth Amendment).

33. 347 U.S. 483 (1954) (ended legal segregation in public schools).

34. 381 U.S. 479 (1965) (ruled that the Constitution protects the right to privacy).

35. PHILIP BOBBITT, CONSTITUTIONAL FATE: THEORY OF THE CONSTITUTION (1984). According to Bobbitt, the modalities are historical, textual, structural, doctrinal, ethical, and prudential.

36. For detailed discussions of philosophy and constitutional theory, *see* THE BLACKWELL GUIDE TO THE PHILOSOPHY OF LAW AND LEGAL THEORY (Martin P. Golding and William A. Edmundson eds., 2005).

37. MICHAEL J. GERHARDT, ET AL., CONSTITUTIONAL THEORY: ARGUMENTS AND PERSPECTIVES 1 (2000).

38. *Green v. Bock Laundry Mach. Co.*, 490 U.S. 504, 528 (1989) (Scalia, J., concurring).

39. ANTONIN SCALIA, A MATTER OF INTERPRETATION: FEDERAL COURTS AND THE LAW 38 (1997). "In this context, speech and press, the two most common forms of communication, stand as a sort of synecdoche for the whole. That is not strict construction, but it is reasonable construction."

40. Mark C. Murphey, *Natural Law Theory*, in THE BLACKWELL GUIDE TO PHILOSOPHY OF LAW AND LEGAL THEORY (Martin P. Golding and William A. Edmundson eds., 2005).

41. CASS SUNSTEIN, THE PARTIAL CONSTITUTION 51 (1993).

42. CHARLES BLACK JR., STRUCTURE AND RELATIONSHIP IN CONSTITUTIONAL LAW (1969).

43. JOHN HART ELY, DEMOCRACY AND DISTRUST: A THEORY OF JUDICIAL REVIEW (1980).

44. SCALIA, *supra* note 39.

45. *Id.* at 12.

46. BLACK, *supra* note 42, at 6.

47. ELY, *supra* note 43.

48. Kimberlé Crenshaw and Gary Peller, *The Contradictions of Mainstream Constitutional Theory*, 45 UCLA L. REV. 1683, 1689 (1998).

49. I am using the term "discursive theme" here to represent repetitive phrases that are found in the Court's dicta. These discursive themes are separate from doctrinal principles in that the Court did not directly base its legal ruling on those themes.

50. DAVID RABBAN, FREE SPEECH IN ITS FORGOTTEN YEARS (1997).

51. *See e.g.*, *Debs v. United States*, 249 U.S. 211 (1919), *Schenck v. United States*, 249 U.S. 47 (1919), *Abrams v. United States*, 250 U.S. 616 (1919). For an extended discussion of these cases, *see* chapters 2 and 7.

52. *See Abrams v. United States*, 250 U.S. 616 (1919). For a historical discussion of the marketplace metaphor, *see* Anna M. Taruschio, *The First Amendment, the Right Not to Speak, and the Problem of Government Access Statutes*, 1001 FORDHAM URBAN L.J. 27, 1006–7 (2000) explaining the origins of the "marketplace of ideas" concept in First Amendment jurisprudence: "Early American jurists and legal theorists incorporated Mill's concept of a marketplace of ideas into their framework for a free society." Taruschio argues that this original Millian perspective of protecting the market to allow for the search for truth later developed into a principle for encouraging "rigorous public debate."

53. 250 U.S. 616 (1919).

54. *Id.* at 630.

55. STEVEN SHRIFFIN, DISSENT, INJUSTICE AND THE MEANING OF AMERICA 7 (1999).

56. For further discussion of Holmes's influence by Mill, *see* H. L. POHLMAN, JUSTICE OLIVER WENDELL HOLMES: FREE SPEECH AND THE LIVING CONSTITUTION (1991): "Holmes was deeply shaped by the philosophy of British empiricism and it is therefore hardly surprising that he adopted Mill's rationale for free speech," at 10.

57. 376 U.S. 254 (1964).

58. *Id.* at 270.

59. RABBAN, *supra* note 50.

60. ZECHARIAH CHAFEE, FREEDOM OF SPEECH (1920); ZECHARIAH CHAFEE, FREE SPEECH IN THE UNITED STATES (1941).

61. ZECHARIAH CHAFEE, FREE SPEECH IN THE UNITED STATES 31 (1941). Chafee, despite this strong sentiment toward protecting speech, was not an absolutist. He argued for a preferred balancing of free speech against other social necessities, such as maintaining order.

62. ALEXANDER MEIKLEJOHN, POLITICAL FREEDOM: THE CONSTITUTIONAL POWERS OF THE PEOPLE (1960).

63. Theories of only protecting political speech later were shown to be problematic because of the difficulty in determining just what speech is necessary for effective self-government. They raised many questions, not the least of which was exactly what speech contributes to the political process. For example, what about academic research? What about literature, or art, or dance? Despite these problems, some theorists, such as conservative jurist Robert Bork, continue to argue for protection of only purely political speech. Robert Bork, *Neutral Principles and Some First Amendment Problems*, 47 IND. L.J. 1 (1971).

64. *See*, for example, HARRY KALVEN JR., A WORTHY TRADITION: FREEDOM OF SPEECH IN AMERICA (1988), Vincent Blasi, *The Checking Value in First Amendment Theory*, 1977 A.B.F. RES. J. 521 (1977), STEVEN SHIFFRIN, THE FIRST AMENDMENT, DEMOCRACY AND ROMANCE (1990).

65. *Id*. KALVEN, at 47.

66. Blasi, *supra* note 64, at 3.

67. THOMAS EMERSON, TOWARD A GENERAL THEORY OF THE FIRST AMENDMENT (1963).

68. *Id*. at 3.

69. *Id*. at 5.

70. C. EDWIN BAKER, HUMAN LIBERTY AND FREEDOM OF SPEECH (1989).

71. MARTIN REDISH, THE VALUE OF FREE SPEECH (1974).

72. LEE BOLLINGER, THE TOLERANT SOCIETY: FREEDOM OF SPEECH AND EXTREMIST SPEECH (1986).

73. KENT GREENAWALT, FIGHTING WORDS: INDIVIDUALS, COMMUNITIES, AND LIBERTIES OF SPEECH (1995).

74. STEVEN SHIFFRIN, DISSENT, INJUSTICE AND THE MEANINGS OF AMERICA (1999).

75. BOLLINGER, *supra* note 72.

76. SHIFFRIN, *supra* note 74.

77. The one exception to this treatment of speech has been broadcast regulation. In broadcast, however, the government regulates not because they don't trust the autonomous individual to make choices about society but because they don't trust the government, which controls the broadcast frequencies, to make those choices.

78. *See*, for example, ROBERTO UNGER, DEMOCRACY REALIZED: THE PROGRESSIVE ALTERNATIVE (1998).

79. *See*, for example, DERRICK BELL, AND WE ARE NOT SAVED: THE ELUSIVE QUEST FOR RACIAL JUSTICE (1987); Richard Delgado, *Words That Wound: A Tort Action for Racial Insults, Epithets, and Name-Calling*, 17 HARV. C.R.-C.L. L. REV. 133 (1982); Charles Lawrence, *If He Hollers Let Him Go: Regu-*

lating Racist Speech on Campus, 1990 DUKE L.J. 431 (1990); Mari Matsuda, *Public Response to Racist Speech: Considering the Victim's Story*, 87 MICH. L. REV. 2320 (1989).

80. CATHARINE MACKINNON, FEMINISM UNMODIFIED: DISCOURSES ON LIFE AND LAW (1987); CATHARINE MACKINNON, ONLY WORDS (1993); NADINE STROSSEN, DEFENDING PORNOGRAPHY: FREE SPEECH, SEX, AND THE FIGHT FOR WOMEN'S RIGHTS (1995); Robin West, *Jurisprudence and Gender* 201, in FEMINIST LEGAL THEORY: READINGS IN LAW AND GENDER (Katharine T. Bartlett and Rosanne Kennedy eds., 1991).

81. For example, *see* ROBERTO UNGER, THE CRITICAL LEGAL STUDIES MOVEMENT (1986) and MARK KELMAN, A GUIDE TO CRITICAL LEGAL STUDIES (1987).

82. *Id.*

83. MARTHA CHAMALLAS, INTRODUCTION TO FEMINIST LEGAL THEORY 73 (1999).

84. DERRICK BELL, AND WE ARE NOT SAVED: THE ELUSIVE QUEST FOR RACIAL JUSTICE (1987).

85. Angela Harris, *Forward: The Jurisprudence of Reconstruction*, 82 CAL. L. REV. 741, 745 (1994).

86. Adrien Katherine Wing, *Introduction*, in CRITICAL RACE FEMINISM: A READER 1 (Adrien Katherine Wing ed., 1997).

87. *Id.*

88. Harris, *supra* note 85, at 474.

89. GERHARDT, *supra* note 37, at 331.

90. MARTHA CHAMALLAS, INTRODUCTION TO FEMINIST LEGAL THEORY (2003).

91. NANCY LEVIT, THE GENDER LINE: MEN, WOMEN AND THE LAW 189–95 (1998).

92. Patricia Smith, *Four Themes in Feminist Legal Theory: Difference, Dominance, Domesticity, and Denial*, in THE BLACKWELL GUIDE TO THE PHILOSOPHY OF LAW AND LEGAL THEORY (Martin P. Golding and William A. Edmundson eds., 2005) 90.

93. Nicola Lacey, *Feminist Legal Theory and the Rights of Women* 17–19, in GENDER AND HUMAN RIGHTS (Karen Knop ed., 2004).

94. For example, the Supreme Court ruled in *Reed v. Reed*, 404 U.S. 71 (1971) that administrators of estates were not permitted to be named in a way that would discriminate between sexes. The Court reinforced this position even further in 1976 in the case of *Craig v. Boren*, 429 U.S. 190. Here, the Court ruled that any sex-based classifications must bear a substantial relationship to an important government interest.

95. Smith, *supra* note 92, at 90.

96. LEVIT, *supra* note 91, at 189.

97. STROSSEN, *supra* note 80, at 31.

98. CHAMALLAS, *supra* note 90, at 39.

99. 417 U.S. 484 (1974).

100. CAROL GILLIGAN, IN A DIFFERENT VOICE: PSYCHOLOGICAL THE-
ORY AND WOMEN'S DEVELOPMENT (1982).

101. *Id*. at 25–26.

102. CHAMALLAS, *supra* note 90, at 57.

103. For example, women are fundamentally different from men in their ability to give birth. This can be seen as a positive difference for women in that it allows them to be more nurturing and more connected to others. It can also be seen as negative because it can make them more vulnerable physically during pregnancy and more dependent on others both during and after pregnancy.

104. Dominance feminists are also referred to as radical feminists or inequality feminists. For the purpose of this book, I will discuss this perspective using the term dominance feminism.

105. MACKINNON, FEMINISM UNMODIFIED, *supra* note 80.

106. Catharine A. MacKinnon, *Feminism, Marxism, Method, and the State: Toward Feminist Jurisprudence*, in FEMINIST LEGAL THEORY: READINGS IN LAW AND GENDER 181 (1991).

107. *Id*. at 182. "This defines our task not only because male dominance is perhaps the most pervasive and tenacious system of power in history, but because it is metaphysically nearly perfect."

108. In 1980 the Equal Employment Opportunity Commission used MacKinnon's framework when developing their guidelines prohibiting sexual harassment.

109. Nancy J. Hirschmann, *Difference as an Occasion for Rights: A Feminist Rethinking of Rights, Liberalism, and Difference*, in FEMINISM, IDENTITY AND DIFFERENCE 29 (Susan Hekman ed., 1999).

110. *See* chapter 3 for an extended discussion of poststructural feminism.

111. *See* chapter 3 for a more detailed discussion of postmodern feminism.

112. Deborah Rhode, *Feminist Critical Theories* 333, in FEMINIST LEGAL THEORY: READINGS IN LAW AND GENDER (Katharine T. Bartlett and Rosanne Kennedy eds., 1991).

113. MARY JOE FRUG, POSTMODERN LEGAL FEMINISM xix (1992).

114. *Id*. Also *see*, Patricia Cain, *Feminist Jurisprudence: Grounding the Theories*, in FEMINIST LEGAL THEORY: READINGS IN LAW AND GENDER 268 (1991) and Mari Matsuda, *When the First Quail Calls: Multiple Consciousness as Jurisprudential Method*, in WHERE IS YOUR BODY? AND OTHER ESSAYS ON RACE, GENDER, AND THE LAW 3 (1996).

115. *Id*. Cain.

116. Kathryn Abrams, *Sex Wars Redux: Agency and Coercion in Feminist Legal Theory*, 95 COL. L. REV. 304 (1995).

117. Tracy Higgins, *Democracy and Feminism*, 110 HARV. L. REV. 1957 (1997).

118. Content neutrality in First Amendment analysis refers to limiting, except in rare, specified situations, the government from restricting speech based on content. *See* chapter 4 for a more in-depth discussion of the history and applicaton of the content-neutrality principle.

Chapter Two

Liberalism and the
Legal History of Free Speech

Michael Kammen identified three spheres of liberty: liberty and authority, liberty and order, and liberty and justice. He made two arguments that are key to the foundation of this study: the concept of liberty is fluid and liberty can best be defined in relation to other qualities, such as authority or justice. Liberty, then, is constructed socially and historically.[1]

Understanding U.S. legal and political conceptions of liberty in a historical context requires not only reconstructing certain specific political or social moments (i.e., the Lochner era or the Warren Court era)[2] but also situating those conceptions of liberty into the meta-context of liberal philosophy. Understanding the tenets that drive that philosophy and the ways in which those tenets have evolved through time leads to a richer comprehension of the development of the liberty inherent in free speech doctrine and also illustrates why linking that liberty to equality becomes problematic inside the current system.

This chapter explores the problematic relationship between liberty and equality by focusing on the liberty of freedom of speech as defined through the First Amendment. Following, I define liberal philosophy by offering a brief historic overview of its development, particularly in U.S. society. I then show the ways in which the tenets of this U.S. liberal pluralism manifest themselves in contemporary First Amendment jurisprudence. Specifically, I will use U.S. Supreme Court dicta and rulings to illustrate the intricate discussions of liberty but also the Court's reliance on the ideas of government suppression and individual autonomy as the guiding concepts that have helped give shape to how that liberty gets conceptualized and applied in free speech cases. Finally, I offer a critique of this system of liberal political thought as it pertains to the role of equality in free speech cases.

DEFINING LIBERALISM

The term liberalism can be defined in ways ranging from defining it as "a distinctive political current" to "the world-view of post-Enlightenment modernity."[3] For purposes of this discussion, the terms liberal and liberalism will refer in the general sense to "the world-view of post-Enlightenment modernity" and in a more specific formulation to "the self-understanding of Western, market-based representative democracies."[4] In the United States,[5] this "self-understanding" is translated into individual autonomy and protection from government interference. Specifically in the area of free speech, the concern is that "there is an inherent and inexorable tendency on the part of all governments to seek to expand their power over speech."[6] In a more general sense, liberals are averse to state power because they feel that power threatens individuals. However, they still maintain a strong reliance on state policy as a promoter of change and progress. This fear of state power is a direct descendant of the initial historical origins of liberal philosophy. And, as we will see later in this chapter, this fear also has major implications for the way in which the First Amendment functions in society.

Liberalism has its earliest origins in the struggles against religious orthodoxy during the sixteenth and seventeenth centuries in Europe. Beginning during the Renaissance period, and building momentum during the Reformation, liberalism would become "one of the main political forces in the Enlightenment."[7] In the eighteenth and nineteenth centuries liberalism would be called upon to offer solutions for class struggles between aristocrats and commoners not only in Europe, but in the United States as well. In the United States, the underpinnings of liberal philosophy have evolved in terms of negative liberties. As political theorist Richard Bellamy explains:

> The emphasis has been on devising general principles of justice, such as bills of rights, and mechanisms, such as the division of powers and the separation of church and state, that serve to exclude disruptive elements from the political sphere so as to allow individuals to exercise their putative "natural" liberty as much as possible.[8]

This current formulation of liberalism has been informed by several of the earlier liberal philosophers and their philosophical descendants.[9] There is, for example, a significant difference between the amount of liberty accorded the sane, rational adult in the classical liberal world of Ludwig von Mises, F. A. Hayek, and Herman Finer and the more egalitarian approaches of Dworkin and Rawls.[10] Despite these varied ways of conceptualizing liberalism, some major themes exist across all permutations of liberalism, uniting them under the "liberal" umbrella. In a broad sense, "all varieties of liberalism, however, share a commitment both to the equal moral worth of persons and to the tolerance of diverse points of view on how lives should be lived."[11] To what extent or degree this commitment is adhered to is what defines different, occasionally competing, versions of liberalism.

I focus here on certain characteristics of liberalism, specifically those that have served as the foundation for Supreme Court interpretations of the First Amendment. These particular traits of liberalism form three broad themes that, once established in this chapter, also will serve in later chapters as the major points of contention in critiquing the shortcomings of First Amendment doctrine and contemporary legal problem-solving in dealing with many of today's social issues. The themes are that the main purpose of organized government is to ensure individual liberties, that the (autonomous) individual is a (most important) factor in political society, and that the government is the major possible threat to the individual. These themes, while existing throughout the history of liberalism, vary depending on the particular national and historical context. The focus of this chapter is on the ways in which U.S. liberalism adheres to these broad themes in the Supreme Court cases in the twentieth century.

BROAD LIBERAL THEMES

The three broad themes of liberalism—a focus on rights or liberties, a reliance on the autonomous, rational individual, and the construction of the government as adversary—are infused in the Bill of Rights. This infusion has created a document through which the relationship between government and individual liberty is a negative one. The First Amendment to the U.S. Constitution operates in this negative way, with the individual's right to free speech being protected from government infringement. As a result, both the discourse and the doctrine presented through First Amendment cases have been in keeping with the basic tenets of liberal political philosophy. Following, I draw on U.S. Supreme Court cases to further illustrate how these three main themes in liberal thought have manifested themselves in First Amendment doctrine. Ultimately, these broad liberal themes shaped the way in which freedom of speech has been defined through the First Amendment.

Liberty and the First Amendment

They [the founding fathers] valued liberty both as an end and as a means. They believed liberty to be the secret of happiness and courage to be the secret of liberty. They believed that freedom to think as you will and to speak as you think

are means indispensable to the discovery and spread of political truth; that without free speech and assembly discussion would be futile . . . that public discussion is a political duty and that this should be a fundamental principle of the
American government.

Justice Brandeis, concurring
Whitney v. California, 1926[12]

While defining exactly what liberties are best for the good life is an ongoing process, certain mechanisms were written into the Constitution to ensure
that the pursuit of liberty could continue throughout later generations. The
First Amendment was written to include freedom of speech and press as both
essential liberties in and of themselves and as means to achieve other liberties. As Justice Brandeis noted in his concurrence in *Whitney v. California*,
1926, the founding fathers "valued liberty both as an end and as a means."[13]

Examining the development of First Amendment doctrine through the sedi-
tion cases beginning in 1919 up through the 1969 case of *Brandenburg v. Ohio*
illustrates to some extent the development of the importance of freedom of
speech as a liberty protected inside of the liberal paradigm. Prior to 1919 the
First Amendment received little more than a passing nod from the Supreme
Court.[14] As Chief Justice Vinson pointed out in 1951 in *Dennis v. United States*,
"No important case involving free speech was decided by this court prior to
Schenck v. United States, 249 U.S. 47 (1919). Indeed, the summary treatment accorded an argument based upon an individual's claim that the First Amendment
protected certain utterances indicates that the Court at earlier dates placed no
unique emphasis upon that right."[15] In other words, freedom of speech has not
been consistently valued through the history of the First Amendment, and in fact
seems to have had virtually no value prior to 1919.[16]

In 1919, the Court decided a trilogy of cases that would serve as the foundation for fifty years of struggling with sedition cases in an attempt to give
shape to the nebulous liberty of free speech. These cases—*Debs v. United
States*, *Schenck v. United States*, and *Abrams v. United States*—made up the
initial conversations in the Supreme Court about the role of the First Amendment in society. In effect, those cases set the stage for our current conceptions
of free speech.[17] All three of these cases dealt with accusations of infringement of the Espionage Act of 1917.[18] While *Debs* brought the issue of free
speech and national security to the table,[19] it was not until *Schenck* that the
Court developed a test to determine at what point the liberty of free speech
could be halted in the name of protection of the democratic government.

In *Schenck v. United States*, Schenck and others were convicted for mailing circulars aimed at obstructing the recruitment and enlistment of men into
the military. Schenck argued that he did not play a pivotal role in the compil-
ing and mailing of those circulars and should be protected by the First

Amendment liberty of free speech. Writing for the Court, Justice Holmes dealt with the contention that the information in the circulars was protected under the First Amendment by applying the "clear and present danger" test, which made it unconstitutional for the government in certain circumstances to deny free speech rights.

The "clear and present danger" test was first mentioned in *Schenck* by Holmes. In a brief statement, Holmes applied the test to a particular category of highly dangerous speech: "The most stringent protection of free speech would not protect a man in falsely shouting fire in a theatre and causing a panic. It does not even protect a man from an injunction against uttering words that may have all the effect of force."[20] Holmes's language in *Schenck* served to construct a test that would ultimately limit the parameters of free speech for several decades. It can be argued that Holmes never intended for "clear and present danger" to become a rigid rule pertaining to all inflammatory speech about the government because in subsequent cases he dissented when "clear and present danger" was applied. Furthermore, in *Schenck* he precedes his statement about "clear and present danger" with a statement explaining that there are specific circumstances in which the test would apply: "We admit that in many places in ordinary times the defendants in saying all that was said in the circular would have been within their constitutional rights. But the character of every act depends upon the circumstance in which it is done."[21] Despite the qualifier by Holmes, "clear and present danger" began to be applied to any cases involving group-organized negative opinions about the government, especially those groups with a communist agenda.[22]

These sedition cases show to some extent the relationship between the liberal theme of rights and the development of the First Amendment. As the "clear and present danger" test was modified and developed over time, so was the definition of where the First Amendment fit into the landscape of constitutional rights. Throughout the following fifty years, discourse in First Amendment cases about the role of free speech in society gained form and power.

In *Abrams v. United States*, the Supreme Court provided the first specific discussion of the value of the right to free speech.[23] In *Abrams*, five Russian-born citizens were convicted under the Espionage Act for publishing and distributing leaflets in New York City that were critical of U.S. involvement in hindering the Russian revolution. In what has become one of the most famous free speech case dissents, Holmes makes a broad statement that has become the foundation for our current free speech doctrine. He wrote:

> But when men have realized that time has upset many fighting faiths, they may come to believe even more than they believe the very foundations of their own conduct that the ultimate good desired is better reached by free trade in ideas—that the best test of truth is the power of the thought to get itself accepted in the competi-

tion of the market, and that truth is the only ground upon which their wishes safely can be carried out. That at any rate is the theory of our constitution.[24]

This quote from Holmes, while running counter to the essence of previous First Amendment rulings like those in *Debs* and *Schenck*, was in perfect keeping with a Millian conception of freedom of speech. Holmes in other cases had supported government regulations because "legislative enactments should be presumed constitutional unless they violated fundamental rights."[25] This support of legislative activity even led Holmes to dissent in *Lochner v. New York* in favor of allowing the states to regulate contract making.[26] For some scholars, then, Holmes's opinion in *Abrams* seems out of place.[27] However, Holmes's Millian conception of why we protect speech could be seen not only in his court opinions, but also in speeches and other writings. For example, at a dinner at a Harvard Law School function in 1913 Holmes said that the law embodied within it "beliefs that have triumphed in the battle of ideas."[28] To Holmes, the First Amendment protected the dissemination of truth in the marketplace of ideas. The marketplace of ideas metaphor, one of the most powerful discursive themes in First Amendment dicta, will be discussed in more detail in this chapter's section on liberal autonomy.

Six years after the *Abrams* ruling, Benjamin Gitlow was charged under a New York statute for participating in "criminal anarchy" by producing and disseminating a communist manifesto.[29] Gitlow's conviction was upheld, but not until after the Supreme Court broke new ground by holding that the First Amendment could be applied to the states through the Fourteenth Amendment. The Court found that "freedom of speech and of the press . . . are among the fundamental personal rights and 'liberties'" protected under the due process clause in the Fourteenth Amendment.[30] Although the historical significance of the Doctrine of Incorporation[31] on the development of free speech doctrine should not be minimized, the "liberty" that the Court describes in *Gitlow* is a very limited one. Almost immediately after making its grand proclamation in the majority opinion, the Court went on to explain in detail that this free speech right is not absolute. The opinion read: "That a state, in the exercise of its police power, may punish those who abuse this freedom of utterances inimical to the public welfare, tending to corrupt public morals, incite to crime, or disturb the public peace, is not open to question."[32] The liberty of free speech described in *Gitlow* is a protected right. But this umbrella of protection does not include "publications or teachings which tend to subvert or imperil the government," "publications promoting the overthrow of the government by force," or "articles which tend to destroy organized society."[33] In other words, the liberty inherent in the First Amendment following *Gitlow* is a highly qualified liberty and one without firm boundaries. For example, the Court does not address how to define what materials would qualify as documents intending to overthrow the government or what they mean by destroying organized society.

The Supreme Court's view of free speech as a fundamental, but much restricted, liberty continued through *Whitney v. California*.[34] In *Whitney*, Charlotte Whitney was charged with five counts of violating the California Criminal Syndicalism Act of 1919.[35] Justice Brandeis, in his concurrence in *Whitney*, discussed freedom of speech as an important part of human liberty. He wrote that, according to the founding fathers, liberty should be valued "both as an end and as a means" and that this liberty is intricately connected to the "freedom to think as you will and to speak as you think."[36] Not only did Brandeis offer a link between liberty and freedom of speech, but he also historically situated this connection by attributing it to the founding fathers. Approximately four years later in *Near v. Minnesota*,[37] Brandeis's sentiments about liberty, free speech, and how they must be historically situated are discussed in Chief Justice Hughes's opinion. *Near* focused primarily on the issue of prior restraint. In deciding the position the Court would take concerning the government's ability to restrain publications before they occur, Hughes referred to the conception of liberty and its place in First Amendment analysis. He wrote:

> Liberty of speech and press is also not an absolute right, and the state may punish the abuse. . . . Liberty, in each of its phases, has its history and connotation and, in the present instance, the inquiry is as to the historic conception of the liberty of the press and whether the statute under review violates the essential attributes of that liberty.[38]

For Hughes, the liberty of freedom of speech and press has always existed as an essential liberty, which would seem to expand the scope of the power of that liberty in First Amendment cases. However, Hughes dealt only with the issue at hand—prior restraint. Building on his assessment of inherent liberty, the majority in *Near* concluded that prior restraint, except in rare circumstances,[39] was "an infringement of the liberty of the press guaranteed by the Fourteenth Amendment."[40] Justice Butler, writing in dissent, argued that the Court in *Near* set a new standard for the way freedom of speech would legally be conceived of as a liberty. He wrote that the opinion "gives to freedom of the press a meaning and a scope not heretofore recognized and construes 'liberty' in the due process clause of the Fourteenth Amendment to put upon the states a Federal restriction that is without precedent."[41] Clearly not all Supreme Court justices had yet accepted freedom of speech as an absolute liberty.

While freedom of speech still continued to be fairly restricted compared to today's standards, particularly in cases dealing with communist rhetoric, the discourse about the importance of freedom of speech to human liberty continued to
develop throughout the next decades. For example, in *Dennis v. United States*
the Court ruled against *Dennis*, yet much of the discourse in the dissent promoted the importance of speech in a free society.[42] In *Dennis*, Justice Frankfurter
wrote in his dissent that "freedom of expression is the well-spring of our civi-
lization."[43] He added, "liberty of thought soon shrivels without freedom of expression."[44] Included in Frankfurter's discourse about freedom of speech, however, was a caution that part of that liberty included Congress's need to limit
certain expression. In *Dennis*, freedom of speech is still supported in word only
and only by the dissent. However, these early kernels of free speech rhetoric
soon would be picked up, elaborated on, and applied by the Warren Court.

In the 1960s, as the period of liberty and justice was beginning to take shape,
Court dicta about the importance of the First Amendment to human liberty became more common in speech and press cases. Also taking shape during this
period was the struggle to balance the First Amendment with other constitutional amendments. As this struggle proceeded, the liberty of freedom of speech
was more sharply defined. For example, in 1967 in *Time, Inc. v. Hill*, a privacy
case, the Court explained that the liberty inherent in free speech was not solely
based on "political expression or comment upon public affairs."[45] While the
Court acknowledged that critique of government is an important reason to protect speech, the majority also was concerned with individual self-fulfillment.
The Court stated: "Exposure of the self to others in varying degrees is a concomitant of life in a civilized community. The risk of this exposure is an essential incident of life in a society which places a primary value on freedom of
speech and of press."[46] What the *Hill* ruling illustrates is that by the mid-1960s,
freedom of speech was not just about seditious libel or prior restraint. Through
a series of cases starting in the early part of that century, a broader conception
of the liberty inherent in freedom of speech had developed.

A year later in *Curtis v. Butts*, a libel case, the Court reiterated this dicta from
Hill.[47] The majority in *Curtis* added that this focus on self-fulfillment was a
prime goal of the founding fathers: "This carries out the intent of the Founders
who felt that a free press would advance 'truth, science, morality, and arts in
general' as well as responsible government."[48] By the early 1970s, freedom of
speech had been firmly defined as a key legal liberty both in discourse and in
Court rulings. For example, in the libel case *Rosenbloom v. Metromedia*, Justice Brennan stated that the liberty of the press is so important in U.S. society
that it is the "more deeply impressed [liberty] on the public mind."[49] Not only
is liberty in general a "bulwark" of American life and government, but freedom
of the press is also a major component of that liberty.

Throughout the course of the past one hundred years, the concept of freedom of speech and press has developed into a liberty that is "deeply impressed on the public mind." From the language in the early sedition cases to the speech-restrictive ruling in *Dennis* to the Warren's Court support of free speech protection, freedom of speech as a liberty has developed and changed throughout U.S. Supreme Court history. The liberty of freedom of speech experienced questionable treatment by the Court during the world wars, but even then members of the Court discussed the importance of the First Amendment. This liberty bestowed through the First Amendment received preferential balancing during the Warren Court era and continues to receive that preference decades later. From cases dealing with hate speech to those involving Internet pornography, the liberty of the First Amendment continues in many cases to trump other constitutional rights and liberties.

What this development to date represents for this study is both disconcerting and promising. Throughout the past one hundred years of First Amendment Supreme Court rulings, the Court has given ever-increasing preference to the liberty of free speech over other liberties. However, the history also suggests, much as Kammen did, that the definition of liberty is fluid, changing as the social, political, and historical context changes. This fluidity offers an opportunity for reconceptualizing liberty in terms of equality, a task that will be addressed in greater detail in chapter 3. Before moving on to how that change may occur, it is first necessary to deal with the conception of the autonomous individual in free speech theory and application and the role of the government in protecting or restricting that freedom. These two issues tie directly to why the liberty of free speech has been constructed the way it has at present.

Liberal Autonomy

> The constitutional right of free expression is powerful medicine in a society as diverse and populous as ours. It is designed and intended to remove governmental restraint from the arena of public discussion, putting the decision as to what views shall be voiced largely into the hands of each of us, in the hope that use of such freedom will ultimately produce a more capable citizenry and more perfect polity and in the belief that no other approach would comport with the premise of individual dignity and choice upon which our political system rests.
>
> Justice Harlan
> *Cohen v. California*, 1971[50]

The liberties protected in the liberal paradigm belong not just to the "individual" members of the citizenry, but to a certain, well-defined type of individual. This individual is one whose faculties allow him to be autonomous from others, even as he participates in an organized society. This individual also is rational, so that he will make the best decisions possible utilizing whatever materials or information are available to him. The liberty of freedom of speech written into the First Amendment was designed to protect just such an individual. This liberty of speech and press "is based on the individual's right to 'think as you will and speak as you think.'"[51] The significance of First Amendment jurisprudence in constructing the individual in this particular fashion can be mapped through both the Supreme Court's discourse about the role of speech in a free society and in First Amendment doctrine. By looking at the development of two major discursive themes—"the marketplace of ideas" and "free and robust debate"—as well as at the development of certain areas of free speech doctrine, I explore the ways in which the liberal characterization of the autonomous, rational individual has shaped free speech protection. What will become apparent throughout this discussion is that a main rationale for how liberty of freedom of speech should operate is located in the construction of this liberal, autonomous individual.

Not until the Espionage Act cases in the early 1900s did the first shadowy outlines of our current conception of the First Amendment appear. From those three early cases—*Debs*, *Schenck*, and *Abrams*—there came not only the first free speech doctrine (the "clear and present danger" test) but also the introduction of one of the longest-running metaphors in U.S. free speech history—the "marketplace of ideas."[52]

Holmes introduced the marketplace metaphor in his dissent in *Abrams* when, in describing the magnitude of the need for the protection of speech in a free democratic society, he stated: "The best test of truth is to get itself accepted in the competition of the market."[53] The marketplace of ideas metaphor has a direct relationship to the autonomous, rational individual described in the writings of philosophers such as Mill and Milton.[54] The marketplace, arguably, is the center of Western capitalist democracy. In the liberal sense, the U.S. marketplace discussed in Holmes's dissent was one in which the citizenry would best be able to succeed by their own devices without government involvement. The marketplace where goods and services are exchanged was self-regulating and so government involvement was not only unnecessary but would likely upset the balance of the market. As the Court had previously decided in the substantive due process case, *Lochner v. New York*, the police power of the state should not unjustly interfere with "the right of the individual to liberty of person and freedom of contract."[55] In the *Lochner* scenario, everyone has an equal opportunity to compete in an open market. The individual is the key player in his own destiny. He can choose to participate in the market or not and he is only limited by his own interest and ability.[56] The figurative marketplace of ideas operates by this same reasoning. Everyone has an opportunity to compete in the marketplace of ideas and that market will self-regulate, leaving the best ideas to rise above the din of the market. This figurative marketplace, as developed by the Court, does not question who has (or does not have) access to the marketplace. It also fails to address in any complex way other possible reasons (i.e., social or economic status) as to why some may have a louder voice. Instead, the marketplace is conceived of as open to all autonomous individuals who can participate equally in the conversations with the best ideas surfacing no matter whose ideas they are.

The marketplace of ideas metaphor remained powerful throughout the next seventy-five years of First Amendment case law and led to the development of other discursive themes about the function of speech in U.S. society, including "the answer to speech is more speech."[57] For example, in 1951 in *Dennis v. United States*, the majority, building on the marketplace of ideas theme, further reinforced the autonomous nature of the liberal citizen.[58] In *Dennis*, several members of the Communist Party were convicted under the Smith Act[59] for advocating the overthrow of the government.[60] The larger issue in this case was whether this particular application of the Smith Act violated the First Amendment because the actions of the party members contained "an element of speech."[61] The Supreme Court found that the Act did not violate the First Amendment because it was "directed at advocacy, not discussion."[62] While Dennis lost, the loss was not the result of the Court's indifference to the First Amendment. In fact, Chief Justice Vinson made a plea to the Court to "pay special heed to the demands of the First Amendment marking out the boundaries of speech."[63] The boundaries of speech in the marketplace of ideas created in *Dennis* became defined as a competitive arena where the answer to speech that an individual or group finds disagreeable is more speech, not government restrictions on that disagreeable speech. The majority in *Dennis* found that "the basis of the First Amendment is the hypothesis that speech can rebut speech, propaganda will answer propaganda, free debate of ideas will result in the wisest governmental policies. It is for this reason that this Court has recognized the inherent value of free discourse."[64] In the marketplace of ideas it is imperative that the individual remain sovereign in his ability to speak and express himself.

During the Warren Court era, despite much skepticism about the laissez-faire economic market,[65] the marketplace of ideas metaphor continued to be used in support of the individual's use of speech. For example, in *Time, Inc. v. Hill*, the Court did not rely on the marketplace of ideas; however, the dissent built most of its argument on the metaphor.[66] Justice Harlan, in his dissent, relied on this metaphor to demonstrate his disapproval of the Court's ruling: "'The marketplace of ideas' where it functions still remains the best testing ground for truth."[67] Later in his dissent, he acknowledged that there are places where "the marketplace of ideas doesn't function." However, his point remained that in public debate there is "a strong likelihood of competition of ideas."[68] In other words, so long as speech is in the public arena, the marketplace metaphor holds true—the individual is free to trade ideas and the First Amendment will protect that trade. This free trade, of course, can only occur between parties equally capable of interacting with and producing the same level of social force, the same level of autonomy. In *Hill*, the Supreme Court continued to rely on the marketplace metaphor as a key discursive theme in the development of free speech liberty, further reinforcing the reliance of the autonomous individual in First Amendment jurisprudence.[69]

In 1974, the Court had an opportunity to reconsider the validity of the then more than fifty-year-old metaphor for free speech protection. In *Miami Herald v. Tornillo*, the Court was compelled to look directly at the implications for the free flow of ideas in the economic marketplace.[70] *Miami Herald v. Tornillo* concerned Florida's right-of-reply statute, which granted political candidates the right of equal space in newspapers to answer criticisms or attacks. Florida's statute was found to impose an unconstitutional infringement on the press under the First Amendment. Newspapers, according to the Court, could not uphold the Florida statute because of the serious economic burden it would place on them. The Supreme Court noted that the economic marketplace of the 1700s was "[a] true marketplace of ideas . . . [with] relatively easy access to the channels of communication."[71] The Court reviewed access advocates' allegations that this type of marketplace no longer exists: "Newspapers have become big business and there are far fewer of them to serve a larger literate population. . . . [T]he result of these vast changes has been to place in a few hands the power to inform the American people and shape public opinion."[72] According to access advocates, a marketplace where a few corporations own media outlets has replaced the image of the open market arena where individuals each compete to be heard above the din and as a result, these few booming voices drown out the quieter voices. The Court discussed its concern: "[T]he First Amendment interest of the public in being informed is said to be in peril because the 'marketplace of ideas' is today a monopoly controlled by the owners of the market."[73] This position by the access advocates is interesting, not just because of their current concerns of ownership patterns, but more so because inherent in their argument is the assumption that at some point in the United States we had an equal, functioning marketplace of ideas. Even a group as critical of First Amendment application as the access theorists still firmly bought into the marketplace constructed throughout earlier Supreme Court decisions.

In a unanimous opinion, the justices rejected the access advocates' minimal critique of the marketplace, reaffirming the marketplace of ideas metaphor as an important discursive theme in First Amendment dicta. In *Miami Herald v. Tornillo*, this metaphor takes on new heights by using it to override possible contamination of the economic market of freedom of speech and of the press. What became the key issue in this case was not the increasing corporate control of media outlets in the economic market, but the negative effect of the government's possible involvement in "compelling editors or publishers to publish that which 'reason' tells them should not be published" in the marketplace of ideas.[74] The press is not a corporation in the marketplace of goods; it is a vessel in the sea of the marketplace of ideas. It is operated not by businessmen eager to make a monetary profit, but by "reasonable" editors and publishers. The Court, using this rationale, concluded that any "government-enforced right of access inescapably 'dampens the vigor and limits the variety of public debate.'"[75] I believe that here we see the extent to which the marketplace of ideas metaphor serves as a hallmark of liberal autonomy. Not only can individuals compete equally in the traditional marketplace, but those same individuals can also exercise equal influence on how the media sets its political and social agendas.

Although legal scholars scrutinized the marketplace of ideas metaphor, it continued to appear sporadically in Supreme Court cases. Even in broadcast cases where the Court more readily supported government restrictions on speech, the metaphor was used. For example, in *Federal Communications Commission v. Pacifica*, 1978,[76] the Court stated: "For it is a central tenet of the First Amendment that the government must remain neutral in the marketplace of ideas."[77] Here, because of traditional regulation of broadcast by government, the marketplace metaphor does not stop the speech from being restricted. However, in this same case, Justice Brennan, in his dissent, conjures up "a public free to choose those communications worthy of its attention from a marketplace unsullied by the censor's hand."[78] For Brennan, the marketplace metaphor was such a strong discursive element in free speech cases that even in the area of broadcast, it must be given weight.

In *Texas v. Johnson*, 1989, the Supreme Court again fell back upon the marketplace of ideas metaphor. In *Johnson*, George Johnson burned a flag in political protest and was convicted under a Texas statute that made it illegal to desecrate the American flag. [79] The Court wrote: "The First Amendment does not guarantee that other concepts virtually sacred to our nation as a whole — such as the principle that discrimination on the basis of race is odious and destructive — will go unquestioned in the marketplace of ideas."[80] A symbol such as the American flag can be discussed in a negative manner, even destroyed in protest, in the open market.

The marketplace of ideas metaphor has been a significant building block of the protection of speech in First Amendment discourse. What is of special significance in this discussion of the metaphor is what it represents—the connection of free speech protection to the role of the autonomous individual. This metaphor served to reinforce the liberal conception of the individual. This liberal idea of the rational, autonomous individual and his role in a free democratic society has been such a strong component in First Amendment doctrine that even when the marketplace metaphor faded away as a viable way of thinking about the relationship between free speech and government neutrality, remnants of the metaphor continued to hang on, cropping up in case law as recently as the late 1980s.[81]

A second touchstone discursive phrase in the development of First Amendment doctrine is "free and robust debate." This theme is most associated with the groundbreaking federal libel case *New York Times v. Sullivan,* 1964.[82] Pivotal to the Court's ruling in *Sullivan* was the idea that open speech among citizens is essential to U.S. democracy. In a much-cited passage, Justice William Brennan wrote: "Thus we must consider this case against the background of a profound national commitment to the principle that debate on public issues should be uninhibited, robust, and wide-open, and that it may well include vehement, caustic, and sometimes unpleasantly sharp attacks on government and public officials."[83] Just as was the case with the marketplace of ideas metaphor, the Supreme Court in *Sullivan* did not directly tie the protection of free and robust debate to the liberal conception of the autonomous individual. However, this relationship was strongly implied. Only an autonomous, rational individual would be able to participate in free debate in a manner that would add to the democratic process or the search for truth and a better society.[84]

The ideas expressed in the "free and robust debate" language existed prior to *Sullivan*. For example in *Near v. Minnesota* in 1931, the majority opinion, quoting James Madison, wrote:

> It has accordingly been decided, by the practice of the states, that it is better to leave a few of its noxious branches to their luxuriant growth, than, by pruning them away, to injure the vigor of those yielding the proper fruits. And can the wisdom of this policy be doubted by any who reflected that to the press alone, checkered as it is with abuses, the world is indebted for all the triumphs which have been gained by reason and humanity over error and oppression.[85]

It would be disingenuous to present the position taken above as one that the Supreme Court has unanimously supported throughout First Amendment history. In *Near*, the dissent directly disputed the value of using the First Amendment to facilitate free and robust debate. The dissenters argued that free and robust debate must be carefully balanced to ensure protection of citizens' reputations, property, and personal safety.[86]

Despite their disagreement over how much speech protection was needed to ensure robust debate, both the majority and the dissent relied on the liberal conception of the autonomous, rational individual. The dissenters in *Near* were concerned with the probability that, rational and autonomous or not, individuals cannot have freedom to speak whenever they wish because other liberties, such as peace and personal safety, must be considered. The dissenters in *Near* feared that by reading the First Amendment too broadly one would not have robust debate but instead would have total mayhem and anarchy. Even in *Sullivan*, the Court was divided over when speech crossed the line from robust to chaotic. Nevertheless, as the majority opinions in both *Near* and *Sullivan* demonstrate, the free and robust debate theme holds a major place in First Amendment discourse. And, although not specifically stated, underlying these cases is the idea that the Court need not determine the line between robust debate and chaos. This job falls to the people, the autonomous individuals that make up society, not to judges and jurists.

Following *Near*, the idea of free and robust speech continued to be fleshed out in various U.S. Supreme Court decisions. For example, in *Dennis v. United States*, the majority looked to "free debate" as a way to ensure the "wisest governmental policies."[87] Almost two decades later in *Red Lion Broadcasting Co. v. FCC*, the Court carried the idea of free debate into the area of broadcast regulation: "In light of the fact that the 'public interest' in broadcasting clearly encompasses the presentation of vigorous debate of controversial issues of importance and concern to the public . . . regulations are a legitimate exercise of congressional delegated authority."[88] The Court ruled that public debate is so important that the government may regulate broadcasters to require them to ensure that at least a certain level of debate occurs on issues of public concern.

Other contemporary speech cases discussed free and robust debate among individuals. In obscenity cases, for example, the need for open debate among informed citizens drove the Court away from censoring obscenity based on moral grounds and instead into a complicated (and frequently convoluted) discussion of a possible need to protect obscenity for what it might offer to public debate. In *Miller v. California*, the Court pointed out that when dealing with obscenity the test to determine what should be protected must be based on the value of the particular speech in relation to overall societal concerns.[89] In trying to strike this balance, the majority found that "the protection given speech and press was fashioned to assure unfettered interchange of ideas for the bringing about of political and social changes desired by the people. . . . But the public portrayal of hard-core sexual conduct for its own sake, and for ensuing commercial gain, is a different matter."[90] Only in the most extreme circumstances should government restrict debate among rational individuals.

Libel serves as another area of contemporary Supreme Court rulings that apply the discursive theme of free and robust debate. The libel cases are exemplary in illustrating the relationship between this discursive theme and the liberal conception of the autonomous individual. Constitutional libel law is premised on the need to balance the protection of the individual's reputation with the need for the exchange of information to occur between individuals about other individuals.[91] This need for the exchange of information and ideas was deemed so important in *Sullivan* that the Court developed a test that would in most cases excuse the release of erroneous information so long as that information was not published with "actual malice."[92] As previously noted, *Sullivan* was also the case that coined the expression "free and robust debate."

In libel cases that followed, the Court reinforced and expanded on this theme. *Gertz v. Welch* followed on the heels of both *Sullivan* and *Rosenbloom v. Metromedia, Inc.*[93] In *Sullivan*, the Court made the distinction that public officials would have to prove not only false information in a defamation suit, but also "actual malice" on the part of the publisher.[94] *Gertz* extended that requirement to cover not only public officials but also public figures,[95] while *Rosenbloom* looked at a third possible provision—whether private individuals could be held to the same standards if the issue being covered by the media was determined to be of interest to the general public.[96] *Gertz*, by creating various levels of public figures, struck a balance between the need to protect "free and robust debate" in the press and the competing need to allow individuals to be compensated for damage to their reputation.[97] In striking this balance, the Court first stated that "under the First Amendment there is no such thing as a false idea. . . . But there is no constitutional value in false statements of fact."[98] The majority further defined this tension between the press and the individual: "The First Amendment requires that we protect some falsehood in order to protect speech that matters. The need to avoid self-censorship by the news media is, however, not the only societal value at issue."[99] In *Gertz*, the autonomous individual is the main focus and the individual's connection to robust debate in a free society is central to the argument of how best to construct a First Amendment libel test.

Other libel cases also addressed the free and robust debate theme. For example, in *Rosenblatt v. Baer*, a case dealing with how to define the public official category, the majority stated: "There is, first, a strong interest in debate on public issues, and, second, a strong interest in debate about those persons who are in a position significantly to influence the resolution of those issues."[100] In *Curtis Publishing v. Butts*, the Court reinforced the role of free and robust debate in free speech doctrine.[101] The majority in *Curtis* used even stronger language to support its position: "It partakes of the nature of both, for it is as much a guarantee to individuals of their personal right to make their thoughts public and put them before the community as it is a social necessity required for the maintenance of our political system."[102] Both *Rosenblatt* and *Curtis*, which focus on the importance of public debate, take as base assumptions that a level of equality exists among possible participants in that debate. *Curtis*'s blatant statement concerning "the individuals . . . personal right to make their thoughts public" shows the Court's predilection for protecting what it sees as an already existing right for already existing equally autonomous speakers.

This conversation about the role of debate in a free society continued in *Time, Inc. v. Hill*.[103] In *Hill*, the Court directly linked the role of the First Amendment to ensuring robust debate and the role of debate in securing a well-functioning political society: "The guarantees for speech and press are not the preserve of political expression or comment upon public affairs, essential as those are to healthy government. Exposure of the self to others in varying degrees is concomitant of life in a civilized community."[104] In *Hill*, the Court makes clear that free and robust debate must be protected even when the discussion is not political or about issues of public concern.

Much of the discourse in Supreme Court First Amendment cases involved two major discursive themes—the marketplace of ideas metaphor first invoked in *Abrams v. United States* and the free and robust debate dicta from *New York Times v. Sullivan*. Both themes serve to exemplify a broader theme in liberal democratic theory in the latter part of the twentieth century. In both the marketplace of ideas metaphor and the free and robust debate discourse, the liberal, autonomous individual is key. Once the Court began to recognize the significance of free speech as a liberty, the justices also began to discuss liberty in relationship to the importance of citizens' speech in society. In the early years of this discussion, in cases such as *Near*, the Court struggled with where to draw the line between the need for unfettered discussion and competing needs of other liberties. By 1964, in *Sullivan*, the Court was firmly in favor of "free and robust debate." Freedom of speech is a liberty that exists only through lively and open discussion among rational, autonomous citizens. Without this conception of the individual, neither the marketplace of ideas metaphor nor the free and robust debate metaphor would make sense as currently construed. Both metaphors assume that freedom of speech exists for all with government's only responsibility being to maintain the space (the marketplace) unfettered from government interference in the dissemination of ideas (free and robust debate). This role of the government in protecting or restricting speech is the second principle embedded in the Court's development of the liberty of freedom of speech.

Government Neutrality in U.S. Liberalism

> The fundamental freedoms of speech and press have contributed greatly to the development and well-being of our free society and are indispensable to its continued growth. Ceaseless vigilance is the watchword to prevent their erosion by Congress or by the States. The door barring federal and state intrusion into this area cannot be left ajar; it must be kept tightly closed and opened only the slightest crack necessary to prevent encroachment upon more important interests.
>
> Justice Brennan
> *Roth v. United States*, 1957[105]

One of the major themes in liberal political thought is that governmental power must be constantly held in check. The government poses the greatest threat to the preservation of people's liberties. One way to ensure fairness in government is by having the government adhere to the principle of legal neutrality. For example, in free speech cases, neither the government nor the judicial system can enforce speech restrictions based on the viewpoint of the speaker.[106] A speaker may be restricted for other reasons, such as the time, place, or manner in which the speech is delivered, but he cannot be silenced because of his ideas. This, according to the liberal approach, constitutes government neutrality in speech law.

Early First Amendment cases give substantial discretion to the government. Shortly after the First Amendment was ratified, Congress enacted the Alien and Sedition Act, which would later be followed by other sedition-based laws, including the Espionage Act (1917) and the Smith Act (1940).[107] However, even while the Supreme Court was upholding seditious libel convictions under these acts, the language the Court used to support those convictions favored a minimal government. In other words, the Court did not support a powerful government per se, but in these early cases it found a great threat that allowed for government intervention—the threat to national security. And so the early sedition cases of *Debs*, *Abrams*, and *Schenck* all attempted to reconcile First Amendment rights with the need to protect the government from being overthrown. This reconciling would continue throughout First Amendment cases, with, as decades passed, an increasing movement away from protecting the government and toward protecting the autonomous individual. For example, in *Gitlow v. New York* in 1925 the tension between the need to protect the government from speech that might affect national security and the need to protect speech from needless government censorship was a major issue in the Court's opinion.[108] The majority gave broad discretion to what would constitute valid government restrictions of speech by ruling that "a state, in the exercise of its police power, may punish those who abuse this freedom by utterances inimical to the public welfare, tending to corrupt public morals, incite to crime, or disturb the public peace, is not open to question."[109] Even as this statement discussed the need to prohibit government suppression of speech, it continued to give wide latitude to what constitutes reasonable justification for government restrictions. However, a commitment to more government neutrality comes through in Holmes's dissent. He wrote: "Every idea is an incitement . . . the only difference between the expression of an opinion and an incitement in the narrower sense is the speaker's enthusiasm for the result."[110] Holmes's concern was that the Court, by failing to apply the "clear and present danger" standard, was in effect supporting government censorship of seditious libel.[111]

In the 1950s, the majority in *Dennis v. United States* continued to try to balance protection of free speech and governmental restrictions on speech during times of societal concerns about communism:

> The demands of free speech in a democratic society as well as the interest in national security are better served by candid and informed weighing of the competing interests, within the confines of the judicial process, than by announcing dogmas too inflexible for the non-Euclidian problems to be solved.[112]

In *Dennis*, the Court still struggled with how to honor liberal philosophy's views of a need for neutral government with growing fears of communism. The Court would not settle in favor of a neutral government until *Brandenburg v. Ohio* in 1969.[113] In *Brandenburg*, the Court, building on free speech rulings during the Warren Court years, stated firmly that government regulations that restrict speech based on its proscription of unpopular societal views would not be permitted under the First Amendment.[114] Contemporary speech law's focus on the need for government neutrality is illustrated by other Warren Court decisions. For example in *Roth v. United States*, one of the earlier obscenity cases, the Supreme Court held that not only should the government not be allowed to restrict speech, but in effect must be constantly monitored to ensure that it does not do so.[115] The majority in *Roth* stated that "ceaseless vigilance" is the only way to ensure that Congress or the states do not encroach on free speech.[116]

In another Warren Court case, *Rosenblatt v. Baer*, the Court attempted to determine how to define a public official in libel cases.[117] In *Rosenblatt*, the Supreme Court now expressed a firm support for the importance of the citizenry to keep government in check through open dialogue and critique:

"Criticism of government is at the very center of the constitutionally protected area of free discussion."[118] *Rosenblatt* also had free speech absolutist Justice Black calling for an "unconditional right" of people to say what they want about public affairs.[119] He saw this as a "minimum" guarantee of the First Amendment. The following year in *Curtis*, the Supreme Court summarized the historical meaning of the First Amendment: "The modern history of the guarantee of freedom of speech and press mainly has been one of a search for the outer limits of that right."[120] In other words, by the second half of the twentieth century the Court had moved to a position that the government should have as little room as possible to censor or punish speech.[121]

In *Time, Inc. v. Hill*, the Court talked explicitly about the "chilling effect" that libel can have on the press: "In this context, sanctions against either innocent or negligent misstatement would present a grave hazard of discouraging the press from exercising the constitutional guarantee."[122] In his concurrence, Douglas spoke of the chilling effect: "Once we narrow the gambit of the First Amendment, creative writing is imperiled and the 'chilling effect' on free expression which we feared in *Dombrowski* is almost sure to take place."[123] *Keyishian v. Board of Regents of the University of the State of New York* also spoke of the possible chilling effect: "The danger of that chilling effect upon the exercise of vital First Amendment rights must be guarded against by sensitive tools which clearly inform teachers what is being proscribed."[124] This concern of the chilling effect on speech is directly connected to a fear of government suppression.

In dealing with broadcast regulation, the Warren Court had to handle problems distinct from print media. With broadcast, there were concerns over scarcity of resources, such as bandwidths. As such, broadcasting required some level of government regulation because the airwaves were not only a limited resource, but a public resource as well.[125] For example, in *Red Lion Broadcasting v. Federal Communications Commission*, the Supreme Court balanced government restrictions on speech and protection of speech differently as a result of the spectrum issues.[126] *Red Lion Broadcasting* established that, despite the First Amendment's commitment to government neutrality, when dealing with broadcasting the government can administer a greater amount of restriction on speech because of the limited nature of the spectrum. In the case of print media, however, any attempt by the government to regulate speech would be considered suspect and held to the highest level of scrutiny.

Miami Herald v. Tornillo raised several questions concerning the government's role in the regulation or the promotion of speech.[127] The opinion listed instances where the Court "foresaw the problems relating to government-enforced access as early as its decision in *Associated Press v. United States*."[128]

Those cases discussed, including *Associated Press v. United States*, *Branzburg v. Hayes*, and *New York Times v. Sullivan*, all dealt with the relationship between the government and the press. Following its discussion of these earlier cases, the majority concluded:

> The choice of material to go into a newspaper, and the decisions made as to limitations on the issue and public officials—whether fair or unfair—constitute the exercise of editorial control and judgment. It has yet to be demonstrated how governmental regulation of this crucial process can be exercised consistent with First Amendment guarantees of a free press as they have evolved to this time.[129]

In his concurrence, Justice Brennan elaborated on the historical significance of this contentious relationship between the First Amendment and the government: "Whatever differences may exist about interpretations of the First Amendment, there is practically universal agreement that a major purpose of that amendment was to protect the free discussion of governmental affairs."[130] Despite this "practically universal agreement," Justice White in his dissent raised concerns that the majority was too fearful of government regulation: "The press is the servant, not the master, of the citizenry, and its freedom does not carry with it an unrestricted hunting license to prey on the ordinary citizen."[131]

Other cases immediately following the end of the Warren Court era continued to rely on government neutrality developed during those years. For example, *New York Times v. United States* marked the height of the Court's view of government as the enemy of free speech.[132] This case involved the government's attempt to stop the *New York Times* and *Washington Post* from publishing the Pentagon papers. The Supreme Court found in favor of the press, reaching back to the founding fathers to support its position that the First Amendment stands in direct conflict with the government: "In the First Amendment, the founding fathers gave the free press the protection it must have to fulfill its essential role in our democracy . . . only a free and unrestrained press can effectively expose deception in government."[133]

This fear of government intrusion continued post-Warren Court in a number of different types of speech cases. For example, in *R.A.V. v. City of St. Paul, Minnesota*, the question considered by the Court was not the possible harmful effects of hate speech, but instead the government's right to regulate possibly harmful speech.[134] In the Internet cases pertaining to, among other things, filtering software in public libraries, the Court again focused not on the possible societal harm caused by Internet pornography, but instead on the government's possible infringement of an adult's right to view pornography.[135]

Throughout the history of the Supreme Court's development of First Amendment doctrine, the concern over government control has appeared both directly and indirectly. Early cases such as *Debs*, *Abrams*, and *Schenck* attempted to reconcile the fear of government control of speech with concerns of national security. This balancing continued throughout the 1960s, ultimately finding that unless the government can show substantial reasons for restricting speech, the First Amendment should win out, even in cases involving the lesser protected broadcast arena.

CONCLUSION

The U.S. judicial system has its foundations in liberal philosophy. While conceptions of what constitutes liberty under this philosophy change depending on the time period, three broad themes emerge that connect different conceptions of liberal philosophy. These themes are a focus on rights or liberties, a reliance on the autonomous, rational individual, and the construction of the government as adversary. In this chapter, I reviewed First Amendment case law in regard to those themes in order to illustrate why privileging equality in free speech cases is problematic under current liberal constructions of the individual in society.

First, I demonstrated how the liberty of free speech came to be defined over an approximate fifty-year period. Prior to the sedition cases in 1919, freedom of speech was not a high priority issue for the U.S. Supreme Court. However, starting in 1919, the Court first began to note the importance of the role of speech in U.S. society, specifically stating in cases such as *Abrams v. United States* that free speech required special attention because of its ability to support the spread of truth in a democratic system. Six years later in *Gitlow v. New York*, the Court furthered its position on the liberty of free speech when it stated that "freedom of speech and of the press . . . are among the fundamental personal rights and liberties." The Court reaffirmed this commitment a year later in *Whitney v. California*, noting that "the freedom to think as you will and to speak as you think" constituted a valued liberty. Throughout those early cases, despite its rhetoric about the importance of free speech, the Court continued to limit that freedom in the name of national security. However, the significance of the discourse in those cases would carry heavy weight in both dicta and decisions by the 1960s. At that time, not only was the liberty of free speech attached to the search for truth and the cornerstone of a functioning democracy, but the Court also was incorporating another liberty into the definition of freedom of speech—that of personal self-fulfillment. By the 1970s, the importance of the liberty of freedom of speech was firmly established and clearly defined by the Court.

The second broad theme that I examined was that of liberal autonomy. I proposed that the liberty of freedom of speech is accorded to a particular type of individual, one that remains autonomous in thought and action even as he participates in society. I then tracked this reliance on the autonomous individual by reviewing two key discursive themes in First Amendment Supreme Court cases—the marketplace of ideas metaphor and the free and robust debate discourse. The marketplace of ideas metaphor made its debut in 1919 at the same time that the Court was beginning to give shape to the liberty of freedom of speech. In his dissent in *Abrams v. United States*, Holmes first introduced the metaphor, stating that "the best test of truth is . . . to get itself accepted in the competition of the market." This metaphor would continue to pick up support throughout the next seventy-five years, being cited in a range of speech cases from broadcast to obscenity to flag burning. The free and robust debate discourse would start in the 1960s during the high point of what Kammen identified as the liberty and justice period. In one of the most quoted passages from free speech cases, the Court in *New York Times v. Sullivan* wrote that public discussion must be "uninhibited, robust and wide-open." This discourse would be repeated throughout various cases from that point on, establishing that as long as speech remained unfettered by government censorship then all individuals would remain autonomous to participate equally in the debate.

Finally, I reviewed the third major liberal theme, the reliance by the Court on government neutrality. From the very beginning, the Court has emphasized the absolute necessity for the government to remain neutral in terms of the liberty of freedom of speech. Even in the case of *Gitlow*, who would ultimately be found guilty of violating an anti-syndicalism act, the Court spent considerable time reinforcing that only in very limited circumstances, such as espousal of overthrow of the government, should one lose this liberty. By the 1960s, the pendulum was swinging in the favor of government neutrality in First Amendment cases such as *Rosenblatt v. Baer*, in which the Court argued for an "unconditional right" for people to say whatever they wanted about public affairs. Two years later in *Keyishian v. Board of Regents of the University of the State of New York* the transformation seemed complete when the Court focused on the concern of the chilling effect of government restrictions on freedom of speech.

Taken together the three overarching liberal themes in First Amendment doctrine assume that a level of equality already exists among members of the citizenry and that so long as the government remains neutral, every autonomous individual will be capable of equally contributing to public debate. However, as I illustrated in chapter 1, not everyone has the same access or ability to engage equally. Social, political, and economic status all play a role in how much authority an individual feels in terms of participating in the debate. The Supreme Court, by creating the illusion of open, equal debate, further disenfranchises and often completely silences those who are already disempowered socially, politically, and economically.

In chapter 3, I reconstruct the individual to be one with limited agency instead of rational autonomy. By redefining the individual in this way, I can then reconsider liberty in terms of equality and thus develop a new framework for free speech case analysis that will open public discussion in a more substantial way to disempowered groups.

NOTES

1. MICHAEL KAMMEN, SPHERES OF LIBERTY: CHANGING PERCEPTIONS OF LIBERTY IN AMERICAN CULTURE (1986).

2. The Lochner era spanned the first thirty years of the twentieth century. The Warren Court existed from 1953 through 1969.

3. JAMES MEADOWCROFT, *Introduction*, in THE LIBERAL POLTICAL TRADITION: CONTEMPORARY REAPPRAISALS 1 (James Meadowcroft ed., 1996). Meadowcroft explains: "[Liberal and liberalism] may be variously associated with a particular habit of mind (characterized perhaps as open and tolerant, or less positively as permissive); with a distinctive political current, which emphasizes individual freedom and rights, and stands opposed to both conservatism and socialism; with the ideological perspective of a specific class (commercial and industrial interests, the bourgeoisie or middle class); with a mode of contemporary political philosophy at loggerheads with 'communitarianism'; with the self-understanding of western, market-based representative democracies; or most comprehensively, with the world-view of post-Enlightenment modernity." *See also*, RONALD DWORKIN, A MATTER OF PRINCIPLE (1985) and TAKING RIGHTS SERIOUSLY (1977); JOHN RAWLS, A THEORY OF JUSTICE (1971) and POLITICAL LIBERALISM (1993); LUDWIG VON MISES, LIBERALISM: THE CLASSICAL TRADITION (Ralph Raico trans., 1996) (1927). In POLITICAL LIBERALISM, Rawls defines U.S. conceptions of liberalism in this way: "Political Liberalism assumes that, for political purposes, a plurality of reasonable yet incompatible comprehensive doctrines is the normal result of the exercise of human reason within the framework of the free institutions of the constitutional democratic regime. Of course a society may also contain unreasonable and irrational, and even mad, comprehensive doctrines. In their case the problem is to contain them so that they do not undermine the unity and justice of society," at xviii.

4. *Id*. MEADOWCROFT.

5. While this chapter will focus only on the forms of liberalism manifest in the U.S. political and legal arena, it should be noted that liberalism in the broad sense is the dominant political ideology in both North America and Western Europe.

6. RODNEY SMOLLA, FREE SPEECH IN AN OPEN SOCIETY 65 (1992).

7. ANDREW KERNOHAN, LIBERALISM, EQUALITY, AND CULTURAL OPPRESSION 2 (1998).

8. Richard Bellamy, *Pluralism, Liberal Constitutionalism and Democracy: A Critique of John Rawls's (Meta)Political Liberalism*, 77 in THE LIBERAL POLITICAL TRADITION: CONTEMPORARY REAPPRAISALS (James Meadowcroft ed., 1996).

9. For example, *see* THOMAS HOBBES, LEVIATHAN (New York: E. P. Dutton & Co. 1914) (1651); JOHN LOCKE, TWO TREATISES OF GOVERNMENT (New York: E. P. Dutton & Co. 1924) (1690); IMMANUAL KANT, KANT'S POLITICAL WRITINGS (1970); JOHN STUART MILL, ON LIBERTY (Emery Neff ed., Intro., 1926) (1859); JOHN MILTON, AREOPAGITICA (Richard C. Jebb ed., 1969) (1644); RONALD DWORKIN, A MATTER OF PRINCIPLE (1985) and TAKING RIGHTS SERIOUSLY (1977); and JOHN RAWLS, A THEORY OF JUSTICE (1971) and POLITICAL LIBERALISM (1993).

10. *See* MISES, *supra* note 3, F. A. HAYEK, THE CONSTITUTION OF LIBERTY (1960), HERMAN FINER, THE ROAD TO REACTION (1945), RAWLS, *supra* note 3, and DWORKIN, *supra* note 3.

11. KERNOHAN, *supra* note 7, at 1.

12. 274 U.S. 357, 1105 (1926).

13. *Id.*

14. Although most First Amendment scholars trace the modern conception of free speech to these World War I cases, some scholarship offers an alternative approach. First Amendment scholar David Rabban, for example, found that "[a]lthough the Supreme Court and other federal courts decided many more free speech cases than Chafee revealed and subsequent scholars assumed, a significantly larger number of cases in state courts even more clearly refutes the conventional wisdom that litigation over the constitutional meaning of free speech began in 1917." DAVID RABBAN, FREE SPEECH IN ITS FORGOTTEN YEARS 131 (1997).

15. 341 U.S. 494, 503 (1951).

16. While the U.S. Supreme Court may not have been reviewing many speech cases during this time, some activity was occurring at the state level. *See, e.g.*, RABBAN, *supra* note 14.

17. *Debs v. United States*, 249 U.S. 211 (1919), *Schenck v. United States*, 249 U.S. 47 (1919), *Abrams v. United States*, 250 U.S. 616 (1919).

18. The Espionage Act (1917), the Trading With The Enemy Act (1917) and the Sedition Act (1918) gave the government far-reaching control during the World War I era. The Espionage Act in part called for the prosecution of "persons who sought to effectuate a place of action which necessarily, before it could be realized, involved the defeat of the plans of the United States for the conduct of the war with Germany, must be held to have intended that result notwithstanding their ultimate purpose may have been to prevent interference with the Russian Revolution," at 250 U.S. 616 (1919).

19. In this case, Eugene Debs was convicted under the Espionage Act after he gave a speech in Canton, Ohio, in 1918 discussing "socialism, its growth, and a prophecy of its ultimate success," at 249 U.S. 211, 212.

20. 249 U.S. 47, 52 (1919).

21. *Id.*

22. For discussions of Holmes and "clear and present danger," *see* James Weinstein, *Symposium: Free Speech and Community: A Brief Introduction to Free Speech Doctrine*, 29 ARIZ. ST. L.J. 461 (1997) (discussing Holmes's realization that "clear and present danger" was an "anemic" way to protect speech); Steven J. Heyman, *Righting the Balance: An Inquiry Into the Foundations and Limits of Freedom of Expression*, 78 B.U. L. REV. 1275 (1998) (discussing Chafee's read of Holmes's intention in "clear and present danger"); and Richard A. Primus, *Canon, Anti-Canon, and Judicial Dissent*, 48 DUKE L.J. 243 (1998) (discussing Holmes and the "clear and present danger" test).

23. 250 U.S. 616 (1919).

24. *Id.* at 630.

25. Timothy W. Gleason, *Freedom of the Press in the 1930s: The Supreme Court's Interpretation of Liberty in a Changing Political Climate* 74 (1983) (unpublished M.A. thesis, University of Washington) (on file with University of Washington library).

26. 198 U.S. 45, 46 (1905).

27. *See*, for example, David Rabban, *Emergence of First Amendment Doctrine*, 40 UNIV. of CHICAGO L. REV. 1259 (1983) (stating that not until *Abrams* did Holmes shift his perspective from a majoritarian emphasis to one that favored protection of speech).

28. OLIVER WENDELL HOLMES JR., COLLECTED LEGAL PAPERS 294–95 (1920).

29. *Gitlow v. New York*, 268 U.S. 652, 654 (1925).

30. *Id.* at 659.

31. The Doctrine of Incorporation allows the First Amendment to be applied to the states through the Fourteenth Amendment. Prior to *Gitlow* and the development of the Doctrine of Incorporation, the First Amendment only applied to federal government.

32. *Id.* at 668.

33. *Id.*

34. 274 U.S. 357 (1926).

35. *Id.*

36. *Id.* at 375.

37. 283 U.S. 697 (1931).

38. *Id.* at 708.

39. The three exemptions put forth by Chief Justice Hughes were times of war, obscenity, and fighting words, at 716.

40. *Id.* at 723.

41. *Id.*

42. The *Dennis* Court further suppressed dissident political speech by changing the "clear and present danger" test to a "clear and probable danger" test. Justice Vinson, using "clear and probable danger," argued that the government had a right to protect itself from being overthrown.

43. *Id.* at 550.

44. *Id.*
45. 385 U.S. 374, at 388 (1965).
46. *Id.*
47. 388 U.S. 130, 147 (1967).
48. *Id.*, quoting letter to the inhabitants of Quebec, 1 JOURNALS OF THE CONTINENTAL CONG. 108.
49. 403 U.S. 29, at 51 (1971).
50. 403 U.S. 13, 24 (1971).
51. TIMOTHY GLEASON, THE WATCHDOG CONCEPT: THE PRESS AND THE COURTS IN NINETEENTH-CENTURY AMERICA, vii (1990) quoting *Whitney v. California*, 274 U.S. 357, 1098.
52. For a discussion of the philosophical underpinnings of the "marketplace of ideas" metaphor and subsequent development in First Amendment discourse *see*, Anna M. Taruschio, *The First Amendment, the Right not to Speak, and the Problem of Government Access Statutes*, 27 FORDHAM URB. L.J. 1001, at 1006–10 (2000).
53. *Abrams v. United States*, 250 U.S. 616, 630 (1919).
54. JOHN STUART MILL, ON LIBERTY (Emery Neff ed., Intro., 1926) (1859) and JOHN MILTON, AREOPAGITICA (Richard C. Jebb ed., Folcroft, Pa.: Folcroft Press, 1969) (1644). Both Mill and Milton grappled with the individual in regard to religion and religious truth. Holmes, on the other hand, focused on the U.S. debate surrounding Socialism and Communism. Despite the different reasons for their concern over the role of the individual, each of these men constructed a citizen that was both rational and autonomous.
55. *Lochner*, *supra* note 26, marked the zenith in the era of laissez-faire economics. *Lochner* dealt with a state statute designed to better working conditions for bakers in the city of New York. The Court in *Lochner* found the statute to be in violation of the Fourteenth Amendment, arguing that "[t]here is no reasonable ground for interfering with the liberty of person or the right of free contract, by determining the hours of labor, in the occupation of a baker (46)." *Lochner* remained the ruling opinion in this area of substantive due process until the late 1930s.
56. This ability to participate freely in the marketplace of the Lochner era was reserved only for men. *See*, 208 U.S. 412 (1908) (ruling that states could infringe on women's rights to make contracts to protect women).
57. Taruschio, *supra* note 52, at 1008: "[T]he concept of 'more speech' is central to the marketplace of ideas. 'More speech' means that under the marketplace of ideas paradigm, more speech, never less, is the remedy for false or untrue speech."
58. 341 U.S. 494 (1951).
59. The Smith Act was a peacetime sedition law established by Congress in 1940 and aimed primarily at persecuting members of the Communist Party in the United States.
60. 341 U.S. 494, 502 (1951).
61. *Id.*
62. *Id.*
63. *Id.* at 503.
64. *Id.*

65. KERNOHAN, *supra* note 7.

66. 385 U.S. 374 (1967).

67. *Id.* at 406.

68. *Id.* at 407.

69. Other cases in which the marketplace of ideas metaphor was invoked include *Keyishian v. Board of Regents of the University of the State of New York*, 385 U.S. 588 (1967), *Red Lion Broadcasting Co. v. Federal Communications Commission*, 395 U.S. 366 (1969), and *Cohen v. California*, 403 U.S. 15 (1971). In *Keyishian*, the Court combined the marketplace of ideas metaphor with the language about robust debate: "The classroom is peculiarly the 'marketplace of ideas.' The Nation's future depends upon leaders trained through wide exposure to that robust exchange of ideas (603)." In *Red Lion Broadcasting*, the Court looked at the area of broadcasting regulation and, while finding that there must be more restrictions on speech there, they worked to set up an open market as well: "No man may be prevented from saying or publishing what he thinks, or from refusing in his speech or other utterances to give equal weight to the views of his opponents (386)." In *Cohen*, the Court relied firmly on the marketplace metaphor, tying it explicitly to the individual: "The constitutional right of free expression is powerful medicine in a society as diverse and populous as ours. It is designed and intended to remove governmental restraints from the arena of public discussion, putting the decision as to what views shall be voiced largely into the hands of each of us (24)."

70. 418 U.S. 241 (1974).

71. *Id.* at 248.

72. *Id.* at 249–50.

73. *Id.* at 250.

74. *Id.* at 256.

75. *Id.* at 257, quoting *New York Times v. Sullivan*, 376 U.S. 254, at 279 (1964).

76. 438 U.S. 726 (1978) (dealt with the airing of comedian George Carlin's monologue "dirty words"). The ruling in this case established certain FCC guidelines concerning at what times of day certain indecent or obscene material could or could not be broadcast.

77. *Id.* at 745. It should be noted that the Court, despite this dicta about government neutrality, did rule in favor of some speech restrictions in this case.

78. *Id.* at 772.

79. 491 U.S. 397, at 418 (1989).

80. *Id.*

81. This metaphor also is still being used in lower court cases, including several that will be discussed in chapter 4.

82. 376 U.S. 264 (1964).

83. *Id.* at 270.

84. *Id.* For example, the Court quotes Justice Learned Hand, who said that the First Amendment "presupposes that right conclusions are more likely to be gathered out of a multitude of tongues." Much like Rawls's reasonable individual, the individuals constructed by the Court in *Sullivan* will come to the "right conclusions" so long as they are free to debate.

85. 283 U.S. 697, 716 (1931), quoting Madison, letter sent by Constitutional Congress (October 26, 1774) to inhabitants of Quebec.

86. *Id.* at 732.

87. 341 U.S. 494, 503 (1951).

88. 395 U.S. 367, at 385 (1969).

89. 413 U.S. 15 (1973).

90. *Id.* at 34–35. The decision in this case was not unanimous. Justice Douglas, in his dissent, argued that virtually all speech has place in public debate, including obscene or pornographic speech: "The idea that the First Amendment permits government to ban publications that are offensive to some people puts an ominous loss on freedom of the press . . . the First Amendment was not fashioned as a vehicle for dispensing tranquilizers to the people. Its prime function was to keep debate open." (44–45)

91. *See New York Times v. Sullivan*, 376 U.S. 254, 270 (1964). "Thus we consider this case against the background of a profound national commitment to the principle that debate on public issues should be uninhibited, robust, and wide-open."

92. *Id.* at 279. "The constitutional guarantees require, we think, a federal rule that prohibits a public official from recovering damages for a defamatory falsehood relating to his official conduct unless he proves that the statement was made with 'actual malice'—that is with knowledge that it was false or with reckless disregard for whether it was false or not."

93. *Rosenbloom v. Metromedia, Inc.*, 403 U.S. 29 (1971).

94. 376 U.S. 254, 270, 279–80 (1963).

95. 418 U.S. 323 (1974).

96. 403 U.S. 29 (1971).

97. This particular balancing of speech occurs in all libel cases. The significance here has to do with where the Court struck the balance in *Gertz*, not simply with the fact that a balance was struck.

98. 418 U.S. 323 (1974).

99. *Id.* at 806.

100. 383 U.S. 75 (1966).

101. 388 U.S. 130 (1967).

102. *Id.* at 149.

103. 385 U.S. 374 (1967).

104. *Id.* at 388.

105. *Roth v. United States*, 354 U.S. 476, 488 (1957).

106. The content-neutrality principle in First Amendment doctrine will be discussed at length in chapter 4.

107. Espionage Act, *supra* note 18.

108. 268 U.S. 652 (1925).

109. *Id.* at 666.

110. *Id.* at 672.

111. *Id.* at 671. In *Gitlow*, Holmes explained that while he had problems with the ways in which the Court applied "clear and present danger" in *Abrams*, he was still

hopeful that the standard could be used to protect the "liberty" of free speech. He wrote in the dissent in *Gitlow*: "If I am right, then I think that the criterion sanctioned by the full court in *Schenck v. United States* applies. . . . It is true that in my opinion this criterion was departed from in *Abrams v. United States*, but the convictions that I expressed in that case are too deep for it to be possible for me as yet to believe that it and *Schaefer v. United States* have settled the law. If what I think the correct test is applied, it is manifest that there was no present danger of an attempt to overthrow the government by force on the part of the admittedly small minority who shared the defendant's views."

112. 341 U.S. 494, 524–25 (1951).
113. 395 U.S. 444 (1969).
114. *Id.* at 448.
115. 354 U.S. 476 (1957).
116. *Id.* at 488.
117. *Rosenblatt v. Baer*, 383 U.S. 75 (1965).
118. *Id.* at 85.
119. *Id.* at 95.
120. *Curtis Publishing v. Butts*, 388 U.S. 130, 148 (1967).
121. *Id.* at 163.
122. *Time, Inc. v. Hill*, 385 U.S. 374, 389 (1967).
123. *Id.* at 401–2.
124. 385 U.S. 588, at 604 (1967).
125. 395 U.S. 367, 375–79 (1969).
126. *Id.* at 389 (1969). The Court in *Red Lion Broadcasting* also discussed the nature of the private sector and its power to regulate speech: "There is no sanctuary in the First Amendment for unlimited private censorship operating in a medium not open to all. Freedom of the press from governmental interference under the First Amendment does not sanction repression of that freedom by private interests" at 392.
127. 418 U.S. 241 (1973).
128. *Id.* at 254.
129. *Id.* at 258.
130. *Id.* at 259.
131. *Id.* at 263.
132. 403 U.S. 713 (1971).
133. *Id.* at 717.
134. 505 U.S. 377 (1992).
135. *See Reno v. ACLU*, 520 U.S. 1113 (1997).

Chapter Three

Agency and the Evolution
of First Amendment Analysis

In chapter 2, I identified the three overarching liberal themes in Supreme Court discourse as the acknowledgement of certain liberties, the reliance on the conception of the autonomous individual, and the assumption of the adversarial role of the government. These themes overlap into one position—the autonomous individual must be protected from the state. Liberty viewed through this prism is constructed in part on the premise that, as previously stated in chapter 1, requires an autonomous individual whose rights will be protected by the government from the government. In chapter 2, it becomes apparent that liberty and autonomy are intricately linked together in First Amendment doctrine. As one legal scholar has noted: "Freedom of expression is not only a right that autonomous individuals should have in a liberal democratic society but is essential for maintaining those individuals' autonomy."[1] To a large degree then, liberal democracy depends on the autonomous nature of individual citizens.

As a result of the importance of individual autonomy to historical conceptions of liberty, the notion of autonomy must be reconfigured in terms of partial agency in order to allow for the construction of a liberty of free speech that privileges equality. While legal scholars already have produced research concerning issues of gender and race discrimination (such as sexual harassment or racial discrimination in the workplace), critical analysis of speech law is one area traditionally ignored by feminist scholars. Aside from pornography, most feminist scholarship has viewed the First Amendment primarily as an ally for the disempowered.[2] Recent research focusing on power and agency, however, allows for a reconsideration of the ways in which the First Amendment operates in relation to disempowered groups. By problematizing issues of power and agency in terms of both societal and governmental power, feminist scholarship has opened the door for critiquing current conceptions of free speech in a democratic society.

Although little feminist scholarship focuses directly on the First Amendment, targeting speech law could be one way to foster spaces for diversity. As feminist scholar Wendy Williams has noted: "We [feminists] are at a crisis point in our evaluation of equality and women and . . . perhaps one of the reasons for the critique is that, having dealt with the easy cases, we [feminists and the courts] are now trying to cope with issues that touch the hidden nerves of our most profoundly embedded cultural values."[3] One answer to this "crisis point" is to find new ways of thinking about and analyzing free speech cases. Specifically, this chapter establishes partial agency as a viable alternative to liberal-based autonomy. This new conceptualization of agency brings to the surface the way in which power operates through speech. Once partial agency has been established, I explain the relationship between power and discourse in poststructural feminist terms, illustrating how these theoretical shifts implicate a different analytical framework for free speech cases.

FROM AUTONOMY TO AGENCY

In chapter 1, I argued that the Court needed to move away from a pairing of liberty with justice, as was established during the Warren Court era, in the direction of a new era of liberty and equality. Establishing this pairing of liberty and equality requires a change in the way we conceptualize free speech. However, evaluating women's (as well as other disempowered groups') equality through the First Amendment can be difficult. The First Amendment has been, at varying levels, a proponent for the disempowered. The First Amendment has, for example, protected speech in a way that has allowed disempowered groups to argue for better political and social treatment. However, the same First Amendment protects hateful speech (targeting those disempowered groups) in a way that either leads to violence[4] or in a more subtle, perhaps more insidious assault, silences members of marginalized groups.[5]

Shifting the focus from justice to equality allows First Amendment doctrine to facilitate more progressive speech rights for disempowered groups without losing the benefits that currently exist.[6] The problem is that this shift becomes difficult, or worse yet futile, within the context of what John Dewey termed the atomic individual.[7] In critiquing the Lockean notion of the individual, Dewey suggested that the individual cannot be considered autonomous from the social circumstances in which he exists.[8] Gerald Dworkin described liberal autonomy as a concept difficult to define.[9] It has been defined as "self-rule or sovereignty" and "sometimes as identical to freedom of will."[10] Joel Feinberg, looking at the roots of the word autonomy, stated: "[I]t is plausible that the original applications and denials of those notions [i.e., self-rule, self-government] were to states and that their attribution to individuals is derivative, in which case 'personal autonomy' is a political metaphor."[11] One feminist scholar has defined the role of the autonomous individual in law as a falsely constructed "atomistic individual" whose construction "fails to recognize the inherently social nature of human beings."[12]

Left out of this liberal-based perspective on individual autonomy are any discussions of the ways in which power and agency can be affected by social influences.[13] Because liberalism assumes an autonomous individual who has to fear power abuses primarily from the state, so long as the government is not allowed to punish speech, then the integrity of the individual remains intact. This, of course, ties directly to Berlin's explanation of negative liberty in chapter 2—you can only lack political liberty if someone intentionally and outrightedly impedes you. In other words, U.S. liberalism's reliance on negative liberty in relation to governmental power further reinforces a reliance on the conception of the autonomous individual. While traditional theorists may leave issues of private power[14] unanswered, feminist legal scholars, particularly those coming from a social constructivist perspective, have critiqued women's place in the legal system for decades, with the most recent feminist legal scholarship focusing on just those issues of private power and agency.[15]

Feminist legal scholars have critiqued the liberal conception of autonomy in various ways.[16] The origins of this critique can be traced to the development of dominance theory in feminist scholarship.[17] As noted in chapter 1, dominance theory emerged in response to the liberal feminist or second-wave feminist movement of the 1970s. Unhappy with the liberal feminist agenda of working toward equality inside of the dominant (patriarchal) paradigm, dominance feminists began to critique the very foundations of liberalism. Theorists, such as Catharine MacKinnon, argued that the autonomous person in liberal philosophy and politics was a construct based on male notions of power and privilege and thus designed to perpetuate patriarchal power relations.[18] Women did not fit the liberal conception of autonomy because of the immense power of patriarchy to condition their choices and perceptions. MacKinnon in effect shifted the focus from autonomy to agency. Building on the dominance theorists' ideas about social construction, postmodern and poststructural scholars have further problematized individual autonomy by conceptualizing individuals with varying levels of political and social agency.

For example, feminist legal scholar Jennifer Nedelsky argues that "feminism requires a new conception of autonomy."[19] She explains that while feminists now critique liberalism for taking "atomistic individuals as the basic units of political and legal theory" those same feminists are not "prepared to abandon freedom as a value, nor, therefore [can they] abandon the notion of a human capacity for making one's own life and self."[20] Nedelsky says that ultimately the problem to be solved is "how to combine the claim of the constituitiveness of social relations with the value of self-determination."[21] Agency needs to be defined both in terms of individual will and in the effect of socialization on individuals based on group identity.

Legal scholar Susan Williams argues that "one of the central problems facing contemporary feminist theory, in and outside of law [is] the difficulty defining and explaining the possibility of a feminist conception of autonomy."[22] She explains that when approaching autonomy from a social constructivist position, the traditional view of the autonomous individual "becomes both incoherent and irrelevant."[23] The paradox revealed by Williams, perhaps one could say a postmodern feminist paradox, is that while the traditional conception of autonomy is made "incoherent" inside of the feminist critique, a feminist critique with no theorization of autonomy at all leaves feminism unable to deal with real-world problems. As Williams explains: "Feminists must retain some possibility for people to be more than mere reflections of their social conditioning for theoretical, practical, and personal reasons . . . without it feminism itself becomes incoherent, futile, and useless."[24] If feminism is to remain faithful to its belief in praxis, it cannot simply abandon some conception of an active, resistant political citizen.

Unlike traditional conceptions of autonomy, agency comes from a poststructural feminist reliance on the social constructivist idea of the interaction of the individual and his/her social environments. The concept of agency embodies a different conception of the self than the liberal individual. The self defined in terms of agency has "no authentic or unified 'original' self which can simply be recovered or discovered as the source of 'autonomous' action."[25] The self and self-identity in terms of agency are relational to their surroundings, to their social and cultural influences. Agency infers a dialectical relationship between our ability to claim some agency and the role of social construction in our identity.

One must be careful not to replace the liberal, autonomous individual with the equivalent of a cultural dupe. As Volpp explains in "Talking 'Culture': Gender, Race, Nation, and the Politics of Multiculturalism": "Women are not subsumed by culture, but are in active negotiation with it."[26] Volpp's agent exists in a space where "culture is contested, and not in a static essence."[27] As a result, replacing autonomy with agency requires widening the focus from merely the "individual" to include the cultural and political negotiations that shape and are shaped by the individual. Agency, viewed in this way, "acknowledges an internal, as well, as an external or outwardly oriented aspect of agency."[28] Agency, as I will refer to it throughout the rest of this book, incorporates the definition set out by Kathryn Abrams in "Sex Wars Redux: Agency and Coercion in Feminist Legal Theory," within which agency is described as a person's ability to "develop and act on conceptions of oneself that are not determined by dominant, oppressive conceptions."[29] Because women (and members of other marginalized groups) must contend with dismantling oppressive institutional power structures, their agency is "necessarily partial and constrained."[30] In trying to act within current societal structures, they must actively resist dominant oppressive conceptions of themselves as individuals.

Moving the focus from autonomy to agency has major implications when considering the relationship between liberty and equality in regard to freedom of speech. First, this shift in focus gets us past some of the liberal dilemmas associated with restricting speech, particularly those tied to the marketplace of ideas metaphor and the discourse about the answer to speech being more speech. For either of those First Amendment themes to be applicable, autonomy is a precondition. For example, the assumption behind "the answer to speech is more speech" is that when one person says something hateful to another person, that person can respond to the hateful remark with more speech. However, in a society where certain individuals are socially constructed to be subordinate based on their group affiliation, speaking can be difficult, even impossible, in certain situations.

While this shift creates opportunities to consider different conceptions of the First Amendment, it also opens new areas of concern not problematic under the traditional approach. The neatness of the Enlightenment project, with its perfectly defined political citizen, its reliance on truth, and focus on a universal concept of progress, is replaced by a much messier postmodern individual. This individual exists in a much more complicated political and social arena where there is no "truth" and no perfect political world waiting to be discovered through rational thought. As Volpp points out, "considering cultural evidence when culture is contested, and not in a static essence, is admittedly a daunting task."[31] Tackling this daunting task will require more than simply applying the broad definition of agency discussed above. Agency must be further formulated to allow for both individuality and social construction. In other words, the power of the individual agent must be reformulated as partial or incomplete. Just how this balance is determined will have great consequences for a new formulation of speech law.

Various feminist scholars have developed different theoretical constructs of a legal/social agent who is "neither fully free nor completely determined."[32] For the purpose of this project, I focus primarily on the conceptions of agency developed by Higgins and Abrams. The work of these two scholars is most closely connected with theorizing power relations and comparing the individual's agency to areas of constitutional law. For example, Higgins's work on agency is concerned with developing a definition that will work within a liberal democratic framework. Abrams, while taking a broader approach to developing her idea of partial agency, offers the most complete description of how to determine agency and how that determination might affect legal outcomes. Following are descriptions of Higgins's and Abrams's conceptions of incomplete or partial agency. Once I have outlined their perspectives, I will use poststructural theories of power to add depth to the conception of partial agency, making it more applicable to speech law.

HIGGINS AND INCOMPLETE AGENCY

Building on a social constructivist foundation,[33] Higgins develops her own conception of incomplete agency. Incomplete agency, according to Higgins, "expresses the idea that, in a range of legal contexts, women's choices should be understood as neither fully free nor completely determined."[34] In other words, incomplete agency means that women are not completely subordinate to men, as dominance theory implies, but they also do not have the power of the individual assumed in the foundation of liberal philosophy. Higgins starts her critique by pinpointing one of the major tensions in constitutional law and theory: how to balance the "respect for majoritarian will and the protection of individual autonomy."[35] She argues, as have other feminist scholars discussed herein, that "mainstream constitutional theory's assumption of individual agency yields a distorted conception of women as citizens."[36] The problem in the legal system lies not in the way the laws are applied, but in the ideological construct of complete agency that supports those applications.

Because of the manner in which the "citizen" is constructed in liberal theory, the development of the individual "lacks a critique of power beyond that exercised by the state."[37] In this system, so long as the citizen remains free from governmental restraint or coercion, the individual remains free. While acknowledging that this conception of freedom seems the correct fit with a commitment to popular sovereignty, Higgins counters: "Nevertheless, whether expressed as the confidence of democrats in the political process or the focus of rights foundationalists on the threat of state power, this assumption of individual agency oversimplifies the relationships between citizenship and democracy by ignoring the interdependence of identity and public power."[38] She suggests that individual agency must critique both political, external constraints and nonpolitical constraints.[39] The nonpolitical constraints are social and cultural constraints that "are cultural and widespread, rather than individualized and specific."[40] As a result, incomplete agency as defined by Higgins mandates that freedom be redefined. Freedom must be seen not as a preexisting condition that comes automatically with democracy, but instead as a socially constructed state that carries with it unequal power relations.[41] For example, she uses the case of *United States v. Virginia (VMI)*[42] to illustrate "the connections among constitutionalism, democracy, and mainstream assumptions about identity."[43] She explains that both Justice Ginsburg's opinion and Justice Scalia's dissent express the same set of assumptions about the individual's agency, concluding that as a result:

> Neither the majority opinion nor the dissent in *VMI* adequately confronted the interdependence of public and private power in the regulation of gender. Whereas Justice Scalia ignored the influence of prior state action on the expression of gender-specific preferences in the democratic process, the majority focused solely on the need to limit such state entrenchment of gender norms. In so doing, the majority opinion calls into question the ability of the state to reshape those norms to promote gender equality.[44]

This focus on state action as the root to gender inequality ignores "the economic and political subordination of women"[45] and consequently fails to address persistent inequality "ranging from the systematic economic disadvantage that women experience due to their disproportionate responsibilities within the family to the persistent threat of gender-based violence in the home and the workplace and on the streets."[46] Higgins sees political freedom as necessary to facilitate individual and social freedom. She calls for the development of "a feminist conception of freedom" in which feminists would distinguish between cultural constraint and individual agency.[47]

To bridge this gap, Higgins focuses on the relationship between freedom and power, a relationship in which power is relational and cultural, not state sanctioned and imposed, "where power dictates freedom not because the powerful escape social construction but because in our society power is socially constructed as freedom."[48] Higgins explains that as a result of this relationship between power and freedom, "freedom must be defined and defended as a set of social conditions, not as the absence of political or social constraints."[49]

For Higgins, even the most basic traditional conception of free speech would fail to facilitate real freedom for marginalized groups. Not everyone begins with the same level of cultural or social freedom, so the First Amendment, as a negative liberty, does not create a "free citizen." In order to create active democratic citizens, the First Amendment would have to be read in a way that would both recognize incomplete agency and facilitate movement toward more complete agency.

In Higgins's analysis women are plagued by both political institutional constraints and social/cultural institutional constraints. However, Higgins's focus remains on the political institutional constraints. While she mentions the need to incorporate the social/cultural effects on individual development, she only hints at how that might happen. While her approach offers a starting point for analyzing the role of agency in the study of freedom and power, she stops short of actually theorizing power in any meaningful way. She offers a directive of what needs to be done—a standard must be developed that would "entail both a substantive conception of equality and a procedural conception of democratic function"[50]—but does not offer a formulation of incomplete agency that would facilitate those substantive and procedural changes.

ABRAMS AND PARTIAL AGENCY

Legal scholar Kathryn Abrams has written two key articles theorizing a form of partial agency. She argues that agency must be reformulated before substantive change can occur in the current patriarchal legal system. Her first article, "Sex Wars Redux: Agency and Coercion in Feminist Legal Theory," published in 1995, was written in reaction to the ways in which feminists at the time constructed a version of women's agency.[51] She offers an historical background of feminist theory's development of partial agency.[52] She explains that "the first distinguishing feature of the emerging critique has been an account that foregrounds questions of agency, more concretely juxtaposing women's capacity for self-direction and resistance on the one hand with often-internalized patriarchal constraint on the other."[53] Abrams retains many of the constructivist suppositions of dominance theory, most notably that women are both "impeded" and "shaped [by] sexualized oppression."[54] As a result of this oppression, women operate with limited or partial agency. However, Abrams takes issue with dominance theory because she believes that it offers little to no room for women to combat oppression.

Abrams sees resistance as difficult, but not impossible. Following from this general theoretical understanding of partial agency, she suggests that there are five possible legal or political strategies available under agency theory.[55] These strategies range from minimal changes to the law in only the most egregious areas of oppression to a complete overhauling of certain major legal rules.[56] She supports using the latter strategy to bring the abstract theory of partial agency to bear on tangible legal issues.[57]

Through this strategy, she encourages a modification to existing legal rules in an effort to remove legal mechanisms that lead to "a dichotomous characterization of women's legal subjectivity."[58] She would deal with this dichotomy by "ordaining legal intervention or mitigation for those who lack the capacity to act for themselves, and denying legal relief to those who demonstrate agency or responsibility."[59] In this way, Abrams uses partial agency as a theoretical wedge to separate rigid liberal notions of total autonomy from equally rigid feminist conceptions of the socially or biologically constructed woman. In this strategy, women's legal subjectivity would need to be considered in a different way. Currently, according to Abrams, women in the legal system are characterized in one of two ways: either they are autonomous, active individuals, or they are powerless, passive victims.[60] Abrams argues that the system needs to be altered in a way that will allow for consideration of more complex subjectivity. The very assumptions of liberal legal subjectivity need to be reconsidered "in accordance with more sophisticated accounts of liberal subjectivity or poststructural accounts of a decentered subject."[61]

As one example of how this version of partial agency could be directly applied to law, Abrams looks at sexual harassment. In the case of sexual harassment law, she explains that one of the key problems in pursuing a sexual harassment claim is the Court's focus on a specified set of reactions of unwelcome behavior. The level or type of resistance that women express in the face of accused sexual harassment becomes determinant, to a certain degree, of whether sexual harassment occurred in the first place. Women must resist in specified legal ways to serve as proof that harassment occurred. Abrams argues that this approach to sexual harassment offers a false dichotomy in which women either react to harassment in the legally acceptable way and thus prove harassment, or they react in a way not recognized by the legal system and so are not able to maintain a sexual harassment case. Women, for example, must voice timely complaints about the harassment or make drastic moves to get away from the harasser in order to show that they were resisting the advances—either active and autonomous or powerless and passive.

Abrams argues that research has shown that often women who are confronted with harassment in the workplace will use "jocularity, changes in subject, or efforts to avoid the perpetrator" as a means of defense instead of a "straightforward, frontal assault" against the perpetrator.[62] For the courts to acknowledge these various acts of resistance, the legal system would have to concede to some level of partial agency:

Acknowledging partial agency means looking for responses outside the range of the autonomous liberal subject or the wholly dominated victim, responses consistent with the broad notion that women strive to affect their environments and direct lives, even when their chances of doing so are limited by structures or relationships of oppression.[63]

While in "Sex Wars Redux" Abrams carefully explains the problematic nature of dichotomous subjectivity in current legal application, she does not discuss how courts might begin to construct a more complex subject. In "From Autonomy to Agency: Feminist Perspectives on Self-Direction,"[64] Abrams shifts the focus more specifically onto the actual construction of a theory of partial agency. In this article, Abrams suggests that there is "a collective dimension to the development and exercise of autonomy," a significantly different view than one supported by conventional liberal doctrine.[65] This group-based approach to agency argues that the individual operates not as an autonomous being but instead as part of a group(s) with which she identifies or is identified. These groups are socially constructed and as such some groups are culturally constructed with less agency or autonomy than others. Agency for socially and politically disempowered groups is formed to a certain degree by the contestation of power relations among various groups. She explains that "practices contributing to socialization may operate not simply on individuals, but on individuals as members of groups."[66] As a result, both individuals and groups can work to resist socially assigned definitions of who they are and what their place should be in society.

Agency then is defined not as a political condition separate from social influences but instead as a contested space where social norms privilege certain groups over others. In the case of women, for example, negative social and cultural norms based on gender are not mere coincidence, but instead "are a product of, and a means by which, women's oppression is perpetuated in particular settings."[67] These cultural norms not only have an adverse affect on the ways in which women view themselves and their choices, but they also have the opposite effect on the more privileged group, allowing members of that group to "see themselves as attractive, competent, and capable in relation to others, permitting them to undertake a wide range of choices and projects."[68] Using this reasoning, Abrams calls for "a feminist theory that underscores the collective dimension of self-definition and self-direction."[69]

Constructing agency in this way sidesteps the uncritically optimistic role of the individual in liberal theory, but also refutes the total pessimism of the controlled subject in dominance theory. Thus, partial agency opens the door to the possibility of an emancipatory movement by individual members of disempowered groups. As Abrams explains, partial agency can "reflect inevitable gaps in the structures that produce oppression, as well as the assertion of a multiple-constructed will: they occur in what we might conceive as the conceptual space between social influence and social determination."[70] In other words, switching from autonomy to agency brings to the surface the negotiated power relations that take place in different contexts and in varying degrees of societal interaction.

Abrams takes this theoretical premise about the mechanics of political and social agency and applies it specifically to legal institutions.[71] She suggests the possibility of two approaches to affecting law: either by "drawing on the explicit prescriptive, or prohibitive, power of legal rules"[72] or by focusing on "the constitutive role of legal ideas and images."[73] Abrams ultimately asserts that by formulating a type of partial agency for disempowered groups one could work to reconstruct the liberal legal system to "comprehend and respond to a human subject whose self-definition and self-direction have more the quality of feminist agency than of liberal autonomy."[74] Self-direction in this type of framework exists on two levels. It can be resistant or transformative. Resistant self-direction occurs when individual members of disempowered groups actively challenge dominant ideological constructs of their group in an effort to achieve their larger individual goals.[75] Those practicing resistant self-direction may not be aware that they are challenging dominant constructions of themselves. They also may not participate in "explicit confrontation," but instead resist in more subtle ways. For example, women who are confronted with sexual harassment on the job often respond, not aggressively, but through more individual resistance such as leaving the room when the behavior occurs or simply avoiding the perpetrator of the harassment whenever possible.[76]

In transformative agency, the individual is aware that they are challenging culturally oppressive norms. This type of agency "may be reflected in resistance aimed at formal political or legal institutions by individuals or groups."[77] One example of transformative agency is the "Take Back the Night" movement. In this movement, women sought to reclaim public spaces where they did not have free access because of fear of danger.[78] Other examples of transformative agency include Catharine MacKinnon's work in sexual harassment law and the production of underground "fanzines" for women.[79]

In the legal arena, Abrams argues that there are two instrumental approaches. Legal actors could use the power of prohibitive legal rules to attempt to foster women's agency. For example, prohibitive rules in the area of pornography could be used to correct unequal power relations that result from patriarchal constructs of women as sexual objects.[80] A second instrumental approach would rely on "the constitutive role of legal ideas and images."[81] In other words, legal rules would need to be changed to acknowledge different levels of individual and group resistance.[82] For example, in the area of sexual harassment, women are currently required to prove that they were clear that the behavior was unwelcome. Changing the constitutive role of law would require courts to reconsider what types of responses by the victim clearly demonstrate to the perpetrator that the behavior in question is unwelcome sexual harassment.

While Abrams outlines an approach for how one might begin to use partial agency to alter current legal applications, she still stops short of actually describing a concrete approach to case analysis. She acknowledges that because partial agency depends so much on the context of oppression involved, no single overarching theory of law can be developed. Each area of law will have to develop independently. In the area of speech law, Abrams does discuss some implications of partial agency theory on the pornography issue. She states these changes may lead to pornography restrictions that "may help foster agency."[83] However, she does not follow through on exactly how that might occur.

Abrams concludes that two things need to occur before theories of agency can be implemented in a legal system based on autonomy. She argues that the legal system would need to both "more fully acknowledge . . . the social formation of the human subject" and "acknowledge variation and contingency, not only in the agency of a given subject, but in other human attributes as well."[84] Ultimately, she concludes that these "transformational steps" would have to occur before notions of agency could have any impact in the legal arena.[85] The following theorization of agency is an attempt to enter into this scenario described by Abrams. By using poststructural feminist conceptions of power, I am able to move Abrams's theory of partial agency to a concrete level of legal application in free speech law.

POWER AND DISCOURSE

In order to discuss partial agency in relation to freedom of speech, the agency of the marginalized groups needs to be accounted for at the outset. Current theories of partial agency are not formulated in a manner that will allow for application in the area of free speech. Abrams comes closest to developing a working model of partial agency; however, she fails to adequately explain the interconnectedness of social or cultural power on the one hand and governmental or constitutional power on the other. The definition of power developed in this section draws primarily from poststructural feminist conceptions. Defining power and discourse is key to reconfiguring Abrams's theory of partial agency to construct an analytical framework for First Amendment free speech cases.

As explained in chapter 1, poststructuralism assumes that there is no authentic self to be recovered, but rather a self that is constructed by various societal elements such as language and discourse. The effects of poststructural theory on feminist studies have been a recognition of the category of gender being constructed by language and that social structures are not fixed, but instead are given meaning through discourses.[86] Instead of being seen as fixed and material, power is relational, historical, and discursive. Power in this scenario is not solely, or even mainly, located in obvious centers of power, such as the government, but is instead diffuse throughout society and, as a result, more difficult to isolate, define, or resist.

This theory of power shifts the focus from government as the key power point to power being located throughout other areas of society as well. This shift in focus offers a radically different approach to the normalized humanist approach in liberal democracy. As Jana Sawicki explains, this shift in the focus of power offers an alternative in which "the classical liberal normative contrast between legitimate power and illegitimate power is not adequate to the nature of modern power."[87] This approach to viewing modern power translates into a system of power in which control is not forceful or overt, but instead is relational and reconstructive. For example, Sawicki, relying on theories of Michel Foucault, explains that by defining power through discursive practices, a "social field" is created in which power "can attach to strategies of domination as well as to those of resistance."[88] In this conception, power is diffuse and exhaustive but also, as a result of its continual production and reproduction, able to facilitate resistance and liberation. Sawicki argues that "[A]ccording to this analysis of power and resistance, freedom lies in our capacity to discover the historical links between certain modes of self-understanding and modes of domination, and to resist the ways in which we have already been classified and identified by dominant discourses."[89] To Sawicki, this translates into opportunities for "refusing to accept dominant culture" and thus the opportunity for creating resistant cultures.[90]

A significant problem for feminist scholars in using this type of poststructural approach is that it makes political and social praxis difficult. The difficulty lies in trying to address oppressive power when those power points are diffuse throughout society, not only institutional but cultural as well. This "diffusion of the political" means that "the power to produce political inequalities emanates not only from the institutions of the political system per se, but from the social, cultural and linguistic practices."[91] As a result of this diffusion, resistance to oppression must occur not only, or even mainly, at the governmental/institutional level, but at the social, cultural, and linguistic level as well.[92]

One way to think about this combination of governmental and social power is through Chantal Mouffe's interpretation of the process of hegemony. Mouffe, building on Antonio Gramsci's conception of hegemony, establishes two ways in which oppressive power is maintained—expansive hegemony and transformative hegemony. In order for the dominant ideology to be maintained, it must expand just beyond the limits of that ideology so as to achieve

active consent from those who are subordinate.[93] Gramsci took the original
Marxist concept of ideology a step further by adding to it the concept of
hegemony.[94] In Gramsci's first elaboration on the process of hegemony, he
explained:

> The proletariat can become the leading [*dirigente*] and the dominant class to the
> extent that it succeeds in creating a system of alliances which allows it to mobi-
> lize the majority of the working population against capitalism and the bourgeois
> State. In Italy, in the real class relations which exist there, this means to the ex-
> tent that it succeeds in gaining the consent of the broad peasant masses.[95]

Hegemony then, broadly defined, refers to the process by which ideologies
are maintained. According to hegemony theory, institutions work together to
enforce dominant ideologies, although not through direct pressure. Subordinate classes willingly buy into their own subordination by accepting dominant ideologies.

Hegemony theory, however, does not claim that only the dominant ideology can be presented. This theory also states that this ideology is constantly
contested and must be "continually reproduced, continually superimposed,
continually negotiated and managed, in order to override the alternative and,
occasionally, the oppositional reading."[96] Gramsci noted that hegemony operates in two ways: through "domination (legal force)" and through "intellectual and moral leadership (political persuasion)."[97] According to Mouffe,
these hegemonic processes can be explained through the terms transformative
or expansive hegemony. Transformative hegemony is the process through
which law is used to maintain majority consensus.[98] Expansive hegemony, on
the other hand, maintains active consent from subordinate groups through
subtle coercion by moral, political, and intellectual leaders.[99] This subtle coercion, for example, may take the form of a policy being constructed that offers some concession to members of the subordinate group but in actuality re-
produces and supports the values and interest of the dominant ideology.

Both Higgins and Abrams addressed the difference between overt legal
power and more discrete social power. Higgins explained that one must consider "the interdependence of identity and public power."[100] This means that
oppressive power exists at both the "political external" level and the "social
and cultural" level.[101] Despite this diffusion of power, both Higgins and
Abrams express the possibility of altering the social, cultural level by taking
action at the political level. In effect, Abrams's development of a theory of
partial agency comes from an attempt to address this contemporary conun-
drum in poststructural feminist theory concerning the usefulness or even possibility of political reformation created by poststructural influences.

Abrams offers a breakdown of societal power similar to that offered by Mouffe, except that while Mouffe focuses on the ways in which dominant, oppressive power is maintained, Abrams focuses on how dominant, oppressive power can be resisted. Abrams uses the terms resistant agency and transformative agency to illustrate how this opposition might occur. As explained earlier, resistant agency occurs at the unaware individual level, while transformative agency occurs through intentional attempts to subvert or overcome gender-based oppression.[102]

In each of these discussions of dominant power and resistance to oppression, the operation of power is complicated by the ability of systems of oppression to maintain and reproduce themselves. However, resistance is not impossible. Resistance in the legal sphere also can be valuable in altering cultural patterns of oppression. Following, I discuss how power operates specifically in free speech and how the First Amendment can be reconceptualized to use transformative agency to facilitate more active resistance by disempowered groups.

POWER, DISCOURSE, AND THE FIRST AMENDMENT

Power in contemporary society is discursive, relational, and historical. This conception of the way in which power manifests itself in society has implications for the ways in which free speech law needs to be reconfigured. Before offering the alternative framework to First Amendment case analysis, I first discuss how discourse connects to the First Amendment and the significance of relational/historical power to free speech.

Studying the power of the discursive nature of the First Amendment has implications for the reconceptualization of agency and its relationship to speech. The power of discourse in modern society lies in its ability to "mask the actual character of modern power and thus to conceal domination."[103] This critique of power in relation to social and cultural normalization allows one to study the discursive role of First Amendment doctrine inside of the normative liberal system. These discursive themes, such as the "marketplace of ideas" or the "answer to speech is more speech" operate to disguise the ways in which modern power functions. The key to these discursive themes is a focus on the need to ensure that the government does not censor speech. This "repressive hypothesis"[104] assumes that "power functions essentially negatively through such operations as interdiction, censorship or denial."[105] However, if power is both repressive and productive, then the "proliferation of liberationist discourse" becomes a way to further mask domination.[106]

This subtle form of domination has implications for the First Amendment and its ability to foster liberty. Modern power operates "not by negating opposing forces but rather, utilizing them, by linking them up as transfer points within its own circuity."[107] In the case of free speech, marginalized speech is not "negated by opposing forces." Instead, this speech is seemingly supported, and yet it is through that seeming support that the power of those unpopular groups is controlled. Through the creation of a discourse about an "untouchable" First Amendment that protects everyone's right to political participation, members of marginalized or disempowered groups, in effect, "retool" themselves. If members of those groups believe that everyone can speak, then the messages that are most often expressed must be the messages that won out in the debate. This system of government-protected speech presupposes a debate that never happens. The power is not in censoring speech. The power is in the illusion of the openness of the debate.

The First Amendment utilizes various discursive elements in the maintenance of this open debate, including discursive themes such as "the answer to speech is more speech" and the "marketplace of ideas." According to the discourse in these themes, the oppressive power to be feared is from direct governmental/legal action. Also inherent in these free speech themes is the idea that by giving the individual the liberty to speak then that individual alone can fight oppressive power. However, that conception assumes that power, both resistant and oppressive, is embedded in the agency of the individual speaker. This discourse, then, does not account for other oppressive power, such as the expansive hegemony described by Mouffe. Nor does it consider the possibility of the type of group-based identity and agency expressed through Abrams's theory of partial agency.[108]

This discourse does not account for how power operates relationally and historically and, as a result, under the guise of free speech for everyone, the First Amendment maintains the status quo of societal power dynamics, reinforcing inequalities among certain disempowered groups. Because power operates relationally it does not exist in the individual speaker but instead in the interstices between speakers. Also, because power is historically created and reinforced, it is not a power between individuals, per se. Instead, the power occurs between individuals as members of socially constructed groups. Social construction is not undirected but instead operates through a process by which "intersecting practices of construction [are] shaped by more powerful groups that tend to socialize less powerful groups to various forms of subordination."[109] As a result, while everyone is to some degree socially constructed, members of subordinate groups are constructed primarily by those groups oppressing them.

A different way to conceptualize the power of free speech is to locate the power not in the individual exerting or resisting it, but instead to the relational space between the speakers. By locating the power in the interstices, the relationship between the Court and free speech changes as well. If power operates between speakers who are members of culturally constructed groups, then the First Amendment can be used to facilitate changes in social power by opening avenues for those disempowered groups.

In Abrams's model, this would be most similar to using an instrumental change in the law to advance the possibility of more transformative agency. However, in Abrams's model transformative agency is focused on getting the government to address specific social inequalities and oppressions. One example of this model would be MacKinnon's work in the creation of sexual harassment law. In the example of the "Take Back the Night" marches, again, the transformative agency involved is focused on a specific issue of gender oppression.

In my model, the government would alter the First Amendment in a much broader sense. Instead of focusing on specific areas of social oppression, such as sexual harassment, my model argues for altering speech law in a manner that would allow for more transformative agency by women to occur without actually having the government directly involved with deciding how that transformation should be accomplished. Using this approach would work to circumvent the problems of expansive and transformative hegemony set out by Mouffe. By offering a solution that is neither totally government-focused (i.e., sexual harassment law) nor totally culturally focused (i.e., "Take Back the Night" marches), this approach to reconfiguring First Amendment case law avoids the hegemonic power in both transformative and resistant agency. For example, according to Abrams, agency and instrumental change are connected in that one can be used to directly affect the other, i.e., sexual harassment law. In Mouffe's model this won't work because those moments of transformative agency, which are so reliant on government/institutional involvement, are swallowed up by the transformative hegemony. The approach I take here argues not that the government should enforce speech for disempowered groups. Instead, because the Court already makes choices concerning what speech to protect or not protect, it can reconfigure the First Amendment to choose to protect or not protect speech based partially on the disempowered status of certain cultural groups. The new space being created by the First Amendment in this scenario does not address a particular type of transformative agency to be taken nor does it give the government the power inherent in Abrams's conception of transformative agency to steer where and how the resistance will occur.

The intricacies of altering the way in which speech law is construed requires the Court to recognize that power is not located in the individual speaking. Power is located in the negotiated space between speakers. What that means needs to be explained in terms of the development and application of the First Amendment. Scholars and jurists who subscribe to traditional notions of the operation of free speech in society locate power in each individual, autonomous speaker. Under the traditional perspective, every speaker has equal power to speak because they have been afforded equal, neutral treatment under the First Amendment. Switching the focus from autonomy to agency necessitates establishing more accurately where power is located during speech moments. Critical theorists have relocated the power but many of them have placed too much emphasis on the person being inflicted or harmed by the speech. Or, at least, their work could be interpreted this way and has been by the Court. For example, much of the scholarly legal work created by critical race theorists in reference to hate speech spoke almost entirely about the power of that speech to silence members of disempowered groups. Placing this much emphasis on the individual harmed leaves the Court room to argue that the First Amendment should not be used to protect the most squeamish among us. It also opens up a space for traditional adherents to find counterexamples of instances where members of disempowered groups have exercised their right of freedom of speech and press. Shifting the focus toward the negotiated space between speakers in specific speech moments moves the discussion past whether the power of free speech is in the speaker or conversely, in the case of some critical theory, in who constitutes the listener. It also allows us to flip the traditional adherent's argument that focuses on those moments when members of disempowered groups do speak. If the power of speech is located in the negotiated space between speakers, then it only follows that on some occasions those speech moments will allow for active engagement by the disenfranchised. Considering this power dynamic in relationship to existing analytical tests for speech cases allows the Court to recognize the way in which power operates between individuals and the way in which individuals are constructed by dominant cultural ideas and values.

Under current First Amendment free speech doctrine, the historical relationship of group identity to individual power cannot be considered, nor the power embedded between individual speakers. As a result, the framework developed here requires a rebalancing of power based on power being read as relational and historical. Specifically, reading power at the interstices that is predominantly based on socially constructed group-identity requires First Amendment analysis to incorporate three elements when considering free speech cases. In place of the traditional focus on whether the regulation in question is content-neutral or content-based,[110] this framework requires a more multifaceted approach. This approach would include a three-part framework that would consider: (1) the character, nature, and scope of the speech restriction; (2) the historical context of the cultural groups involved in the speech at issue; and (3) the individual power relations occurring at the particular speech moment.

Current free speech analysis is based in large part on content neutrality. However, as will be discussed in detail in chapter 4, this principle creates a two-dimensional approach that has been interpreted in so many different ways as to leave the principle an inconsistent test. This principle developed out of a concern for government censorship of speech based on favoritism or hostility to the ideas being expressed. While the application of this principle has not worked consistently, the fear of government suppression of unpopular speech cannot be ignored. So, the framework suggested here first replaces the two-dimensional content-neutrality principle with a consideration of the character, nature and scope of the speech.[111] By reviewing the restriction in terms of the character of the speech (i.e., political speech, commercial speech), the nature of the restriction (i.e., content-based, viewpoint-based) and the scope of the restriction (i.e., a total ban, a partial ban), the Court can offer a more encompassing consideration of the government's reasons for censoring or restricting speech.

The second prong of the test to be considered is historical context. Specifically, the Court would consider the historical context based on culturally constructed group identity when reviewing whether to restrict speech. If speech has the power both to oppress and to resist oppression, then depending on the history of a person's group identity, the speaker will feel more or less social power and so will feel more or less entitlement to speak. Unless the First Amendment is applied in accordance with the way this power operates, free speech laws will continue to work as part of the hegemonic process, allowing only brief moments of temporary change that ultimately will be rearticulated in terms of the dominant group. Groups that currently are privileged by dominant power structures will continue to have more cultural and political value than those who have been and continue to be disempowered.

The final prong of the framework is the relational nature of the power between speakers. By focusing on this relational power, my framework requires a consideration of the power dynamic of the specific speech situation. Taking this element alone would not be sufficient reason to override another person's speech rights. Doing so would put the Court in the situation of also protecting individuals based on levels of individual vulnerability. If the most vulnerable or sensitive individuals become the benchmark for free speech, then very little speech would be protected. However, using this individual power dynamic as one part of a multilayered analytical test would allow the Court to consider how speech is occurring relationally in certain circumstances. If the Court switched to a framework that not only allows them to consider individual power relations, but actually requires them to do so, then free speech analysis would have to consider the actual person or persons involved in the speech moment, not some liberally constructed "reasonable" person. The reasonable person standard previously has allowed the Court to favor the dominant group and their values over those of disempowered groups.[112]

These three elements of analysis for free speech cases would be applied to create a more well-rounded approach to considering speech and power in contemporary U.S. society. Each element would be considered in the Court's reasoning. For example, this new framework would give the Court a more nuanced approach to handling complex power dynamics in speech issues such as hate speech. Currently, hate speech regulation is unconstitutional under the First Amendment predominantly because those regulations are content-based. Framing speech law in terms of the negotiated space between speakers does not remove concerns about government control. However, instead of focusing on the content restricted by the government, the Court first would have to consider the character, nature, and scope of the regulation in question, followed by the other two prongs of the framework outlined above. This new framework would allow the Court to in some cases consider restricting the hateful speech, while still maintaining the hate group's right to their hateful viewpoints. The end result would be to facilitate the greatest amount of speech possible for all groups concerned.

CONCLUSION

The concept of individual autonomy is intricately connected both to liberty in general and more specially to First Amendment doctrine. As a result, a new perception of the individual must be recognized before the First Amendment can privilege equality as a major component of the liberty of free speech. Specifically, the concept of the autonomous individual must be replaced with a partial agent, a person who lives with varying levels of political and social agency. Partial agency assumes an ability to resist cultural and political oppression while recognizing the role of social construction in simultaneously reinforcing oppression.

While several feminist scholars, including many feminist legal scholars, discuss conceptions of agency, I focused on research conducted by Kathryn Abrams. Abrams juxtaposes "women's capacity for self-direction and resistance, on the one hand, with often-internalized patriarchal constraint, on the other hand."[113] Abrams's research is concerned with finding a way to reconcile self-direction and constraint through legal change. In order for the legal system to accommodate real change for disempowered groups, Abrams says, the system will have to acknowledge the role of group identity in determining an individual's level of social agency. If laws are restructured to recognize the role of cultural identity on individual agency, then the legal system can function effectively as a conduit for social change.

The First Amendment has a complicated relationship with disempowered groups. Unlike areas of law such as sexual harassment where the discriminatory practice is direct and obvious, the oppressive power of the First Amendment is hidden and seemingly passive. To unmask the oppressive elements of the First Amendment, the link between power and free speech must be considered discursively, historically, and relationally.

The power of discourse in modern society lies predominantly in its ability to mask the true character of modern power and as a result to conceal domination. In the case of the First Amendment, discursive themes pertaining to individual autonomy and open debate serve to perpetuate a system of inequality in which those in positions of social and political dominance continue to have more power to speak than members of disempowered groups. This discourse does not account for the social construction of individuals based on group identity. Nor do these discursive themes consider that oppression of free speech does not always occur through government action. In effect, First Amendment discourse does not take into consideration that power is both historically and relationally created and maintained.

To correct these erroneous conceptions of power in First Amendment discourse, I developed a three-prong framework for free speech case analysis. This framework recognizes concerns of possible government abuse through content-based speech restrictions. However, it also maintains that societal speech restrictions are equally, if not more, problematic for historically disempowered groups. The framework will replace current case analysis tests in areas of free speech law that affect directly or indirectly the speech rights of disempowered groups. The three prongs of this analytical approach to case review are: (1) the character, nature, and scope of the speech restriction; (2) the historical context of the cultural groups involved in the speech at issue; and (3) the individual power relations occurring at the particular speech moment. In chapters 4 and 5, I illustrate how this framework would alter First Amendment case analysis in the area of hate speech. In chapter 6, I apply this framework to both pornography in general and more specifically Internet pornography. Finally, in chapter 7, I attempt to address the current move toward regulating political speech by showing how the framework could be used to further define the incitement standard.

NOTES

1. Filimon Peonidis, *Freedom of Expression, Autonomy, and Defamation*, 17 LAW AND PHILOSOPHY 1 (1998).

2. For example, cultural feminist legal scholar Robin West argues that no application of the First Amendment's protection of speech has ever been overtly discriminatory against women and many applications have allowed women a voice that is not available under other countries' speech laws. In *The Difference in Women's Hedonic Lives: A Phenomenological Critique of Feminist Legal Theory*, 3 WIS. WOMEN'S L.J. 138 (1987), West concluded: "First Amendment principles further more than they hinder feminist goals."

3. Note *Feminist Legal Analysis and Sexual Autonomy: Using Statutory Rape Laws as an Illustration*, 112 HARV. L. REV. 1065 (1999).

4. For a recent example of legal scholarship discussing the relationship of hate speech to acts of violence *see*, Alexander Tsesis, *The Empirical Shortcomings of First Amendment Jurisprudence: A Historical Perspective on the Power of Hate Speech*, 40 SANTA CLARA L. REV. 729 (2000). For an earlier example *see*, Richard Delgado and David H. Yun, *Pressure Valves and Bloodied Chickens: An Analysis of Paternalistic Objections to Hate Speech Regulation*, 82 CAL. L. REV. 871 (1994).

5. For an example of the psychological effects of hate speech *see*, Richard Delgado, *Words That Wound: A Tort Action for Racial Insults, Epithets, and Name-Calling*, 17 HARV. CR.-C.L. L. REV. 133 (1982).

6. The benefits that the First Amendment has offered in giving a certain level of voice to disempowered groups should not be ignored. As liberal feminist legal scholar Nadine Strossen has noted: "All censorship measures throughout history have been used disproportionately to silence those who are relatively disempowered and who seek to challenge the status quo. Since women and feminists are in that category, it is predictable that any censorship scheme—even one purportedly designed to further their interests—would in fact be used to suppress expression that is especially important to their interests." NADINE STROSSEN, DEFENDING PORNOGRAPHY: FREE SPEECH, SEX, AND THE FIGHT FOR WOMEN'S RIGHTS 31 (1995). Although Strossen's position is based on an oversimplified version of societal power and agency, her warning remains a powerful check on the complicated nature of the relationship between the First Amendment and power relations among differently situated groups in society.

7. John Dewey, *The Inclusive Philosophical Idea*, in THE ESSENTIAL DEWEY: VOLUME I: PRAGMATISM EDUCATION, AND DEMOCRACY 308 (Larry Hickman and Thomas Alexander eds., 1998).

8. *Id*. at 315.

9. Gerald Dworkin, *The Concept of Autonomy*, in THE INNER CITADEL: ESSAYS ON INDIVIDUAL AUTONOMY 54 (John Christman ed., 1989).

10. *Id. See also*, GERALD DWORKIN, THE THEORY AND PRACTICE OF AUTONOMY (1988).

11. Joel Feinberg, *Autonomy*, in THE INNER CITADEL: ESSAYS ON INDIVIDUAL AUTONOMY (John Christman ed., 1989).

12. Jennifer Nedelsky, *Reconceiving Autonomy: Sources, Thoughts and Possibilities*, 1 YALE J.L. & FEMINISM 7, 8 (1989).

13. Several feminist legal scholars have critiqued traditional liberal conceptions of autonomy as starting from a false set of assumptions, which include the assumption that individual action is autonomous, that it occurs from within the individual. For example, Susan Williams writes: "The traditional notion of autonomy focuses on a distinction between action originating within the person, which is autonomous and action in response to external compulsion. . . . This traditional notion of autonomy breaks down, however, if the desires of the person—the most common internal origin for action—are themselves not autonomous, that is, they do not originate in the person, or are in some meaningful sense, not her own." *A Feminist Reassessment of Civil Society*, 72 IND. L. JOURN. 417, 426 (1997). In RELATIONAL AUTONOMY: FEMINIST PERSPECTIVES ON AUTONOMY, AGENCY, AND THE SOCIAL SELF 5 (2000), a similar critique is offered: "For Rawlsian liberals, autonomy is understood in Kantian terms as the capacity for rational self-legislation and is considered to be the defining feature of persons. . . . Notions of autonomy as individual choice or as political right flow from, and are derivative of, this defining characteristic."

14. By "private power" I mean institutional power other than governmental (public) power.

15. In chapter 1, I discussed feminist legal scholarship from its earlier position in the sameness/difference debate to the more current theories dealing with social construction, diversity, and different assessments of partial agency.

16. Not all feminist scholars critique the liberal conception of autonomy. Liberal feminists, in particular, base their theoretical work on the ideas inherent in liberal political philosophy.

17. As noted in chapter 1, dominance theory holds the same essentialist view of women as radical feminism.

18. CATHARINE MACKINNON, FEMINISM UNMODIFIED: DISCOURSES ON LIFE AND LAW (1987).

19. Nedelsky, *supra* note 12, at 7.

20. *Id.* at 8.

21. *Id.* at 9. Nedelsky explains that while this is a problem faced by communitarian scholars as well, it is a particularly acute one for feminists because of their relationship to the "traditions of theory and of society." She says: "It is worth restating the problem in terms of these complex and ambivalent relations. Feminists angrily reject the traditional conception of liberal theory that has felt so alien, so lacking in language and ability to comprehend reality, and that has been so successful in defining what the relevant questions and appropriate answers are. . . . The values we cherish have come to us embedded in a theory that denies the reality we know: the centrality of relationships in constituting the self." She is, in effect, trying to negotiate the space, much like Kathryn Abrams, between autonomy and agency.

22. Susan H. Williams, *A Feminist Reassessment of Civil Society*, 72 IND. L.J. 417, 425 (1997).

23. *Id*. at 426. For a more in-depth discussion of autonomy from Williams, *see* TRUTH, AUTONOMY, AND SPEECH: FEMINIST THEORY AND THE FIRST AMENDMENT (2004).

24. *Id*. at 427.

25. Jean Grimshaw, *Autonomy and Identity in Feminist Thinking*, in FEMINIST PERSPECTIVES IN PHILOSOPHY, 106 (Morwenna Griffiths and Margaret Whitford eds., 1988).

26. Leti Volpp, *Talking "Culture": Gender, Race, Nation, and the Politics of Multiculturalism*, 96 COLUM. L. REV. 1573, 1585 (1996).

27. *Id*. at 1592.

28. Kathryn Abrams, *Sex Wars Redux: Agency and Coercion in Feminist Legal Theory*, 95 COLO. L. REV. 304, 306 (1995).

29. *Id*.

30. *Id*.

31. Volpp, *supra* note 26, at 1592.

32. Tracy Higgins, *Democracy and Feminism*, 110 HARV. L. REV. 1957, 1660 (1997) (discussing "incomplete agency"). Other feminist legal scholars who have studied the effects of individual agency in the U.S. legal system include Jennifer Nedelsky, *supra* note 12 (discusses "relational autonomy"), Susan H. Williams, *supra* note 22 (discusses "a narrative model of agency"), and Kathryn Abrams, *supra* note 28 (discusses "partial agency"). Nedelsky's term "relational autonomy" also has been used for a collected edition of articles about autonomy and agency, in RELATIONAL AUTONOMY: FEMINIST PERSPECTIVES ON AUTONOMY, AGENCY, AND THE SOCIAL SELF (2000).

33. *Id*. at 1690. Higgins explains that "social construction posits a self that simultaneously determines and is determined by culture (including politics, law, and the constitutional order.) Thus, feminists who employ social construction theory have been concerned not so much with the way patriarchy limits women (implying external constraints) but by the way it creates or defines women (implying internal as well as external constraints)," at 1691.

34. *Id*. at 1691.

35. *Id*. at 1658.

36. *Id*. at 1660.

37. *Id*.

38. *Id*. at 1666.

39. *Id*. 1697.

40. *Id*.

41. *Id*. at 1697.

42. 116 S.Ct. 2264 (1996).

43. Higgins, *supra* note 32, at 1667.

44. *Id*. at 1670.

45. *Id*. at 1673.

46. *Id*. at 1674.

47. *Id*. at 1695.

48. *Id*. at 1697.

49. *Id.*

50. *Id.* at 1695.

51. Abrams, *supra* note 28, at 306.

52. *Id.* Abrams traces the development of dominance theory as developed by MacKinnon and reviews responses to that theory by a group she refers to as "sex radicals." These sex radicals argued against dominance feminism because of its hard stance that any type of heterosexual sex was a form of male dominance. The subsequent debate between dominance theorists and sex radicals eventually led to anti-essentialist work by groups including black feminists and lesbians.

53. *Id.* at 346.

54. *Id.* at 354.

55. *Id.* at 355.

56. *Id.* at 356.

57. *Id.*

58. *Id.*

59. *Id.*

60. *Id.* at 374.

61. *Id.* at 376.

62. *Id.*

63. *Id.* at 366.

64. Kathryn Abrams, *From Autonomy to Agency: Feminist Perspectives on Self-Direction*, 20 WM & MARY L. REV. 805 (1999).

65. *Id.* at 821.

66. *Id.* at 823.

67. *Id.* at 826.

68. *Id.*

69. *Id.* at 822.

70. *Id.* at 837.

71. *Id.* at 840. Abrams explains why we should study law: "Legal institutions are not, of course, the only institutions that might be used to foster agency. In fact, the social constructivist assumption that law is simply one factor among many producing oppression suggests that this might not even be the most important place to start. Yet legal rules can bring the coercive arm of the state to bear on practices perpetuating oppression; moreover, they represent a discrete source of social meaning on which it is possible to focus in a coherent way."

72. *Id.*

73. *Id.* at 842.

74. *Id.* at 840.

75. *Id.* at 832.

76. *Id.* at 833.

77. *Id.* at 836.

78. *Id.* at 837.

79. *Id.*

80. *Id.* at 841.

81. *Id.* at 842.

82. *Id*. at 843. "Drawing on the constitutive or representational role of law is not always easy, or even possible, because courts formulate legal rules to resolve particular cases (or, more broadly, give social direction), not to represent human subjects in particular ways. Yet feminist advocates who are alert to representational issues may help shape legal rules in ways that serve both litigants and the larger groups of which they are a part."

83. *Id*.

84. *Id*. at 845.

85. *Id*. at 846.

86. H. Leslie Steeves, *Trends in Feminist Scholarship in Journalism and Communication: Finding Common Ground Between Scholars and Activists Globally*, presented at Annual Conference of Association for Educators in Journalism and Mass Communication, Washington, D.C., August 2001.

87. JANA SAWICKI, DISCIPLINING FOUCAULT: FEMINISM, POWER, AND THE BODY 24 (1991).

88. *Id*. at 43.

89. *Id*.

90. *Id*.

91. Abrams, *supra* note 64, at 832.

92. *Id*.

93. CHANTAL MOUFFE, GRAMSCI AND MARXIST THEORY 182–83 (1979).

94. LIESBET VAN ZOONEN, FEMINIST MEDIA STUDIES 24 (1994).

95. MOUFFE, *supra* note 93, at 178, quoting Antonio Gramsci.

96. Todd Gitlin, *Prime-Time Ideology: The Hegemonic Process in Television Entertainment*, 26 SOCIAL PROBLEMS 251 (1979).

97. ANTONIO GRAMSCI, PRISON NOTEBOOKS (Joseph A. Buttigieg ed., New York: Columbia University Press, 1992).

98. MOUFFE, *supra* note 93.

99. *Id*.

100. Higgins, *supra* note 32, 1666.

101. *Id*. at 1697.

102. Abrams, *supra* note 64, at 832–36.

103. NANCY FRASER, UNRULY PRACTICES: POWER, DISCOURSE, AND GENDER IN CONTEMPORARY SOCIAL THEORY 27 (1989).

104. *Id*. at 27. The "repressive hypothesis . . . assumes that power functions essentially negatively, through such operations as interdiction, censorship, and denial. Power, in this view, just says no. It says no to what are defined as illicit desires, needs, acts, and speech."

105. *Id*. at 27.

106. *Id*.

107. *Id*. at 24.

108. For a more complete discussion of Abrams's views on group-based agency, *see supra* notes 64–69.

109. *Id*. at 821.

110. For an in-depth discussion of content and viewpoint neutrality, *see* chapter 4.

111. For further discussion of character, nature, and scope, *see* chapter 4's review of Justice Stevens's concurrence in *R.A.V. v. City of St Paul, Minnesota*, 505 U.S. 377 (1992).

112. CAROLINE FORELL AND DONNA M. MATTHEWS, A LAW OF HER OWN: THE REASONABLE WOMAN AS A MEASURE OF MAN (2000).

113. Abrams, *supra* note 28, at 346.

Chapter Four

Rethinking Hate Speech:
Skokie and *R.A.V.*

In the previous three chapters, I laid out the current state of First Amendment doctrine by examining the main legal theories associated with it. I rigorously investigated the problematic underlying liberal principles, illustrating the ways those principles have been rearticulated and reaffirmed through nearly one hundred years of Supreme Court opinions. Having identified the problems associated with the traditional approach to First Amendment doctrine, I constructed an alternative framework for analysis embedded predominately in postmodern and poststructural feminist legal theory. Ultimately, this framework is designed to add equality to the liberty of freedom of speech. In this chapter, I test that framework in the highly contentious area of hate speech regulation.

Hate expressed against people based on their group affiliation has been a problem throughout U.S. history and remains a serious contemporary social issue. Data show the existence of 803 hate groups in 2005, a number that is up 203 from groups counted five years prior.[1] Organized groups established to oppose hate groups, as well as the leaders in those hate groups, agree that the economic slump in the early years of the twenty-first century has created a moment where membership will more than likely increase in hate-based organizations.[2] This hatred gets expressed through actions, words, or a combination of the two. While there is no empirically proven cause and effect link of hate speech leading to hate crimes,[3] there is a strong correlation between the two.[4] Past attempts by states to regulate hate speech, as well as recent case law, substantiate a connection between certain crimes and hate bias motives.[5]

In addition to the possibility of hate speech leading to hate crimes, hate speech in and of itself can have devastating effects.[6] For example, hate speech can silence those who are its targets.[7] For this reason, hate speech is a separate injustice from physical hate crime acts. The United Nations recognizes the need to constrain hate speech through the International Convention on the Elimination of All Forms of Racial Discrimination.[8] Other countries have enacted statutes to punish the use of such speech.[9] However, in the United States the First Amendment has traditionally protected hate speech. As Kent Greenawalt explains in *Fighting Words: Individuals, Communities and Liberties of Speech*,[10] hate speech finds protection in the First Amendment because of a basic premise in free speech doctrine to not restrict speech based on the message or content:

> The fundamental idea is that some messages should not be favored over others. Certain differences in content are a permissible basis of distinction; a message directly urging someone to commit a crime may be treated differently from a message urging someone to obey the law. But, in general, differences in viewpoint are not a permissible basis for distinction.[11]

Under First Amendment doctrine, dissident speech, even if it is hateful, must be protected from the tyranny of the majority. Speech must be judged based on its possible value in general, not on its specific harmful effects—even if agreement could be reached on what constitutes a harmful effect. The repercussions could mean that the majority would restrict any speech that criticized them, thus silencing dissident or minority groups.

This traditional approach to hate speech fails to take into account the harmful effects of hate speech or to even accept the premise that hate speech causes harm. Because of the pervasiveness and the seriousness of hate crimes and because of the connection of hate crime to hate speech, this chapter focuses on current hate speech rulings. By applying the framework described in chapter 3, an alternative approach to First Amendment case analysis is provided in regard to hate speech. This new approach allows First Amendment doctrine to foster equality not just among individuals but among groups within communities as well. By restricting some hateful speech, certain groups will feel less fear and thus more entitlement to speak.[12] This reassessment calls for a shift in the legal treatment of hate speech, a shift that will allow for the restriction of hate speech in certain circumstances depending on the power relationship between the speaker and the target of the speech.

This chapter first outlines the history of the contemporary hate speech debate in U.S. society. Because traditional foundations of First Amendment thought have already been examined in chapter 2, the historical review focuses primarily on alternative approaches to regulating hate speech. The historical review is followed by a discussion of the content-neutrality principle and its relationship to fighting words doctrine—two key elements in the discussion of the constitutionality of hate speech regulation. I will analyze two hate speech cases—*Village of Skokie v. the National Socialist Party of America*[13] and *R.A.V. v. City of St. Paul, Minnesota.*[14] *Skokie* is a state supreme court case that deals with the village's refusal to allow a rally based on the hateful nature of the organization requesting it. *R.A.V.* is one of the most significant U.S. Supreme Court cases in the area of hate speech regulation. The discussion of both *Skokie* and *R.A.V.* will contain a description of the case facts and ruling followed by a critique of the rulings based on the framework developed in chapter 3. Specifically, I ask for a reassessment of the content-neutrality principle. This reassessment will lead to a more multifaceted approach to considering content-based regulations.

HISTORY OF THE DEBATE

The debate concerning the regulation of hate speech flared in the late 1980s, primarily focusing on campus hate speech codes that were being enacted throughout the country.[15] Supporters and foes of hate speech regulations can be divided roughly into two groups: those who view hate speech regulation as a necessary step toward social equality and those who see hate speech regulations as a detrimental abridgment to the fundamental right of free speech.

The traditional legal position seems obvious: speech must be valued as one of the most important elements of a democratic society. Those traditional scholars see speech as a fundamental tool for self-realization and social growth and believe that the remedy for troublesome speech is more speech, not more government regulation of speech. For example, liberal theorist Nadine Strossen argues that restricting hate speech is an unrealistic solution to a complex problem.[16] Strossen, relying to some degree on Mill's connection between speech and the search for truth, argues that restricting hate speech will only mask hatred between groups, not dissipate it.[17] While traditional liberal theorists for the most part support protection of hate speech under the First Amendment, not all liberal theorists agree on the extent of that protection. For example, Steven Shiffrin proposed that some hateful speech, particularly speech targeting individuals, could be restricted in a manner that meets constitutional scrutiny.[18]

Proponents of hate speech regulation, on the other hand, see no value in protecting bias-motivated speech against certain already oppressed groups[19] and question the necessity and logic of using the First Amendment to protect speech that not only has no social value but is socially and psychologically damaging to minority groups. These proponents for the regulation of hate speech suggest a new balance between free speech and social equality.[20]

For example, Mari Matsuda, a leader in the move to restrict hate speech, discussed in her article "Public Response to Racist Speech: Considering the Victim's Story" some of the arguments against regulation, mainly those derived from supposed conflicts with the First Amendment. Matsuda wrote: "[U]nder our system there is 'no such thing as a false idea.' All ideas deserve a public forum, and the way to combat anti-democratic ideas is through counter-expression. When all ideas are voiced freely, we have the greatest chance that the right results will obtain."[21] She explained that under traditional First Amendment reasoning, the strongest argument against legalized restriction of racist speech is that this type of restriction would be content-based. The content-based regulation argument, according to Matsuda, states that racist speech regulation "puts the state in the censorship business, with no means of assuring that the censor's hand will go lightly over 'good' as opposed to 'bad' speech," leading most probably to a slippery slope of regulating speech merely because the government finds it offensive.[22]

Matsuda suggested the creation of a legal doctrine that would define restrictable hate speech based on three identifying characteristics: (1) the message is one of racial inferiority, (2) the message is directed against a historically oppressed group, and (3) the message is persecutorial, hateful, and degrading.[23]

Other scholars took similar approaches to offering hate speech regulations that would pass constitutional muster.[24] For example, in 1992, Richard Delgado, another well-known proponent for the restriction of hate speech, wrote one of the first law review articles to call for regulation of racist speech. In "Words That Wound: A Tort Action For Racial Insults, Epithets, and Name-Calling," Delgado proposed a way in which hate speech regulation could be written in accordance with the free speech clause.[25] He began with a detailed account of the psychological, sociological, and political effects of racial insults. Relying heavily on social scientific data, he outlined the harm caused to the individual by racism and racist speech[26] and then, much like the reasoning presented in *Brown v. Board of Education* in favor of desegregation,[27] made the connection between the problems of the individual and the larger effect that these problems have on a democratic society. Delgado explained:

> Racism is a breach of the ideal of egalitarianism, that "all men are created equal" and each person is an equal moral agent, an ideal that is a cornerstone of the American moral and legal system. A society in which some members are regularly subjected to degradation because of their race hardly exemplifies this ideal.[28]

In effect, hate speech is anti-democratic and reinforces inequalities.

Delgado not only made his arguments in favor of hate speech regulation, but also addressed the possible counterarguments, especially those based in traditional First Amendment discourse.[29] After determining that hate speech can and should be regulated under the fighting words doctrine,[30] he then applied Thomas Emerson's four values of speech[31] to racial insults and concluded that regulation of these types of insults would be in keeping with the basic tenets of First Amendment theory.[32]

The Court effectively closed the door on these alternative legal solutions in *R.A.V. v. City of St. Paul, Minnesota.* In 1992, the U.S. Supreme Court in *R.A.V.* ruled on a city ordinance prohibiting bias-motivated disorderly conduct.[33] The statute read in part:

> Whoever places on public or private property a symbol, object, appellation, characterization or graffiti, including, but not limited to, a burning cross or Nazi swastika, which one knows or has reasonable grounds to know arouses anger, alarm or resentment in others on the basis of race, color, creed, religion or gender commits disorderly conduct and shall be guilty of a misdemeanor.[34]

The Supreme Court struck down the St. Paul ordinance, ruling that the ordinance was facially unconstitutional because it was content-based, imposing a special prohibition on particular disfavored subjects of race, color, or creed.[35] Immediately following *R.A.V.*, several hate speech codes were struck down across the country.[36] No legislation directly trying to restrict hate speech has been reviewed by the U.S. Supreme Court since the 1992 decision.

DEFINING CONTENT NEUTRALITY

The key component in the reasoning in both *R.A.V.* and *Skokie* depended on whether restricting hate speech violated the doctrinal principle of content neutrality. Because of the significance of the content-neutrality principle to those cases, the historical development of content neutrality in First Amendment case law must be reviewed prior to discussing those cases.

The Supreme Court specifically discussed the content-neutrality principle in 1972 in *Police Department of Chicago v. Mosley.*[37] The Court ruled: "Above all else, the First Amendment means that government has no power to restrict expression because of its message, its ideas, its subject matter, or its content."[38] As a result of this focus on content neutrality, any attempt by the government to restrict speech based on content would be impermissible under the First Amendment. However, the Court's reliance on content neutrality as a crucial factor in free speech cases began long before *Mosley*. The concept of content neutrality can be traced to the creation of specific doctrinal approaches to reviewing speech cases including time, place, and manner restrictions and the categorical approach. Under time, place and manner analysis, the government can restrict speech based on the above criteria, but not on the content of the message. The first of the time, place, and manner cases occurred in 1939[39] and the approach has been expanded since[40] to explicitly require that all time, place, and manner restrictions be content-neutral.[41]

In 1942 in *Chaplinsky v. New Hampshire*,[42] the Court developed the categorical approach to permissible speech restrictions. Under the categorical approach, certain groups of speech, such as fighting words, obscenity, and defamation, could be restricted by the government because those categories of speech have been found to have no social value whatsoever. Chaplinsky was arrested under a New Hampshire statute[43] for saying to City Marshall Bowering, "You are a God damned racketeer" and "a damned fascist and the whole government of Rochester are Fascists or agents of Fascists."[44] Supreme Court Justice Murphy delivered a unanimous Court decision upholding both Chaplinsky's arrest and the New Hampshire statute.[45] In doing so, Murphy described what would become the categorical approach. Murphy noted: "There are certain well-defined and narrowly limited classes of speech, the prevention of which have never been thought to raise any constitutional problem. These include the lewd and obscene, the profane, the libelous, and the insulting or 'fighting words.'"[46]

Murphy not only gives voice to the categorical approach, but also in effect creates the category of hate speech. Relying on Zechariah Chafee's work *Free Speech in the United States*,[47] Murphy writes of fighting words: "It has been well-observed that such utterances are no essential part of any exposition of ideas, and are of such slight social value as a step to truth that any benefit that may be derived from them is clearly outweighed by the social interest in order and morality."[48] He further explains that the test for fighting words would be "what men of common intelligence would understand would be words likely to cause an average addressee to fight."[49]

Reading this unanimous opinion could lead one to believe that the Court intended to firmly create a category in which certain insulting speech would not receive First Amendment protection. However, in cases following *Chaplinsky*, the Court continued to narrow its definition of fighting words.[50] Trying to determine what content to include in the fighting words grouping became more problematic as more fighting words cases came before the Court. With each new case, the Court further limited what could be considered fighting words unworthy of First Amendment protection.[51] For example, in *Speiser v. Randall* (1958)[52] the Court stated that even in the category of fighting words "the line between speech unconditionally guaranteed and speech which may legitimately be regulated, suppressed, or punished is finely drawn."[53] The Court reiterated this in *NAACP v. Button* (1963), saying that "because First Amendment freedoms need breathing space to survive, government may regulate only with narrow specificity."[54]

By 1972, the Court seemed poised to completely overturn the fighting words doctrine.[55] In *Gooding v. Wilson*, the Court found a Georgia statute regarding fighting words to be unconstitutionally overbroad.[56] The Court in *Gooding* distinguished the Georgia statute from the New Hampshire statute in *Chaplinsky* by focusing on two words in the Georgia statute definition. Justice Brennan, writing for the majority, said: "The dictionary definitions of 'opprobrious' and 'abusive' give them greater reach than 'fighting' words."[57] Justices Burger and Blackmun dissented in *Gooding*, accusing the majority of "merely paying lip service to *Chaplinsky*."[58] Blackmun, in his dissent, added: "If this is what the overbreadth doctrine means, and if this is what it produces, it urgently needs reexamination. The court has painted itself into a corner from which it, and the States, can extricate themselves only with difficulty."[59] The categorical approach based on the content-neutrality principle has led to a line of cases in which the category of fighting words is virtually meaningless.

By the late 1970s, and continuing today, the Court had determined that not even two of the most heinous, aggressive types of speech—the swastika[60] and the burning cross[61]—could be considered part of the category of fighting words. In *Village of Skokie v. the National Socialist Party of America*,[62] a state court, relying heavily on *Cohen v. California*,[63] wrote:

> [T]he principle contended for by the state [in restricting the wearing of the swastika] seems inherently boundless. How is one to distinguish this from any other offensive word (emblem)? Surely the state had no right to cleanse public debate to the point where it is grammatically palatable to the most squeamish among us. . . . Indeed, we think it is largely because governmental officials cannot make principled distinctions in this area that the Constitution leaves matters of taste and style so largely to the individual.[64]

The court, adhering to the content-neutrality principle, ruled that the government could not base rules on the feelings of "the most squeamish among us" and that the wearing of swastikas was "a matter of taste and style."[65]

What the lower court hinted at in *Skokie*, the Supreme Court made clear in *R.A.V. v. City of St. Paul, Minnesota*.[66] As previously discussed, the majority in *R.A.V.* ruled that the fighting words doctrine could not be used to regulate particular kinds of offensive speech.[67] The majority placed most of its emphasis on the need for content neutrality in First Amendment doctrine and the way in which fighting words were content neutral, but particular hateful speech was not.[68]

The fighting words doctrine introduced in *Chaplinsky* in the name of enforcing content neutrality in speech regulation attempted to expand First

Amendment law to include a new category of unprotected speech. By the 1950s, however, the Court already was beginning to have difficulty in determining where to set the parameters of the category created in *Chaplinsky*. By the 1970s, *Chaplinsky* was for the most part dead doctrine, and by the 1990s, the Court was refusing the use of the fighting words doctrine as a vehicle for restricting hate speech. As will be illustrated in the following examination of *Skokie* and *R.A.V.*, the content-neutrality principle is ineffective in balancing the protection of speech against the need to occasionally restrict speech. Therefore, an alternative approach would supply a more adequate balance.

VILLAGE OF SKOKIE V. THE NATIONAL SOCIALIST PARTY OF AMERICA

In 1977 members of the National Socialist Party of America (NSPA) asked to hold a demonstration in the community of Skokie, Illinois.[69] The NSPA is a group that is "dedicated to the incitation of racial and religious hatred directed principally against individuals of Jewish faith or ancestry and non-Caucasians."[70] Members of the party pattern themselves after the German Nazi Party, wearing storm trooper uniforms emblazoned with swastikas.[71] The party requested permission from Skokie officials to allow them to demonstrate by marching in front of the village hall, carrying signs stating "Free Speech for the White Man" and "Free Speech for White America."[72]

The community of Skokie had approximately seventy thousand residents at the time, with approximately 40,500 of those residents being members of the Jewish community. Of that population, five thousand to seven thousand people were survivors of Nazi concentration camps. Because of the high population of Jewish people, village leaders sought to enjoin the demonstration from occurring. Two separate rulings were handed down before the state supreme court offered yet a third ruling in the case. The court ruled that the NSPA had a First Amendment right to demonstrate in Skokie.

The circuit court issued the original order enjoining the party from "marching, walking or parading in the uniform of the National Socialist Party of America," displaying the swastika, or distributing pamphlets promoting hatred against Jewish people.[73] The appellate court modified the order, allowing the group to demonstrate but not display the swastika during the demonstration.[74] The question then before the state supreme court was whether the appellate court order concerning the swastika was a violation of the party's First Amendment rights.[75]

The court first established that "public expression of ideas may not be prohibited merely because the ideas are themselves offensive to some of their hearers."[76] The listener's feelings cannot be considered as valid reasons for prohibiting speech. However, the court also noted that there are certain categories of speech (i.e., obscenity, defamation, fighting words) that can be restricted because of the content of the speech. In these cases, the government still maintains "the heavy burden of justifying the imposition of a prior restraint upon the defendants' right of freedom of speech."[77] To decide this particular case, the court looked at the category of fighting words to see if the restraint on speech could be considered constitutional.

As previously noted, the category of fighting words originated in *Chaplinsky* and basically is defined as those words that inflict injury or incite immediate violence.[78] The court decided, however, not to use the definition from *Chaplinsky* but to use the modified version from *Cohen v. California*.[79] In *Cohen*, a person was convicted in the 1970s for wearing a jacket that said "Fuck the Draft" into a Los Angeles County courthouse. The Supreme Court refused to find the words on the jacket to be fighting words. The majority in that case explained that under the "premise of individual dignity and choice upon which our political system rests" government restriction should be avoided except in the most severe circumstances.[80] "[V]erbal tumult, discord, and even offensive utterances" do not rise to that level of severity.[81]

Relying on this reasoning from *Cohen*, the state supreme court in *Skokie* found that it would be impossible for the government to determine which offensive words and symbols did not merit First Amendment protection and which invectives were worthy of it. The court noted that "one man's vulgarity is another's lyric" and as a result "the Constitution leaves matters of taste and style so largely to the individual."[82] In *Skokie*, the court ruled that the government could not choose what is acceptable public discourse based merely on the fact that certain symbols cause anger or resentment on the part of the listener. The swastika could not be considered fighting words, nor could audience reaction be a justifiable reason for restricting speech.[83]

Two issues were key in the state supreme court's decision. First, the court focused on the fear of government suppression of ideas. As a result, the swastika, an emblem associated with hate targeted at a specific group, was equated with the slogan "Fuck the Draft." Both the swastika and the slogan were specific content-based expressions. Under content neutrality, neither form of expression could be restricted by the government. Second, the majority privileged the individual's right to speak over the group's right to not be targeted by hate speech. Issues of possible group harm did not justify infringing upon the individual's right to express himself. This individualistic emphasis firmly supported a content-neutral approach in which all invectives, no matter what the message, are for the most part considered equally "trifling and annoying."[84] This approach led the court in *Skokie* to conclude that it is the individual citizen's responsibility to "avoid the offensive symbol if they can do so without unreasonable inconvenience."[85]

As discussed in chapter 3, however, this focus on fear of government censorship and the autonomous individual is problematic in terms of the way in which power operates in society. The government is not the only oppressive institution and focusing on individual rights ignores the ways in which individuals are constructed and oppressed based largely on their group membership. In this case, applying the three-part framework developed in chapter 3 would lead the court to uphold the order enjoining the group from publicly demonstrating in front of the village hall.

Part one of the framework requires the court to shift its focus from the two-dimensional content-neutral versus content-based approach to the multifaceted consideration of the character of the speech, the nature of restriction, and the scope of the ban on the speech. The character of the speech in question could be viewed as political speech. It certainly expresses a particular political standpoint—that white people's rights should take precedent over the rights of non-Caucasians. However, the restriction on the speech was based to a large degree on the manner in which this political perspective was being expressed. So, the character of the speech in question can be considered based on the mode of expression chosen, not necessarily the ideas themselves. The NSPA is not being restricted from holding or expressing their views of racial superiority. Instead, certain content, specifically the swastika, is being restricted.

The nature of the restriction, according to the Skokie officials, was to protect the largely Jewish population from being targeted by a group that exists to perpetrate hatred of Jewish people. The Village of Skokie does not merely contain some Jewish members. The village contains a large number of Jewish people, with thousands of those residents being former Nazi concentration camp survivors. The initial order prohibited the group from demonstrating at all in the village because it was clear that the NSPA was targeting the Jewish population. The restriction was based on the specific population demographic involved, not merely the unpleasant racial and anti-Semitic ideas associated with the NSPA.

As for the scope of the speech restriction, this prohibition is a total ban on this particular way of expressing ideas in that community. Other options to express those opinions might exist, such as holding a rally in a building where it would be less confrontational or holding a demonstration on private property. The second order only enjoined the use of the swastika, so the ban was significantly less in scope than the original order.

Looking at only these three elements, the court would find itself in the similar situation of only focusing on content. The review of the character, nature, and scope offer proof that while the restriction in question was content-based (sometimes permissible under the First Amendment), it was not viewpoint-based (never permissible). The next question to be resolved is whether the content restriction is warranted. For one thing, the Skokie ban on certain content in the NSPA demonstration raises concerns about the government's role in possibly favoring one group over another. As the court in *Skokie* pointed out, "one man's vulgarity is another's lyric."[86] However, considering character, nature, and scope opens the possibility for further review of whether the government's content ban is justified in this particular instance. Looking at the other two prongs of the framework offers the context to allow the court to rule in favor of the Village of Skokie.

First, the historical context of the relationship between the two groups is well documented. Prosecution of Jewish people by the German Nazi Party can easily be supported by factual evidence. The connection between ideas of the German Nazi Party and the National Socialist Party of America can be found in the group's own writings and also can be implied by the NSPA's adoption of the Nazi uniform and swastika. As a result, while the restriction may seem questionable under the first prong, it is definitely more justifiable when taken together with the second prong.

In terms of historical context, Skokie seemingly offers an interesting dilemma. While obviously in 1978 it was easy to determine the historical disempowerment of the Holocaust survivors in the small town of Skokie, how would this look thirty years later? By mere passage of time, the majority of those survivors would no longer be alive, leaving a community that may still be predominantly Jewish but may not have lived through the Holocaust. And what about societal views of Nazis, or, in today's terms, of neo-Nazis? Certainly those proscribing the Nazi philosophy are fewer in numbers today, although the very existence of the term neo-Nazi is proof that the movement has not died away. In essence, *Skokie* raises the question: At what level is a group considered disempowered—how should the court measure this and when does a group once considered disempowered cease to be so?

At first glance these questions seem to point to a possible flaw in my alternative framework; however, just the opposite is true. First, what *Skokie* serves to illustrate is the fluidness of the historical context prong. Just because a group was at one time a disempowered group does not mean that the group will forever have to be considered as such. The historical framework prong actually necessitates a constant reexamination of the speakers involved in light of current social status. For example, thirty years ago, the disempowered status of the Holocaust survivors in *Skokie* was easy to establish. If a similar situation were to arise today, the Court, under my framework, would need to consider the entirety of the group's history—both where they stood then, as well as any changes in social status that have occurred since.

Secondly, diving into the entirety of the group's history requires a much more complex level of proof and analysis than was needed thirty years ago. It requires the Court to reassess both the status of Jewish people in U.S. society as well as the status of neo-Nazis. On the one hand, it could be argued that the level of disempowerment experienced by Jewish people today is significantly less and that neo-Nazi groups are not considered socially acceptable by today's standards, that members of those groups are social outcasts. On the other hand, though, there has been a rise in anti-Christian sentiment post-9/11 and an increasing proliferation of Nazi groups on the Internet. I do not intend here to make a decision one way or the other. This decision would need to be deliberated by the Court after extensive review of documentation. So, while applying this piece of the framework does leave the Court with a certain level of subjective judgment, it is still less problematic than the current standard of content neutrality. As already discussed, content neutrality masks the fact that the decisions made under it uniformly privilege the dominant class. Certainly, the Court could choose to do that again in this case, but in order to do so they would have to acknowledge openly the assumptions and logic behind that choice.

The third prong of analysis involves reviewing the individual speech moment occurring. In this case, the speech moment is occurring in a public space in a small city that is predominantly Jewish. The speech in question combines an anti-Semitic hate group using three elements of expression—marching, carrying signs, and wearing the Nazi storm trooper uniform and swastika. The intensity of a demonstration of this sort in this particularly community could be documented through psychological research to prove traumatic for the members of the targeted group, possibly to the point of silencing their ability to speak. Examples of the types of support studies could include those focusing specifically on the psychological effects of surviving the Holocaust in Germany, those focusing more generally on the psychological and social effects of hate speech on members of targeted groups, and studies demonstrating the power of hateful images (such as the swastika). Using research on possible effects of hate speech on traumatized groups, combined with the historical evidence, would enable the Village of Skokie to constitutionally prohibit the demonstration in their community.

R.A.V. V. CITY OF ST. PAUL, MINNESOTA

In 1990 several teenagers taped broken chair parts together to form a crudely made cross and proceeded to burn the cross inside the fenced yard of a black family.[87] The teenagers were charged under the St. Paul, Minnesota, Bias-

Motivated Crime Ordinance.[88] This ordinance prohibited the display of a symbol "which one knows or has reason to know arouses anger, alarm or resentment in others on the basis of race, color, creed, religion or gender."[89] R.A.V. claimed that the ordinance was overbroad and impermissibly content-based and as such was unconstitutional under the free speech clause of the First Amendment.[90] The trial court, agreeing with R.A.V., dismissed the charges on the ground that the ordinance prohibited expressive conduct, which violated the First Amendment.[91] The Minnesota Supreme Court, however, reversed the ruling.[92]

The Minnesota court found that the ordinance did not prohibit constitutionally protected expressive conduct[93] because the language in the ordinance only reached proscribable fighting words and as a result was not impermissibly content-based.[94] The court focused on overbreadth doctrine, which states that restrictions on speech content that encompass both proscribable and non-proscribable speech will be held facially unconstitutional under the First Amendment.[95] According to the court, the St. Paul Bias-Crime Motivated Ordinance was not overbroad because it covered only fighting words.[96] The court also argued that the state had a "compelling interest" in prohibiting this particular class of fighting words because it is the "obligation" of "diverse communities to fight hatred and violence based on racial supremacy."[97] The court noted:

> There are certain symbols and regalia that in the context of history carry a clear message of racial supremacy, hatred, persecution, and degradation of certain groups. The swastika, the Klan robes, the burning cross are examples of signs—like all signs—that have no meaning on their own, but that convey a powerful message to both the user and the recipient of the sign in context.[98]

In other words, the ordinance in question in *R.A.V.* was not impermissibly content-based under the First Amendment because it fit into a proscribable category of speech and served a compelling government interest of protecting diverse groups in the community. Content, such as swastikas and burning crosses, can be restricted in certain circumstances (where they can cause "anger, alarm or resentment") because in those circumstances the speech exists only to "inflict injury" or "incite an immediate breach of the peace."[99]

In 1992, the U.S. Supreme Court overturned the state court's ruling.[100] The majority explained: "The dispositive question in this case, therefore, is whether content discrimination is reasonably necessary to achieve St. Paul's compelling interest; it is not."[101] The Court found that the St. Paul ordinance was impermissibly content-based because while it did restrict proscribable fighting words it only restricted a subset of fighting words based solely on the content of the speech.[102] On the surface, this case appeared to be about whether St. Paul's ordinance restricted legally prohibited fighting words. However, much of the majority's opinion, as well as the concurring opinions, focused less on the fighting words category per se and more generally on how the Court does or should define and apply the principle of content neutrality in First Amendment cases.

The majority explained that content-based regulations are presumptively invalid under the First Amendment unless the speech being regulated fits into a proscribable category, such as obscenity, fighting words, or defamation.[103] These proscribable categories consist of "a few limited areas" which are "of such slight social value as a step to truth that any benefit that may be derived from them is clearly outweighed by the social interest in order and morality."[104] According to the majority, the "freedom of speech" that is protected by the First Amendment "does not include the freedom to disregard these traditional limitations."[105] In other words, certain categories of speech can be restricted or prohibited "because of their proscribable content."[106]

In *R.A.V.*, the majority argued that even inside of the proscribable categories established by the Court there are two reasons why speech might still be protected: (1) if the reason for the speech being restricted is based on content discrimination not related to the proscribable content of the category,[107] and (2) if the speech is being restricted only because of secondary effects.[108]

In the first exception, the speech restriction in question must be targeting speech as a means of "content discrimination unrelated to [the] proscribable content."[109] Even though certain areas such as fighting words can be restricted based on content, they still have some First Amendment protection. The speech in those categories can be restricted only on the basis of the proscribable nature of the speech, not as a backdoor way to allow the government to promote or show disfavor to certain specific topics. The majority offered several examples of how this works. In libel, for example, the category "libel" may be restricted but restricting libel only against the government would be impermissible content discrimination.[110] The majority offered an example of how obscenity in general can be restricted, but not only obscene government speech: "The proposition that a particular instance of speech can be proscribable on the basis of one feature (e.g., obscenity) but not on the basis of another (e.g., opposition to the city government) is commonplace and has found application in many contexts."[111]

When applying this reasoning to the category of fighting words, the Court noted that in this category a level of expressive content does exist and so that category of speech is not worthless or undeserving of First Amendment protection in every instance. This speech may at times warrant protection because "we have not said that they [fighting words] constitute 'no part of the expression of ideas,' but only that they constitute 'no essential part of any expression of ideas.'"[112] In this sense, the proscribed categories of speech such as fighting words are content-neutral categories because in restricting the speech neither the specific words themselves nor the ideas they expressed are important. Instead, fighting words, according to the majority, can be restricted based on the mode of expression. To further explain this distinction, the majority compared the regulation of fighting words with the regulation of the volume of a noisy sound truck: "[B]oth can be used to convey an idea; but neither has, in and of itself, a claim upon the First Amendment. As with the sound truck, however, so also with fighting words: The government may not regulate use based on hostility—or favoritism—to the underlying message expressed."[113] The government may restrict speech based on the time, place, or manner of the speech, but not based on the particular ideas expressed.

In the case of the noisy truck, the noise element can be restricted but the government cannot restrict based on only particular messages different sounds might convey. For example, the government could not pass a constitutional regulation that would prohibit the sound truck from playing rock music while permitting it to play country music. According to the majority, prohibition in the category of fighting words follows a similar line of reasoning. Fighting words can be restricted not because their content, but based instead on "essentially a non-speech element of communication."[114]

While stating that these categories are not content-based, the majority offered a caveat that some content discrimination is acceptable under First Amendment, particularly in areas that the Court recognizes as proscribable. The Court explained that the rationale for prohibiting content discrimination is the concern that through this type of speech restriction "the Government may effectively drive certain ideas or viewpoints from the marketplace."[115] In the case of proscribable categories of speech, this fear is less, particularly if "the basis for the content discrimination consists entirely of the very reason the entire class of speech at issue is proscribable."[116] Under this rationale, obscenity that is restricted for being excessively prurient in nature would be an acceptable form of content discrimination because obscenity is prohibited in the first place because of prurient interest. To restrict obscenity that critiques the government, on the other hand, would raise concern about the content distinction because this is not inherently a main component of why obscenity is restricted.[117]

The second way in which even a content-defined subclass of proscribable speech may be treated differently is if the content distinction is based on certain secondary effects. The restriction is tied not specifically to the content of the speech although part of the restriction includes a specific area of content. For example, to protect children, the government might permit every type of live obscene act, except those involving children. Certainly in this scenario, the content of the speech—obscene speech involving children—is key to the speech being restricted. However, it is not a problem with the message of the speech per se that has led to the restriction, but an "incidental" restriction on the speech to protect children from being used to produce obscene material.[118]

The majority offered a more detailed example involving the speech restrictions that occur as a result of Title VII's general prohibition against sexual harassment in the workplace. Restrictions on sexually harassing speech under Title VII are aimed at the illegal conduct of harassment, not at an illegal message. The majority explained:

> [S]ince words can in some circumstances violate laws not directed against speech but against conduct, a particular content-based subcategory of a proscribable class of speech can be swept up incidentally within the reach of a statute directed at conduct rather than speech.[119]

Speech that is intertwined with illegal conduct will not be protected merely because it is speech. Restricting speech in those circumstances is constitutionally permissible because the government restriction of the speech is only a secondary effect of what the government is attempting to prohibit. In the case of fighting words, some words may be proscribable because of secondary effects while other "equally offensive" words may not.[120] The test is whether the nature of the content discrimination in question is the result of "the realistic possibility that official suppression of ideas is afoot."[121]

Looking specifically at the St. Paul ordinance, the Court first found the ordinance to be content-based. The St. Paul ordinance applied only to that speech that caused "alarm, anger or resentment" of people based on their "race, color, creed, religion or gender."[122] These restrictions only applied to hateful epithets spoken to certain disempowered groups with no explanation as to why those groups should be protected, but not other groups such as gays and lesbians. The majority wrote:

> Displays containing abusive invective, no matter how vicious or severe, are permissible unless they are addressed to one of the specified disfavored topics. Those who wish to use "fighting words" in connection with other ideas—to express hostility, for example, on the basis of political affiliation, union membership, or homosexuality—are not covered.[123]

According to the majority, it is this selectivity that makes the St. Paul ordinance content-based.

Applying the two "valid" reasons elaborated on by this Court for allowing content-based discrimination of proscribable categories, the St. Paul ordinance does not meet constitutional requirements. According to the majority, the St. Paul ordinance falls neither under the "mode of expression" exception of the noisy truck nor the secondary effects exception of the Title VII example. In the category of fighting words, words should be protected no matter what ideas they express; only the mode of expression can be restricted. The Court argued that because the St. Paul ordinance relies directly on the message, "messages of racial, gender or religious intolerance," the ordinance directly conflicts with the rationale for the content-neutrality principle in First Amendment law.[124] The majority explained: "Selectivity of this sort creates the possibility that the city is seeking to handicap the expression of particular ideas."[125] This content discrimination, according to the majority, is not permissible, even in a proscribable class such as fighting words.

In regard to the "secondary effects" issue, the majority argued that this is not a case in which the speech is being restricted as a side effect to a permissible, non-speech government regulation. According to the majority, unlike the Title VII example where sexual harassment is being targeted and speech pertaining to that conduct is "incidentally" swept up with the restriction, this ordinance directly targets speech as the conduct being restricted.

The majority concluded by assessing that the Minnesota Supreme Court erred in finding that despite possible content discrimination, the discrimination was justified because of compelling state interest in ensuring "the basic human rights of members of groups that historically have been subjected to discrimination."[126] The Court did not argue that the state does not have an interest in this area, but that the interest does not override the "danger of censorship" that this content-based statute brought with it.

Justice White, concurring, found the St. Paul ordinance to be fatally overbroad because "while it reached categories of speech that are constitutionally unprotected" it also encompassed constitutionally protected speech.[127] White's disagreement with the majority concerned the way in which the majority applied content neutrality to proscribable categories of speech. White specifically disagreed with the majority's position that in those proscribable categories there was a subset of speech that still garnered constitutional protection. White stated:

> [T]his Court has long held certain discrete categories of expression to be proscribable on the basis of their content. . . . Today, however, the Court announces that earlier Courts did not mean their repeated statements that certain categories of expression are "not within the area of constitutionally protected speech."[128]

In these categories decisions are based on content but the speech is proscribable because "the evil to be resisted so overwhelmingly outweighs the expressive interest."[129] White explained that the majority's logic concerning a subset of protected speech in those categories was contradictory. The contradiction is that if a proscribable category is created because "the content of the speech is evil" then a subset of that evil speech would be "by definition worthless and undeserving of constitutional protection."[130] To White, there is no question that content restrictions are permissible in the case of nonproscribable speech.[131]

White heavily endorsed the categorical approach to ranking speech (i.e., political speech receives most protection, while certain categories of speech, such as libel or obscenity, receive little or no protection). He explained that decisions about these categories are "content-based" and that this content-based approach has "provided a principled and narrowly focused means for distinguishing between expression that the government may regulate freely and that which it may regulate on the basis of content only upon a showing of compelling need."[132] He accused the majority of creating a "simplistic, all-or-nothing approach" that conflates protection of viewpoint with protection of content.[133] This approach would not allow for the restriction of any fighting words, a point that White feels "confuses the issues."[134]

White explained that in the case of fighting words, for example, fighting words might be "quite expressive (quoting majority)" but are not "a means of exchanging views, rallying support, or registering a protest; they are directed against individuals to provoke violence or inflict injury."[135] According to White, certain fighting words can be banned constitutionally if their only aim is to "provoke violence or inflict injury" and that this ban could take place without "creating the danger of driving viewpoints from the marketplace."[136] Included in this group of proscribable fighting words could be hate speech, so long as the restrictions on the speech were narrowly tailored to meet the government's compelling interest.[137]

Specifically, White argued that both of the majority's reasons for protecting usually proscribable speech and the reading of "secondary effect" were built on flawed reasoning. First, White demonstrated that under the majority's analysis of Title VII, the sexual harassment regulation would either have to fail along with hate speech regulations or the sexual harassment regulations as described by the majority would serve as proof that hate speech regulations are constitutional. As White explained, Title VII pinpoints not workplace harassment in general, but harassment based on a particular "disfavored topic" of sexual harassment.[138] According to White, not only does sexual harassment make content distinctions but it focuses on the effect of the speech on the listener, something the majority claimed was an unconstitutional use of secondary effect.[139]

Ultimately, White argued that the majority was attempting to create an entirely new First Amendment doctrine based on an "underbreadth" principle.

In other words, the majority, according to White, was setting up a system in which one would have to restrict all speech in a category or no speech in that category.[140] He concluded that this approach runs counter to traditional over-breadth doctrine and leaves the legislature with little room to prosecute certain harms.[141]

Justice Blackmun, concurring, also took issue with Scalia's discussion of fighting words and content-neutral categories. He emphasized the Court's prior support of the categorical approach. He explained that if the courts are "forbidden to categorize" speech, then all speech becomes lessened in the process. Despite these concerns, Blackmun also found the St. Paul ordinance facially overbroad. However, he did not want to leave it impossible for future hate crime legislation to be enacted that would pass constitutional scrutiny. He concluded:

> I see no First Amendment values that are compromised by a law that prohibits hoodlums from driving minorities out of their homes by burning crosses on their lawns, but I see great harm in preventing the people of Saint Paul from specifically punishing the race-based fighting words that so prejudice their community.[142]

For Blackmun the possibility does exist to construct a hate speech ordinance that would pass First Amendment scrutiny.

Justice Stevens's concurrence also focused predominantly on how to interpret and apply content neutrality. He disagreed with both the majority and White's concurrence, finding both to be absolutist in their approaches.[143] Stevens began by critiquing the majority's analysis of subsets of protected speech inside of proscribable categories. He argued that the majority's example of obscene anti-government speech was not a valid example because obscenity by its very definition "lacks serious ... political ... value."[144] Secondly, Stevens expressed concern that the majority was attempting to develop a system that supports a ban on all content regulation.[145] According to Stevens, despite dicta in certain cases to the contrary,[146] content-based distinctions are "far from being presumptively invalid" and "are an inevitable and indispensable aspect of a coherent understanding of the First Amendment."[147] He argued that, in fact, "our entire First Amendment jurisprudence creates a regime based on the content of speech."[148] He offered as an example that merely deciding what speech falls into a proscribable or a non-proscribable category must be determined by its content.

Stevens disagreed with White's reliance on the categorical approach to speech restriction, though. Stevens argued that this approach is fundamentally inadequate because "it does not take seriously the importance of context."[149]

For Stevens the content must be judged to some degree on the situation in which it is being used. In the case of hate speech, for example, he finds that specific circumstances may lead to the need for special rules. He explained:

> Lighting a fire near an ammunition dump or a gasoline storage tank is especially dangerous; such behavior may be punished more severely than burning trash in a vacant lot. Threatening someone because of her race or religious beliefs may cause particularly severe trauma or touch off a riot . . . such threats may be punished more severely than threats against someone based on, say, his support of a particular athletic team. There are legitimate, reasonable, and neutral justifications for such special rules.[150]

He called for "a more subtle and complex analysis" that could include both content- and viewpoint-based restrictions, so long as the state can meet a strict standard of scrutiny.[151] Stevens explained that the Court should review multiple elements when considering the importance of content neutrality in attempts of government restriction on speech. These elements include reviewing the content and character of the speech involved (i.e., political speech is treated differently than commercial speech), the nature of the contested restriction (i.e., is the restriction subject-based or viewpoint-based?) and the scope of the regulation (i.e., is it a complete ban on a particular type of speech?).[152] Considering these three elements in the case of the St. Paul ordinance, Stevens found the ordinance to be overbroad, but not unconstitutionally content-based. According to Stevens's analysis, the ordinance bars "either side from hurling fighting words at the other on the basis of their conflicting ideas."[153] From Stevens's perspective, neither side of the argument is privileged.

Analyzing *R.A.V.*

The Court in *R.A.V.* held that the St. Paul ordinance was facially unconstitutional because it attempted to restrict fighting words based on content. The reasoning in *R.A.V.* was based entirely on the doctrinal principle of content neutrality and the traditional approach to restricting speech based on certain categories. The issue of how to determine content neutrality was the point of contention between the state supreme court and the U.S. Supreme Court, as well as among the four opinions in the U.S. Supreme Court decision.

The way in which the majority defined the principle of content neutrality makes it virtually impossible for any ordinances restricting hate speech to be held constitutional. According to the majority, even inside of proscribable categories of speech, a subset of protected speech exists. If the speech is being restricted for some reason other than why the category was developed in the first place or if the secondary effect standard is not met, then the speech in that proscribable category will be constitutionally protected.

Justice White's concurrence accused the majority of creating an all-or-nothing situation in which content and viewpoint are conflated and as a result no content-based restrictions could be held constitutional. Basically, White argued that once a category of speech is found to have no value, the Court cannot decide that certain speech inside that category deserves protection. According to White, the content-neutrality principle in First Amendment doctrine only works if the integrity of the categorical system is maintained.

Stevens argued that analysis based on content neutrality should encompass a consideration of three factors: the character of the speech, the nature of the speech restriction, and the scope of the restricted speech. Stevens claimed that when considering content neutrality, the Court should examine each of these factors in its determination: "Such a multi-faceted analysis cannot be conflated into two dimensions. Whatever the allure of absolute doctrines, it is just too simple to declare expression 'protected' or 'unprotected' or to proclaim a regulation 'content-based' or 'content-neutral.'"[154] Several factors then must be considered when determining whether a speech restriction is unconstitutionally content-based. According to Stevens, these factors are more important than relying on the categorical approach.

In addition to the various opinions in the U.S. Supreme Court, the Minnesota Supreme Court also had a different interpretation of application of the content neutrality principle. The court found the ordinance to be content-based, but also found that content to be subsumed in the fighting words category. The court ruled that the ordinance was not overbroad and as a result was constitutional in accordance with First Amendment application.

Five different justices in three different courts relied on the content-neutrality principle as their guides in ruling in *R.A.V.* The results of their individual analyses were five different applications of the same standard and five different opinions concerning the St. Paul ordinance specifically and hate speech restrictions more generally. These, the "traditional limitations"[155] and "traditional categorical exceptions"[156] tied to the content-neutrality principle, are not as firmly established and consistently applied as Supreme Court dicta would indicate.

The content-neutrality principle does not guarantee government neutrality in First Amendment cases. It actually only guarantees that the Court, and not the state, will be able to determine what content can be restricted and what content cannot be restricted. The Court makes these decisions without acknowledging the value-laden nature of the choice. For example, using content neutrality the Court determined that fighting words targeted at individuals had no value, while fighting words targeted based on group membership expressed important social ideas. The Court in this scenario is relying on a specific construction of the individual and is placing the focus on individual identity not group-based identity.

This focus on content neutrality as the key principle in the *R.A.V.* ruling fails to take into consideration the ways in which modern power operates in society. My framework acknowledges that government censorship based on hostility or favoritism toward ideas is a genuine concern. However, this framework also acknowledges that the government is not the only oppressive power operating in U.S. society. The content-neutrality principle as currently applied cannot adjust for this different conception of power. As a result, when considering a hate speech regulation, the Court needs to review that regulation based on three criteria: (1) character, nature, and scope; (2) historical content; and (3) relational power.

The first criteria, the consideration of the character of the speech, nature of the restriction, and scope of the speech restricted comes from Stevens's concurrence. Despite Stevens's assertion that this is the standard way that the Court decides issues of content neutrality, none of the other opinions took this approach.[157] However, the reasoning behind considering character, nature, and scope is that it helps protect against biased government restrictions, while leaving room to consider context more complexly. In the case of *R.A.V.*, my reading of this first criteria of my framework would be similar to Stevens's findings, although not offering the same conclusion that Stevens's analysis does.

Stevens concluded that the character of the speech being restricted was "only low value speech."[158] Also, the speech being restricted was expressive conduct, not the written or spoken word, and so less deserving of constitutional protection.[159] Similar to the *Skokie* case, an argument could be made, and was made in fact by the majority in *R.A.V.*, that the burning cross was expressive political speech. In *Skokie*, I argued that although the Swastika conveyed a message, restricting that particular use of the swastika in the Village of Skokie was more similar to restricting a mode of expression of a message, not the message itself. In *R.A.V.*, the "low-value" nature of the speech is even more apparent. In *R.A.V.*, the ordinance was written only to restrict fighting words, a category that by its very nature is low-value.

In considering the nature of the speech, Stevens explained that in distinguishing this element, the Court should be much more concerned about viewpoint distinctions over content distinctions.[160] In the case *R.A.V.*, Stevens found the restriction in the St. Paul ordinance to be "subject matter–based," not viewpoint-based.[161] The ordinance would not "drive certain ideas or viewpoints from the marketplace."[162] Instead, only speech that contained specific hateful expressions and content would be restricted. Hate could still be expressed just not against specified disempowered groups and not in specified ways.

As for the scope of the ordinance, Stevens found the restriction to be narrowly tailored because it "does not ban all 'hate speech,' nor does it ban, say, all cross burnings or all swastika displays."[163] The St. Paul ordinance was designed to restrict only that speech that the city believed it had a compelling interest to restrict.

In Stevens's analysis the above criteria would constitute a legitimate ban on hate speech per se, if not on the exact way in which the St. Paul ordinance constructs the category. However, in my framework this criteria only shows that the restriction, being content-based and applied primarily to low-valued expression, merely is not as severe a limitation on free speech as it could be (say if it were viewpoint-based and/or restricted political speech). However, more context needs to be considered before deciding what type of hate speech restriction might permit protection of targeted groups while still protecting the rights of the group holding and expressing those hateful views.

The other two criteria in my framework, historical content and relational power, add the needed context. Considering these two additional elements leads to a finding of the St. Paul ordinance as problematic and ultimately unconstitutional.

The ordinance specifically lists only "race, color, creed or gender" as group identities to be protected from hate speech. There is no discussion in the ordinance as to why these groups deserve protection in the city of St. Paul, but other disempowered groups, such as gays and lesbians, do not. Are gays and lesbians historically welcomed and empowered in St. Paul? The city sets up no discussion of the historical disempowerment of the groups it chooses to protect, neither in regard to overall U.S. history nor local St. Paul history. Not providing the proof of historical disempowerment gives the government too much room to make arbitrary decisions about what groups deserve protection from hate speech and what groups do not. As a result, the St. Paul ordinance fails to meet the requirement of the second prong of the framework.

Application of the third prong of the framework also finds the St. Paul ordinance problematic in its lack of definition of the relational nature of power involved in the speech situations restricted by the ordinance. The ordinance calls for restricting speech or symbols "which one knows or has reasonable grounds to know arouses anger, alarm or resentment in others." Why "alarm" and not "fear?" Why "anger" and not "silencing?" Inherent in the terms "anger," "alarm," and "resentment" is the ability of the target of the speech to act out against the hateful speech. If both groups involved in the speech situation have power to address each other, then the restriction in effect would be limiting "one side of the debate"[164] while protecting the other. In constructing ordinances or enjoining orders to restrict hate speech, the focus needs not to be on the anger caused but on the silencing of disempowered groups that occurs as a result of being targeted by someone's speech.

In the end, applying my analytical approach to *R.A.V.*, the ordinance still would be unconstitutional but for a different reason. The ordinance offered no consideration of context based either on historical power imbalances or the power dynamic involved between the individual speakers. Furthermore, the ordinance limits its protection to only certain disempowered groups. The city offers no justification as to why only those particular groups should be protected from hateful speech. Also, the ordinance relies on the assumption that the hearer will be able to respond to the speech assault, thus leading to favoring one person's voice over another's.

Based on the framework developed in chapter 3, a hate speech ordinance could be constructed that would withstand First Amendment scrutiny. Preparing an ordinance of this type would require proof of historical disempowerment. In addition to supplying evidence of social oppression, the government also would need to supply some support for how the speech being restricted might effect those groups being targeted by the speech. Because of the possibility for government abuse in this type of legislation, the government bears a heavy burden of proving compelling interest and narrowly tailoring the ordinance.

Using an analytical framework based in partial agency would allow for all viewpoints, even those that are distasteful or hate-based. The framework would allow for government restriction on speech only when the hateful speech was targeted to a person or group based on their group identity and only when the speech operated to silence that person or group. As a result, this framework offers a way to balance concerns about biased government censorship by requiring the government to support its compelling interest through historical context and individual power relations.

CONCLUSION

Hate expressed against people because of their group membership continues to be a serious problem in the United States. This hatred gets expressed both through action and through speech. Traditional theoretical suppositions about the First Amendment do not allow for restricting hate speech. Under those frameworks, speech rights are "individual-based" and speech cannot be restricted based on harm to the listener.[165]

In chapter 3, I elaborated on why modern power dictates that assumptions about free speech need to be reconsidered, ultimately altering First Amendment case analysis. In the instance of hate speech specifically, this different conception of power requires the Court to think about the role of group identity in shaping the individual and, as a result of that culturally constructed individual, consider that speech has the power both to be resistant and oppressive.

Two significant hate speech cases were reviewed to illustrate how current doctrine fails to adequately address modern power and to offer a different framework for case analysis that might correct this inadequacy. *Village of Skokie v. the National Socialist Party of America*, an Illinois Supreme Court case, concerned a neo-Nazi organization wanting to demonstrate in a predominantly Jewish community.[166] The U.S. Supreme Court in *R.A.V. v. City of St. Paul, Minnesota*, questioned whether an ordinance restricting hate-based speech was constitutional under the First Amendment.[167] In both cases the courts ruled in favor of the speakers. Also in both cases, the various courts involved applied the content-neutrality principle when determining whether the government's restrictions were constitutional.

However, what content neutrality should mean in First Amendment cases was dealt with differently in every ruling. In *Skokie*, the district court ruled in favor of the total ban requested by village officials, the court of appeals modified the ban to only include a ban on the swastika, and the state supreme court overruled both lower courts, finding in favor of the demonstrators. In *R.A.V.*, not only did three levels of courts disagree, but the Supreme Court's decision also consisted of three concurrences. Each of the opinions in that case took a drastically different view of content neutrality.

These opinions in both cases taken together exemplify the problems inherent in judicial application of the content-neutrality principle. I applied the multifaceted framework developed in chapter 3 in place of the two-dimensional question of whether the restriction in question is content-based or content-neutral. The alternative framework requires the courts to consider three factors: (1) character, nature, and scope of the restriction; (2) historical context of the groups involved; and (3) the relational nature of the individual speech moment.

Applying this framework in the *Skokie* case led to a reversal of the Illinois Supreme Court's ruling. The National Socialist Party of America would not be permitted to show the swastika during its demonstration. In *R.A.V.*, the Supreme Court's ruling would be upheld. The St. Paul Bias-Motivated Crime Ordinance is fatally flawed no matter what analytical framework is applied. However, where the majority's reasoning in *R.A.V.* makes it virtually impossible to have a hate speech restriction that would pass constitutional review, my framework offers a different scenario. Under this alternative framework, the government could use historical evidence and psychological studies to create effective hate speech regulations that would not unfairly privilege one side of the debate[168] or "drive certain ideas or viewpoints from the market-place."[169]

NOTES

1. For more information concerning the location of these groups and their specific hate group affiliation (i.e., Ku Klux Klan, Neo-Nazi, Neo-Confederate, etc.), *see* the website maintained by the Southern Law Poverty Center: www.splcenter.org/intel/intpro.jsp.

2. Southern Poverty Law Center: Intelligence Report, Spring 2001. This report first quotes Joe Roy, director of the Intelligence Project: "If the economy goes sour, we can expect more scapegoating violence, especially against immigrants." Also included in this report is a quote from William Pierce, leader of the neo-Nazi Alliance: "[T]he rise in membership numbers that began two years ago continues, and a recession next year should cause membership to rise even more rapidly." www.splcenter .org/intelligenceproject/ip-4q4.html.

3. Hate speech can be defined as speech that expresses hatred toward or otherwise denigrates a group of persons based on their group affiliation, such as race, gender, religion, and ethnic origin. Hate crimes can be defined as illegal activities (such as trespassing or assault) that are motivated by hatred based on group affiliation.

4. This correlation between the two is supported by various state's legislation that enhances criminal sentences if hate speech is part of the criminal act.

5. *See Wisconsin v. Mitchell*, 508 U.S. 476 (1993). In this case, the Supreme Court ruled that hate speech could be considered as a factor when determining the prison sentence for another, related crime.

6. For earlier discussions of this connection *see* Richard Delgado, *Words That Wound: A Tort Action for Racial Insults, Epithets, and Name-Calling*, 17 HARV. C.R.-C.L. L. REV. 133 (1982) (Delgado outlines various psychology studies conducted linking hate speech to hate crime). For a more recent article, *see* Catherine B. Johnson, *Stopping Hate Without Stifling Speech: Re-Examining the Merits of Hate Speech Codes on University Campuses*, 27 FORDHAM URB L. J. 1821 (2000) (discussing more recent studies of the psychological effects of hate speech on its targets).

7. *See, e.g.*, Laura Leets and Howard Giles, *Words as Weapons—When Do They Wound? Investigations of Harmful Speech*, 24 HUM. COMM. RES. 260 (1997); Gloria Cowan and Cyndi Hodge, *Judgments of Hate Speech: The Effects of Target Group, Publicness, and Behavioral Responses of the Target*, 26 J. OF APPLIED PSYCHOL. 355 (1996); and Phyllis B. Gerstenfield, *Smile When You Call Me That: The Problem with Punishing Hate Motivated Behavior*, 10 BEHAV. SCI. & L., 259 (1992).

8. The United Nations adopted CERD in 1965, at which time it was ratified by more than 125 countries. In part it reads: "[D]issemination of ideas based on racial superiority or hatred . . . should be punished by law." (Article 4) International Convention on the Elimination of All Forms of Racial Discrimination, 660 U.N.T.S. 195, January 4, 1969. Countries have taken different approaches to considering CERD in accordance

with the Universal Declaration of Human Rights that holds in part that everyone "has the right to freedom of thought . . . [and] to freedom of opinion and expression." (Article 18 and 19) General Assembly resolution 217A (III), December 10, 1948.

9. For a discussion of various countries' approaches to hate speech, *see* ROBERT TRAGER AND DONNA L. DICKERSON, FREEDOM OF EXPRESSION IN THE 21ST CENTURY 127–30 (1999).

10. KENT GREENAWALT, FIGHTING WORDS: INDIVIDUALS, COMMUNITIES, AND LIBERTIES OF SPEECH 16 (1995).

11. *Id.* at 16.

12. Delgado, *supra* note 6.

13. *Village of Skokie v. the National Socialist Party of America*, 373 N.E.2d 21 (Ill. 1978).

14. *R.A.V. v. City of St. Paul, Minnesota*, 505 U.S. 377 (1992).

15. For detailed accounts of these early debates, *see* Richard Delgado, *Words That Wound: A Tort Action for Racial Insults, Epithets, and Name-Calling*, 17 HARV. C.R.-C.L. L. REV. 133 (1982); Donald A. Downs, *Skokie Revisited: Hate Group Speech and the First Amendment*, 60 NOTRE DAME L. REV. 629 (1985); David Kretzmer, *Freedom of Speech and Racism*, 8 CARDOZO L. REV. 445 (1987); Mari Matsuda, *Public Response to Racist Speech: Considering the Victim's Story*, 87 MICHIGAN L. REV. 2320 (1989); Charles Lawrence, *If He Hollers Let Him Go: Regulating Racist Speech on Campus*, 1990 DUKE L.J. 431; KENT GREENAWALT, FIGHTING WORDS: INDIVIDUALS, COMMUNITIES, AND LIBERTIES OF SPEECH (1995); RICHARD DELGADO AND JEAN STEFANCIC, MUST WE DEFEND NAZIS? HATE SPEECH, PORNOGRAPHY, AND THE NEW FIRST AMENDMENT (1997); NICHOLAS WOLFSON, HATE SPEECH, SEX SPEECH, FREE SPEECH (1997); Catherine B. Johnson, *Stopping Hate Without Stifling Speech: Re-Examining the Merits of Hate Speech Codes on University Campuses*, 27 FORDHAM URB L.J. 1821 (2000).

16. Nadine Strossen, *Regulating Racist Speech on Campus: A Modest Proposal*, 1990 DUKE L.J. 484.

17. *Id.* "Most importantly, this article maintains that equality will be served most effectively by continuing to apply traditional, speech-protective precepts to racist speech, because a robust freedom of speech ultimately is necessary to combat racial discrimination."

18. STEVEN SHIFFRIN, DISSENT, INJUSTICE AND THE MEANINGS OF AMERICA 49 (1999).

19. Although not every proponent of hate speech regulation agrees on the groups to be covered by this type of regulation, some of the oppressed groups usually included are racial/ethnic minorities, women, and gays/lesbians.

20. Many discussions about hate speech regulation include a belief that there is an imbalance by the legal system in the way it views the free speech clause in the First Amendment and the equal protection clause in Fourteenth Amendment.

21. Matsuda, *supra* note 15, at 2349.

22. *Id.* at 2351.

23. *Id.* at 2357.

24. For example, Charles Lawrence proposed that the fighting words doctrine was definitely applicable to hate speech. He wrote: "The fighting words doctrine anticipates that the verbal 'slap in face' of insulting words will provoke a violent response with a resulting breach of peace. When racial insults are hurled at minorities, the response may be silence or flight rather than a fight, but the preemptive effect on further speech is just as complete as with fighting words." Charles Lawrence, *If He Hollers Let Him Go: Regulating Racist Speech on Campus*, 1990 DUKE L.J. 431.

25. Delgado, *supra* note 6.

26. For discussions about the harms of hate speech to other minority groups, *see* CATHARINE MACKINNON, ONLY WORDS (1993) (looking at the speech versus equality argument in relation to women) and Sandra J. Lowe, *Words Into Stones: Attempting to Get Beyond the Regulative Hate Speech Debate*, 1992 LAW AND SEXUALITY 11 (discussing hate speech regulation in regard to gays and lesbians).

27. 347 U.S. 483 (1954).

28. Delgado, *supra* note 6, at 140.

29. In addition to First Amendment arguments against regulating hate speech, Delgado also discusses other legal arguments including the difficulty of measuring damages inflicted by hate speech, the difficulty of apportioning those damages, and the possible problem of fraudulent claims and a flood of litigation. Delgado, *supra* note 6, at 166–72.

30. In *Chaplinsky v. New Hampshire*, 315 U.S. 568, 572 (1942), the Supreme Court ruled that words which "by their very utterance inflict injury or tend to incite an immediate breach of the peace" have no value and so are not protected by the First Amendment. It was from the opinion in this case that the fighting words doctrine was developed.

31. THOMAS EMERSON, TOWARD A GENERAL THEORY OF THE FIRST AMENDMENT (1963). The four values of the press as developed by Emerson are individual self-fulfillment, ascertainment of truth, participation in decisionmaking, and the balance between stability and change.

32. Delgado, *supra* note 6, at 175.

33. *Id.* Also, *see* Bias-Motivated Crime Ordinance, St. Paul, Minn., Legis. Code 292.02 (1990).

34. *Id.* at 380.

35. While the Court in *R.A.V.* delivered a unanimous opinion in this case, it is important to understand that four of the justices—White, Blackmun, Stevens, and O'Connor—all filed separate concurrences. The major point of contention between the majority opinion and the concurrences revolved around the constitutional validity of content-based regulations. In the Court's opinion, Justice Scalia argued that there is no place in the constitutional treatment of speech for any type of content-based regulation. In the concurrences, however, the justices disagreed, citing areas such as child pornography and obscenity. The concurring justices found the St. Paul statute unconstitutional based on overbreadth, not lack of content neutrality.

36. *See* In re Steven S., 31 Cal. Rptr. 2d 644 (Ct. App. 1994); In re M.S. 22 Cal. Rptr. 2d 560 (Ct. App. 1993), aff'd 896 P.2d 1365 (Cal. 1995); *State v. Ramsey*, 430 S.E.2d 511 (S.C. 1993); *State v. Sheldon*, 629 A.2d 753 (Md. 1993); *State v. T.B.D.*,

638 So. 2d 165 (Fla. Dist. Ct. App. 1994), rev'd, 656 So. 2d 479 (Fla. 1995); *State v. Talley*, 858 P.2d 217 (Wash. 1993); and *State v. Vawter*, 642 A.2d 349 (N.J. 1994). The Court did uphold a Wisconsin law that added sentence time to crimes if it could be proven that hate against groups was a motivating factor. For further discussion of these types of speech-plus laws (laws that punish speech when it occurs with an illegal action), *see Wisconsin v. Mitchell, supra* note 5.

37. 408 U.S. 92 (1971). Although this principle may have been discussed earlier in lower court cases, for the purposes of this study, I will focus only on Supreme Court rulings.

38. *Id.* at 95.

39. *Schneider v. New Jersey*, 308 U.S. 147 (1939).

40. More recent time, place and manner cases include *Globe Newspaper Co. v. Beacon Hill Architectural Commission*, 100 F.3d 175 (Mass. 1996); *Gold Coast Publications, Inc. v. Corrigan*, 42 F.3d 1336 (Fla. 1995); *Miller v. City of Laramie*, 880 P. 2d 594 (1994); *Multimedia Publishing Co. of South Carolina, Inc. v. Greenville-Spartanburg Airport District*, 991 F.2d 154 (1993).

41. The rules for time, place, and manner restrictions include that the restriction must be content-neutral, must not constitute a complete ban on speech, must have a substantial state interest, and must be narrowly tailored.

42. 315 U.S. 568 (1942).

43. *Id.* Chapter 378-2, of the Public Laws of New Hampshire read: "No person shall address any offensive, derisive or annoying word to any other person who is lawfully in any street or other public place, nor call him by any offensive or derisive name, nor make any noise or exclamation in his presence and hearing with intent to deride, offend or annoy him, or to prevent him from pursuing his lawful business or occupation."

44. *Id.* at 569.

45. *Id.*

46. *Id.*

47. *Id.*, citing ZECHARIAH CHAFEE, FREE SPEECH IN THE UNITED STATES (1941).

48. *Id.*

49. *Id.* at 573. The full text describing what constitutes fighting words, reads as follows: "The test is what men of common intelligence would understand would be words likely to cause an average addressee to fight. . . . The English language has a number of words and expressions which by general consent are 'fighting words' when said without a disarming smile. . . . Such words, as ordinary men know, are likely to cause a fight. So are threatening, profane, or obscene revilings. Derisive and annoying words can be taken as coming within the purview of the statute as heretofore interpreted only when they have this characteristic of plainly tending to excite the addressee to a breach of the peace."

50. *See*, for example, *R.A.V. v. City of St. Paul, Minnesota*, 505 U.S. 377 (1992); *Village of Skokie v. the National Socialist Party of America, et al.*, 373 N.E.2d 21 (Ill. 1978); *Gooding v. Wilson*, 405 U.S. 518 (1972); *Cohen v. California*, 403 U.S. 15 (1971); *Speiser v. Randall*, 357 U.S. 513 (1958).

51. The categorical approach has proved to be difficult to use in other areas as well. For example, in the area of obscenity, courts have not been able to agree on exactly what does or does not constitute proscribable obscene content. So, the category exists, but jurists remain unsure about what speech fits into it.

52. 357 U.S. 513 (1958) (states cannot require citizens to take an oath not to attempt to overthrow the government because it violates their right to free speech).

53. *Id.*

54. 371 U.S. 415, at 433 (ruled that the First Amendment protects both abstract discussion and vigorous advocacy).

55. *See*, for example, *Gooding v. Wilson*, 405 U.S. 518 (1972) and *Cohen v. California*, 403 U.S. 15 (1971).

56. *Gooding v. Wilson*, 405 U.S. 518 (1972), citing Georgia Code Ann. 26-6303 which reads: "Any person who shall, without provocation, use to or of another, and in his presence . . . opprobrious words or abusive language, tending to cause a breach of peace . . . shall be guilty of a misdemeanor."

57. *Id.* at 525.

58. *Id.* at 537. Burger wrote: "For me, *Chaplinsky v. New Hampshire* was good law when it was decided and deserves to remain as good law now. A unanimous Court, including among its members Chief Justice Stone and Justices Black, Reed, Douglas, and Murphy, obviously thought it was good law. But I feel by decisions such as this one and, indeed, *Cohen v. California*, the Court, despite its protestations to the contrary, is merely paying lip service to *Chaplinsky*."

59. *Id.* at 537.

60. 373 N.E.2d 21 (Ill. 1978). Although *Skokie* was not a Supreme Court case, the state court's reasoning has been cited in several Supreme Court decisions, most notably in *R.A.V.*

61. 505 U.S. 377 (1992).

62. 373 N.E.2d 21 (Ill. 1978).

63. 403 U.S. 15 (1971).

64. 373 N.E.2d 21, 24 (Ill. 1978).

65. *Id.*

66. 505 U.S. 377 (1992).

67. *Id.* at 378. The majority stated: "A few limited categories of speech such as obscenity, defamation, and fighting words, may be regulated because of their constitutionally proscribable content. However, these categories are not entirely invisible to the Constitution, and government may not regulate them based on hostility or favoritism toward a non-proscribable message they contain."

68. *Id.* at 387.

69. 373 N.E.2d 21 (Ill. 1978).

70. *Id.* at 22.

71. *Id.*

72. *Id.*

73. *Id.*

74. *Id.*

75. *Id.* at 23.

76. *Id.* at 21.

77. *Id.* at 23.

78. *Chaplinsky v. New Hampshire*, 315 U.S. 568, 572 (1942).

79. 403 U.S. 15 (1971).

80. *Village of Skokie v. the National Socialist Party of America*, 373 N.E.2d 23 (Ill. 1978), quoting *Cohen v. California*, 403 U.S. 15 (1971).

81. *Id.* at 24.

82. *Id.*

83. *Id.* at 26.

84. *Id.* at 24.

85. *Id.* at 26.

86. *Id.* at 24.

87. The initials R.A.V. are used in place of the juvenile's full name.

88. *R.A.V. v. City of St. Paul, Minnesota*, 505 U.S. 377 (1992).

89. *Id.* at 378. The St. Paul Bias-Motivated Crime Ordinance, Legis. Code 292.02 (1990) read: "Whoever places on public or private property a symbol, object, appellation, characterization or graffiti, including, but not limited to, a burning cross or Nazi swastika, which one knows or has reasonable grounds to know arouses anger, alarm or resentment in others on the basis of race, color, creed, religion or gender commits disorderly conduct and shall be guilty of a misdemeanor."

90. Both overbreadth doctrine and the content-neutrality principle are explained during the discussion of the Supreme Court opinion in *R.A.V.*

91. *R.A.V. v. City of St. Paul, Minnesota*, 505 U.S. 377, 379.

92. In re *R.A.V.*, 464 N.W.2d 507 (Minn. Sup. Ct. 1991).

93. *Id.* at 509. The Minnesota Supreme Court distinguished the ordinance in *R.A.V.* from the statute in Texas: "Unlike the flag desecration statute at issue in *Texas v. Johnson*, the challenged St. Paul ordinance does not on its face assume that any cross burning, irrespective of the particular context in which it occurs, is subject to prosecution."

94. *Id.* at 508.

95. *Id.* at 509.

96. *Id.* at 508. The Minnesota Supreme Court relied on the definition of fighting words from *Cohen v. California*, 403 U.S. 15 (1971).

97. *Id.* at 507.

98. *Id.*

99. *Id.* at 508.

100. *R.A.V. v. City of St. Paul, Minnesota*, 505 U.S. 377 (1992).

101. *Id.* at 395.

102. *Id.* at 378.

103. *Id.* at 382.

104. *Id.* at 383, quoting *Chaplinsky v. New Hampshire*, 315 U.S. 568 (1942).

105. *Id.*

106. *Id.*

107. *Id.* at 387.

108. *Id.* at 389.

109. *Id.* at 385.

110. *Id.*

111. *Id.* at 385.

112. *Id.*, quoting *Chaplinsky v. New Hampshire*, 315 U.S. 568 (1942).

113. *Id.* at 2545. Scalia builds his example from a similar one offered by Justice Frankfurter in *Niemotko v. Maryland*, 340 U.S. 268, 282 (1951). Frankfurter in that case recognized that both fighting words and the noisy truck are a "mode of speech."

114. *Id.* at 388.

115. *Id.* at 387.

116. *Id.* at 388.

117. *Id.*

118. *Id.* at 389. The majority also mentions treason as another area where the content of the speech is restricted but the reason is not to restrict content but to protect national security.

119. *R.A.V. v. City of St. Paul, Minnesota*, 505 U.S. 377, 389 (1992).

120. *Id.* at 390.

121. *Id.*

122. St. Paul Bias-Motivated Crime Ordinance, St. Paul, Minn., Legis. Code 292.02 (1990).

123. *R.A.V. v. City of St. Paul, Minnesota*, 505 U.S. 377, 391 (1992).

124. *Id.* at 394.

125. *Id.*

126. *Id.* at 395.

127. *Id.* at 413.

128. *Id.* at 400, quoting *Roth v. United States*, 354 U.S. 476 (1957).

129. *Id.*

130. *Id.* at 401.

131. *Id.* at 400.

132. *Id.*

133. *Id.* at 401.

134. *Id.* at 408.

135. *Id.* at 401.

136. *Id.*

137. *Id.* at 402.

138. *Id.* at 409.

139. *Id.* at 410.

140. *Id.* at 405.

141. White explained that the majority's reasoning in this case "leaves two options to law makers attempting to regulate expressions of violence: (1) enact a sweeping prohibition on an entire class of speech (thereby requiring 'regulation for problems that do not exist'); or (2) not legislate at all."

142. *Id.* at 416.

143. *Id.* at 417.

144. *Id.* at 418.

145. *Id.* at 419.

146. *Id.* at 420. Stevens specifically mentions *Police Department of Chicago v. Mosley*, 408 U.S. 92 (1972), in which the Court stated that content-based restrictions are "never permitted."

147. *Id.*

148. *Id.*

149. *Id.* at 426.

150. *Id.* at 416.

151. *Id.* at 428–31.

152. *Id.* at 429–31.

153. *Id.* at 435.

154. *Id.* at 431.

155. *Id.* at 383.

156. *Id.*

157. *Id.* at 428.

158. *Id.* at 432.

159. *Id.*

160. *Id.* at 430.

161. *Id.* at 432.

162. *Id.* at 387.

163. *Id.* at 436.

164. *Id.* at 392. Scalia stated: "St. Paul has no such authority to license one side of the debate to fight freestyle, while requiring the other to follow Marquis of Queensbury rules."

165. For examples of this, see discussion of court rulings in *R.A.V. v. City of St. Paul, Minnesota*, 505 U.S. 377 (1992) and *Village of Skokie v. the National Socialist Party of America*, 373 N.E.2d 21 (Ill. 1978).

166. 373 N.E.2d 21 (Ill. 1978).

167. 505 U.S. 377 (1992).

168. *Id.* at 392.

169. *Id.* at 387.

Chapter Five

Virginia v. Black: An Evolution in First Amendment Doctrine?

The 2003 Supreme Court ruling in *Virginia v. Black*[1] appears to offer an opening for the regulation of hate speech not thought possible following the ruling in *R.A.V.* While Justice O'Connor distinguished the facts in *Black* from those in *R.A.V.*,[2] other members of the Court disagreed.[3] In any case, the Virginia ruling allows for the restriction of some types of hate speech in very specific circumstances. On the surface, *Black* appears to be a step in the same direction as the one I am suggesting. The Court relies on discussion of historical disempowerment and takes into account that speech needs to be considered in terms of the relationship between the speaker and spoken to in individual encounters. However, the ruling is problematic in that it implicitly relies on the criteria outlined in my alternative framework but does not do so directly. In other words, the ruling in *Black* offers no direction as to how courts might apply those principles in subsequent cases. In this chapter, I outline the ruling in *Virginia v. Black* and then, through application of my alternative framework, I establish that the Court still needs to directly address those principles in order to ensure the possibility of more uniform application by the lower courts.

VIRGINIA V. BLACK

In 1988, Barry Black held a Ku Klux Klan rally on his private property, a rally that culminated in the burning of a cross approximately 300 to 350 yards away from a public road and within the vicinity of eight to ten houses. Black was subsequently charged with violating a Virginia statute 18.2-423, which stated:

> It shall be unlawful for any person or persons, with the intent to intimidate any person or group of persons, to burn, or cause to be burned, a cross on the property of

121

another, a highway or other public place. Any person who shall violate any provision of this section shall be guilty of a . . . felony.[4]

Also in 1988, Richard Elliott and Jonathan O'Mara were charged under the Virginia cross-burning statute. Elliott and O'Mara burned a cross in their African-American neighbor's yard after the neighbor had complained about loud target practice at the Elliott and O'Mara yard.

Black, Elliott, and O'Mara all were found guilty by trial and had their convictions upheld by the Court of Appeals of Virginia. Each respondent appealed to the Supreme Court of Virginia, arguing the statute was facially unconstitutional. The state supreme court combined the three cases and overturned the lower courts' rulings, finding that the statute was "analytically indistinguishable from the ordinance found unconstitutional in *R.A.V.*"[5] The court found the statute to be content-based because it singled out cross burnings and overbroad because the prima facie provision would enhance the possibility of conviction and ultimately chill free expression. The U.S. Supreme Court granted certiorari in the case and in an extremely divided ruling in 2003 affirmed in part and remanded in part.

Justice O'Connor wrote the plurality opinion in which the court found that Virginia could prohibit cross burning without violating the First Amendment. To make this argument, O'Connor first established why cross burnings constitute true threats and then distinguished the Virginia statute from the statute struck down in *R.A.V.* Relying on *Watts v. United States*, 349 U.S. 705 (1969), the Court defined true threats as "those statements where the speaker means to communicate a serious expression of an intent to commit an act of unlawful violence to a particular individual or group of individuals."[6] In addition, the plurality noted that the speaker need not actually intend to commit the violence but that the individuals being targeted may feel fear of violence. As O'Connor explained:

> Intimidation in the constitutionally proscribable sense of the word is a type of true threat, where a speaker directs a threat to a person or group of persons with the intent of placing the victim in fear of bodily harm or death.[7]

O'Connor composed a lengthy history of the role of cross burning in the United States to establish that "while a burning cross does not inevitably convey a message of intimidation, often the cross burner intends that the recipients of the message fear for their lives. And when a cross burning is used to intimidate, few if any messages are more powerful."[8] As a result of this reasoning, the state can restrict cross burning; however, cross burnings on their face do not constitute intimidation. While cross burnings can be used to intimidate, they also can be used "as potent symbols of shared group identity and ideology."[9] The plurality concluded that the cross burned on Black's property was for ideological reasons and so overturned his conviction. In respect to Elliott and O'Mara, the plurality vacated the judgment and remanded for consideration minus the prima facie clause.

In the plurality opinion, O'Connor also distinguished *Black* from *R.A.V.*, explaining that in *R.A.V.* the Court found the Minnesota statute unconstitutional because it allowed the city to "impose special prohibitions on those speakers who express views on disfavored subjects."[10] However, this ruling did not mean that "the First Amendment prohibits all forms of content-based discrimination within a proscribable area of speech."[11] O'Connor outlined several areas from *R.A.V.*, such as threats against the president, that the Court noted could be constitutionally restricted true threats. In addition, while the statute in *R.A.V.* focused on specified targets of the hate speech, the statute in *Black* focused instead on a "specific subset of intimidating messages."[12]

Justice Scalia, who wrote the majority opinion in *R.A.V.*, concurred in part and dissented in part. He agreed with the majority that the state can restrict cross burnings under the Virginia statute, but dissented in part because he felt that the prima facie language also passed constitutional muster.[13] He argued that under "the established meaning in Virginia," the term prima facie evidence seems to fit.[14]

Justice Thomas, who joined with the majority in *R.A.V.*, dissented in *Black*, arguing first that the statute in question deals only with conduct and so does not fall under First Amendment analysis.[15] Secondly, even if it did warrant First Amendment analysis, Thomas still took issue with the plurality, primarily concerned with the opinion's reasoning that there are times when cross burnings are not threatening. As Thomas noted, "Considering the horrific effect cross burning has on its victims, it is also reasonable to presume intent to intimidate from the act itself."[16] To support this position, Thomas cites drug laws in which mere possession of a certain amount of drugs makes one guilty of intent to distribute and statutory rape laws in which the government does not have to prove that the child did not consent: "Because the prima facie clause here is an inference, not an irrebuttable presumption, there is all the more basis under our Due Process precedents to sustain this statute."[17] He concluded that the plurality had erred by saying that cross burnings at times are merely "unwanted communication."[18] According to Thomas, cross burnings must always be viewed as physical threats.

Analyzing *Black*

The 2003 Supreme Court ruling in *Black* appears to offer an opening for the regulation of hate speech not thought possible after the 1992 ruling in *R.A.V. v. City of St. Paul, Minnesota*. The ruling allows for the restriction of some

types of hate speech in very specific circumstances. However, while Justice
O'Connor distinguishes the facts in *Black* from those in *R.A.V.*, the ruling was
a split decision with three of the justices disagreeing with the majority's application of the precedent set in *R.A.V.* Specifically, Justice Souter, joined by
Justices Kennedy and Ginsburg, stated:

> I agree with the majority that the Virginia statute makes a content-based dis-
> tinction within the category of punishable intimidating or threatening expres-
> sion, the very type of distinction we were considering in *R.A.V. v. St. Paul*. I dis-
> agree that any exception should save Virginia's law from unconstitutionality
> under the holding in *R.A.V.* or any acceptable variation of it.[19]

Souter argued that although there are differences in the *R.A.V.* statute and the
Virginia statute, the Virginia statute still focuses on one type of content, the
burning cross, out of an entire category of intimidating messages.[20] This position mirrors the one taken by the majority in *R.A.V.* when Justice Scalia explained that one cannot single out a subcategory of speech for restriction based
on the content of that speech.[21] As a result, Justice Souter further reinforced
the Court's reliance on the content-neutrality principle. Justice Thomas, in his
dissenting opinion, went so far as to argue that this case deals with only conduct, not expression: "And, just as one cannot burn down someone's house to
make a political point and then seek refuge in the First Amendment, those who
hate cannot terrorize and intimidate to make their point."[22] By relying on the
speech/conduct distinction,[23] Thomas evaded altogether the issue of content
neutrality raised in *R.A.V.*

In *R.A.V. v. City of St. Paul, Minnesota*, the Court relied primarily on the
content-neutrality principle to overturn the St. Paul Bias-Motivated Crime
Ordinance.[24] This principle, while well accepted in First Amendment analysis, fails to take into account the ways in which modern power operates in society because it only deals with governmental power. The majority in *Black
v. Virginia*, still relying predominantly on traditional conceptions of content
neutrality, ignores the contentious points in *R.A.V.* by focusing on the intimidating nature of cross burning. However, because the majority tried to defend
the validity of the statute under traditional conceptions of the content-neutrality principle, the Court in *Black* was severely split in its ruling and the ruling itself is limited only to burning crosses. In other words, the ruling does
little, if anything at all, to direct lower courts on what other types of hate
speech might be constitutionally restricted.

The ruling in *Black* raises several important questions. For example, what
about other forms of hateful symbolic speech, such as the swastika? And, even
more so, beyond certain emblematic speech, is there any way to restrict purely
verbal forms of hate speech? If so, does that mean the Court is willing to con-

cede that content-neutral doctrines (such as the true threats doctrine) should be read with some level of positive liberty when dealing with speech targeting members of disempowered groups? The Court fails to adequately address any of those questions. When considering the larger issue of hate speech, the Court must rely on a more complex test to assess restrictive statutes. Specifically, the Court needs to review the regulation based on three criteria: (1) character, nature, and scope; (2) historical context; and (3) relational power.

Applying the first criterion of the alternative analytical framework—the consideration of the character of the speech, the nature of the restriction, and the scope of the speech restricted—would offer a similar reading as that of the plurality. O'Connor found that in certain circumstances—those of threats—cross burnings are a low value form of speech. As she explained, cross burnings at times can be nothing more than the expression to commit an unlawful act. Cross burnings cannot be restricted in all circumstances, however, because they can be used as "potent symbols" of shared ideology, as the expression of ideas.[25]

In considering the nature of the speech restriction, the Court is much more concerned with viewpoint restrictions than content restriction. While both are constitutionally problematic, case law has held that the state may sometimes be able to support the suppression of certain content (i.e., obscenity or fighting words) but can never restrict viewpoint. O'Connor, by distinguishing between different motivations for the speech, also made a distinction about the nature of the restriction. The restriction of cross burnings that are true threats is only content-based, while restricting all cross burnings is viewpoint-based because it also restricts the expression of certain ideological positions. As for the scope of the ordinance—the amount of speech restricted—the plurality found the restriction to be narrowly tailored once the prima facie clause was removed. O'Connor supported this position by explaining that the ordinance in *Black* only restricted cross burnings as true threats, a specific subset of intimidating messages.

What is problematic about only applying prong one is that this same framework was used by both Souter and Thomas to make their rulings. In other words, by only considering the issue of content neutrality, three completely different conclusions were reached. O'Connor used it to defend the plurality, Thomas used it to determine that by its very nature a burning cross is always a threat, and Souter used it to argue that, just as in *R.A.V.*, the Virginia statute attempts to single out one content area of speech for special treatment. The other two criteria in the framework—historical disempowerment and relational power—add the needed complexity to have more uniformity in the Court's rulings in hate speech cases.

The plurality in *Black* applied what appeared to be a socio-historic analysis in rendering its ruling. Justice O'Connor offered an in-depth discussion of the historic symbolism of the burning cross in the United States.[26] She concluded that, "To this day, regardless of whether the message is a political one or whether the message is also meant to intimidate, the burning of a cross is a symbol of hate."[27] Specifically, O'Connor ends up considering the entirety of the history of the symbol of the burning cross, supporting my position in regard to *Skokie* that the entirety of a group's place in society, both historically and currently, must be taken into consideration. Through her discussion of significance of the history of cross burning, O'Connor is able to discern that despite social, political, and economic advancement for African Americans, certain hateful speech can still be particularly, and legally, threatening to that group. As previously mentioned though, what remains problematic about the opinion in *Black* is that the entire discussion focused solely on cross burnings, leaving no direction as to what other, if any, types of hateful speech may cross that same line. Regardless, historical disempowerment is considered and the Virginia statute is found to be constitutional.

The third prong of the framework calls for an assessment of the individual speech moment occurring, specifically proximity and degree. For example, a Nazi rally in New York City would have a significantly different silencing effect than one held in a small, predominantly Jewish town. The Virginia statute, by making all cross burnings unprotected speech, ignores completely the question of proximity and degree. In *Virginia v. Black*, the plurality did strike a balance between protecting and restricting free speech based on the particular speech moment occurring. In explaining why the prima facie clause was unconstitutional, O'Connor stated:

> The act of burning a cross may mean that a person is engaging in constitutionally proscribable intimidation. But that same act may mean only that the person is engaged in core political speech. . . . It [the Virginia statute] does not distinguish between a cross burning at a public rally or a cross burning on a neighbor's lawn. It does not treat the cross burning directed at an individual differently from the cross burning directed at a group of like-minded believers.[28]

In other words, according to O'Connor, the Court should be able to draw distinctions between when and where hateful speech might cross the line from protected to unprotected. In this way, the Court begins to consider proximity and degree. However, what is problematic about the ruling is that the discussion is brief and leaves little direction for how lower courts might interpret application. For example, what if the Klan rally occurs on a Klan member's property located in the middle of a predominantly black neighborhood? Or what if the cross that is set on fire is large enough for several people of color in the community to observe? The Court addresses part of the degree issue by focusing on the difference between ideology and threats; however, the question of proximity remains to be answered.

In the end, applying my analytical framework to *Black*, I would concur with the Court's ruling. The Virginia statute was good intentioned and for the most part constitutionally sound, restricting one of the most historically prominent forms of hate speech. The prima facie clause was problematic because it failed to distinguish proximity and degree. In other words, by applying prima facie to all cross burnings, the statute in effect ignored the third criteria of the alternative framework, the relational speech moment occurring. The Court's ruling, however, failed to address the totality of hateful speech, focusing on the history of the burning cross without considering the history of the disempowered group in general. It is predominantly for that reason that O'Connor's opinion does not hold up against the framework being considered here.

CONCLUSION

The Supreme Court in *Virginia v. Black* made two important strides toward a more equitable approach to the constitutional treatment of hate speech. First, the majority reopened the debate concerning whether or not hate speech could be legally restricted at all. While it appeared in 1992 that no restrictive measures could pass constitutional muster, the *Black* opinion made it clear that some level of restriction is possible—at least in regard to banning certain types of cross burnings. Secondly, the majority created a distinction between ideological hate speech and threatening hate speech, a distinction that moves the constitutional treatment of hate speech a step closer to the alternative three-prong framework supported in this book. In the following chapter, I will address yet another problematic and contentious area of free speech—pornography.

NOTES

1. 583 U.S. 343 (2003).
2. *Id.* at 361. ("The fact that cross burning is symbolic expression, however, does not resolve the constitutional question. The Supreme Court of Virginia relied upon *R.A.V. v. City of St. Paul, Minnesota*, to conclude that once a statute discriminates on the basis of this type of consent, the law is unconstitutional. We disagree.")
3. Justice David Souter, joined by Justices Anthony Kennedy and Ruth Bader Ginsburg, concurring in part and dissenting in part, wrote: "I agree with the majority

that the Virginia statute makes a content-based distinction within the category of punishable intimidating or threatening expression, the very type of distinction we considered in *R.A.V. v. City of St. Paul, Minnesota*. I disagree that any exception should save Virginia's law from unconstitutionality under the holding in *R.A.V.*, or any other acceptable variation of if." *Id*. at 380–81.

4. *Id*. at 344.

5. *Id*. 351.

6. *Id*. at 359.

7. *Id*. at 360.

8. *Id*. at 357.

9. *Id*. at 356.

10. *Id*. at 360.

11. *Id*.

12. *Id*. at 362. "Unlike the statute at issue in *R.A.V.*, the Virginia statute does not single out for opprobrium only that speech directed toward 'one of the specified disfavored topics.' It does not matter whether an individual burns a cross with intent to intimidate because of the victim's race, gender, or religion or because of the victim's 'political affiliation, union membership, or homosexuality.'"

13. *Id*. at 368.

14. *Id*. at 369.

15. *Id*. at 394. "A conclusion that the statute prohibiting cross burning with the intent to intimidate sweeps beyond a prohibition on certain conduct into the zone of expression overlooks not only the words of the statute but also reality."

16. *Id*. at 397–98.

17. *Id*. at 398.

18. *Id*. at 400.

19. *Id*. at 380–81.

20. *Id*. at 381.

21. 505 U.S. 377 (1992) at 385. The majority argued that even inside of the proscribable category of fighting words, the speech restriction in question must be targeting speech as a means of "content discrimination unrelated to [the] proscribable content."

22. *Id*. at 394.

23. For an in-depth review of the significance of the speech/conduct distinction in free speech cases, *see* HOWARD SCHWEBER, SPEECH, CONDUCT, AND THE FIRST AMENDMENT (2003).

24. For an in-depth discussion of the application of content neutrality in *R.A.V.*, *see* chapter 4.

25. *Id*. at 356.

26. *Id*. at 352–157.

27. *Id*. at 357.

28. *Id*. at 336.

Chapter Six

The Internet: (Re)Assessing the Pornography Question

In chapters 4 and 5, I examined the issue of hate speech restriction under the First Amendment and found that the content-neutrality principle served as an impediment to speech protection. In this chapter, I examine another contentious free speech topic—Internet pornography. Just as with the hate speech issue, the current level of protection for pornography serves to further silence socially disempowered members of U.S. society.

This chapter begins with a brief history of the development of the Internet in the United States. Prior to discussing the issue of pornography, I address the problem of hate speech on the Internet. By reviewing that area of Internet hate speech, I establish that problematic speech issues on the Internet will not be solved unless those speech areas in general are first dealt with. For the remainder of the chapter, I review the issue of pornography, specifically looking at how the Court could possibly restrict some Internet pornography.

THE INTERNET IN THE UNITED STATES

When work began on ARPANET in 1969 nobody had begun to imagine the possibilities of the Internet. ARPANET was initially developed primarily to enable computers operated by the military, defense contractors, and universities conducting defense-related research to communicate with one another by redundant channels. This type of system would allow communication to continue even if some portions of the network were damaged during times of war. While ARPANET no longer exists today, it provides an early example of the development of a number of civilian networks.

The Internet began to be used as a commercial venture in the early 1990s and has since become a pervasive force in society.[1] Today, there are more than six hundred million Internet users in more than 150 countries.[2] From the very beginning, the Internet has been hailed as "a unique and wholly new medium of worldwide human communication."[3] Throughout the past two decades the accolades have continued.[4] Despite these glowing statements about the wonderful effects of the World Wide Web, the Internet also has introduced a myriad of completely new problems, including cyberstalking, cybersquatting, Internet fraud, and spam. Scholars, such as Robert McChesney, remain concerned about the role of corporate interests overriding the democratic possibilities of the Internet.[5] As he noted recently, "The fourth myth is that the Internet will set us free."[6] More disconcerting for First Amendment scholars is the way in which the Internet has added a much more complicated twist to preexisting problems such as hate speech and pornography.[7]

HATE SPEECH

As I discussed in chapters 4 and 5, hate speech has a long history of contentious court rulings, and has generated much debate about whether or not it should be protected by the First Amendment in all circumstances, some circumstances, or no circumstances. While this debate had already caused major splits among First Amendment theorists, free speech activists and the courts, the Internet ushered in additional problems both in the context of the United States and in the global arena. For example, the Internet makes it difficult to determine who the Internet user is that is violating the law and, if the user can be identified, jurisdictional issues can arise. In addition, there is nothing to stop a user from moving or routing through a jurisdiction with more lenient speech laws. As one scholar notes: "The global nature of the Internet results in those countries with less civilized Internet standards becoming havens for actors who wish to continue their 'savage' manners untouched by the laws of the objecting country."[8]

Previous hate speech cases in United States, such as *Wisconsin v. Mitchell*[9] and *Virginia v. Black*[10] have relied predominantly on true threats doctrine to restrict or punish hate speech in very defined circumstances. True threats are defined as "those statements where the speaker means to communicate a serious expression of an intent to commit an act of unlawful violence to a particular individual or group of individuals"[11] In cases applying this test, the Court has relied on a component of close physical proximity, an in-person, one-to-one call to action. As a result, the true threats doctrine is difficult to apply to the more anonymous, removed context of Internet hate speech.

To date, the U.S court system has heard only one case that relates to Internet hate speech. In 2002, the Ninth Circuit Court of Appeals handed down a ruling in the case *Planned Parenthood of Columbia/Willamette, Inc. v. American Coalition of Life Activists*, otherwise referred to as the Nuremberg Files case.[12] The case involved a website run by the American Coalition of Life Activists.[13] This website contained names, photos, and home addresses of doctors who were known to have performed abortions. The photos were featured in three ways. If the doctor was still alive, the photo was in color; if he was wounded, the photo was in gray; and if he was dead, the photo had a slash through it. All of the photos were set up like wanted poster ads. In 1997, four Oregon doctors sued after their pictures appeared on the website. The doctors argued that the sites "robbed the doctors of their anonymity and gave violent anti-abortion activists the information to find them."[14] Based on this, they argued that the websites constituted "true threats."

The court ruled in favor of the doctors, applying first the federal FACE law.[15] The court relied predominantly, however, on the true threats standard developed in 1969 in *Brandenburg v. Ohio*.[16] According to the *Brandenburg* test, speech is not protected if it is "directed to inciting or producing imminent lawless action and is likely to incite or produce such action."[17] While this case found the website to be in violation of the First Amendment, it does little in terms of overall hate speech on the Internet, predominantly because the U.S. Supreme Court did not hear the case.

While the U.S. Supreme Court continues to ignore the issue of Internet hate speech, the proliferation of hate groups and hate crimes continues to climb, in part due to the Internet.[18] In the global arena, the American stance on hate speech, embedded in traditional conceptions and application of the First Amendment, is even more problematic. The immense amount of free speech protection that has always set the United States apart from the rest of the world is continuing to do so—this time with possible long-term adverse affects and major legal ramifications.[19] A key question to consider is: "[S]hould the Internet be thought of as an 'American Environment'?"[20] Several countries are arguing that it should not.[21] The First Amendment has served as a barrier to U.S. participation in international hate speech legislation, such as Article 4 of the International Convention on the Elimination of All Forms of Racial Discrimination[22] and the Internet hate speech protocol in the Convention on Cybercrime.[23] By looking at current U.S. rulings pertaining to hate speech and the United States' lack of commitment to international Internet laws, it is easy to see that there is "a fundamental and inescapable difference between the legal treatment afforded racist and xenophobic speech under the First Amendment and U.N., E.U. and German law."[24] This situation will continue in terms of Internet law unless the United States reconsiders its views on hate speech in general.

Hate speech on the Internet, then, is just as problematic as hate speech in general. As a result, this area deserves further exploration. Even if, as suggested in chapters 4 and 5, hate speech per se could be restricted, applying the new analytical framework to the Internet raises additional questions concerning how to define harm when Internet users are not physically in proximity to their targets. The issue of pornography is similar to that of hate speech in terms of legal treatment under the First Amendment. Pornography itself, which is currently protected, would have to be reconsidered by the Court before the problem of Internet pornography could be adequately addressed.

INTERNET AND PORNOGRAPHY

Pornography in general is presumptively legal under the First Amendment. To fall into a legally proscribable category, pornography must be either obscene or involve children in the production of it. The key test determining unprotected obscenity came out of the 1973 Supreme Court ruling in *Miller v. California*.[25] The test in *Miller*, which built on an earlier Court decision,[26] established that material was legally obscene if:

> (1) An average person, applying contemporary local community standards, finds that the work, taken as a whole, appeals to prurient interest; (2) the work depicts in a patently offensive way sexual conduct specifically defined by applicable state law; and (3) the work in question lacks serious literary, artistic, political or scientific value.[27]

In addition to the ruling in *Miller*, the Court also has established some laws prohibiting indecent speech.[28] Unlike obscenity, which is legally proscribable in all circumstances, indecent speech is protected by the First Amendment, except in limited circumstances. The Court has ruled in several cases that the government may limit public indecent speech so long as the government meets strict scrutiny requirements.[29] For example, in the late 1970s in *Federal Communications Commission v. Pacifica*, the Court ruled that the government has a compelling interest to restrict broadcasts of indecent material.[30] Four years later in *New York v. Ferber*, the Court determined that indecent speech deserved less First Amendment protection and that this speech could be prohibited so long as the government has a strong interest in doing so.[31] *Ferber* also established that any material containing child pornography could be restricted regardless of whether or not that material is legally obscene under the *Miller* test.[32]

These earlier decisions were not established with the Internet in mind and, as a result, have been difficult to apply to Internet-related cases.[33] Despite these shortcomings in current case law, or perhaps because of them, Internet pornography continues to be a contentious issue. The contention can generally be divided into two camps: those who believe that pornography should be restricted on the Internet almost entirely and those who stand by traditional legal arguments concerning adults' rights to consume pornographic material.

Those in opposition to pornography on the Internet point to the increasing amount of Internet pornography, studies showing the detrimental effects of Internet pornography on society, and the invasive nature of the medium of the Internet.[34] The arguments in favor of protecting Internet pornography are grounded in pre-Internet case law and supported by a series of Supreme Court rulings throughout the past decade dealing specifically with the Internet. Not long after the Internet became available to the general population, Congress began passing laws to protect children from sexual images and content on the Internet: "From its inception, child pornography law has attempted to reconcile two powerful interests: the First Amendment and the prevention of sexual exploitation of children."[35] In this balance, the First Amendment has served as a barrier for any of these laws protecting children with the exception of the Children's Internet Protection Act.[36] As one law journal noted: "As a by-product of the American principles of constitutionality and free speech, any promulgation of sexual content that does not cross the bounds into criminally prohibited obscenity is deemed possible."[37]

The first of these laws was included in the Telecommunications Act of 1996. This act was comprised of seven titles, six of which were the result of extensive committee hearings.[38] One of those titles, the Communications Decency Act (CDA), had two provisions written with the purpose of protecting minors from "indecent" and "patently offensive" communications on the Internet. The CDA prohibited the knowing transmission of indecent content to anyone under the age of eighteen.[39] The prohibited material was sexually explicit but not legally defined as obscene.[40] In 1997 in *Reno v. ACLU*,[41] the U.S. Supreme Court reviewed the CDA, examining the issue of whether the indecency provision and the patently offensive provision in the CDA were unconstitutional under the freedom of speech clause in the First Amendment.[42] In order to address that question, the Court first had to determine what type of medium the Internet should be treated as.[43]

The government based its argument in favor of the CDA on three cases: *Ginsberg v. New York* (1968),[44] *Federal Communications Commission v. Pacifica* (1978),[45] and *Renton v. Playtime Theatres* (1986).[46] All three of these cases restricted obscene and/or indecent speech when it was available to minors. In what the *New York Times* hailed as "as messy a product as the court has brought forth in years," Justice Stevens's majority opinion focused not on the indecency cases regarding minors, but instead on determining whether or not the Internet should be treated more like broadcast or print.[47] The majority found that the Internet did not have the qualities of broadcast—there was no scarcity of frequencies and the Internet was not as invasive as radio and television.[48] As a result, the Court applied the strict scrutiny standard and found that the CDA was not narrowly tailored and that the government had failed to supply a compelling state interest. In a 7–2 decision, the Court found the questionable provisions of the CDA to be unconstitutional under the First Amendment.

Almost immediately following the ruling in *Reno v. ACLU*, Congress began to fashion another federal law that would sidestep the unconstitutional issues in the CDA. In 1998, the legislature passed the Child Online Protection Act (COPA). COPA prohibited "commercial websites from knowingly transmitting to minors (under the age of 17) material that is harmful to minors."[49] Proponents of the law felt that it sufficiently corrected the overbreadth and vagueness issues in the CDA. First, unlike the CDA, COPA only applied to commercial speech, not all speech, and so narrowed the scope of the restriction. Secondly, the phrase "harmful to minors" was added in COPA to correct the vagueness problem. Specifically, COPA restricted:

> Any communication, picture, image, graphic file, article, recording, writing, or other matter of any kind that is obscene or that (A) the average person, applying contemporary community standards, would find, taking the material as a whole and with respect to minors, is designed to appeal to, or is designated to pander to, the prurient interest, (B) depicts, describes, or represents, in a manner patently offensive with respect to minors, an actual or simulated sexual contact, an actual or simulated normal or perverted sexual act, or a lewd exhibition of the genitals or post-pubescent female breast; and (C) taken as whole, lacks serious literary, artistic, political, or scientific value for minors.[50]

In essence, Congress modeled the language in COPA after the test established in *Miller v. California*.[51]

Despite these safeguards, the ACLU and sixteen other organizations sued, claiming that COPA violated the First Amendment.[52] What ensued were a series of court rulings, including three U.S. Supreme Court cases.[53] Finally, in June of 2004, the U.S. Supreme Court issued its final ruling concerning COPA. In *Ashcroft v. ACLU II*,[54] the Court ruled 5–4 that COPA failed the strict scrutiny analysis by not offering the least restrictive means available.[55] The intricacies of this case will be discussed later in this chapter.

While COPA was still being considered by the courts, federal legislators passed the Children's Internet Protection Act (CIPA) in 2000.[56] CIPA, enacted as part of the Consolidation Appropriations Act, required libraries in the LSTA and E-rate (government programs that give funding to libraries) to show that they were using certain filtering software. Specifically, libraries had to use filtering software on their computers to protect against visual depictions that would be considered obscene to children, that would be considered child pornography, or that would be harmful to minors.[57] The act would permit libraries to disable these filters for adults who were doing bona fide research or for other lawful purposes. The filters could not be disabled for any reason if the patron was a minor. Almost immediately, the American Library Association (ALA), along with groups representing libraries, patrons, web publishers, and others, filed suit claiming that CIPA was unconstitutional under the First Amendment.[58] The general concern was that this regulation would limit adults' abilities to access legally protected speech. Specifically, the concerns included worries that the filtering technology would block more content than just pornography, that librarians would be burdened by having to deal with requests to unblock website access on a case by case basis, and that the cost of the filtering software itself would place an undo burden on libraries.[59] In its lawsuit, the ALA argued that CIPA "is facially invalid because it effects an impermissible prior restraint on speech by granting filtering companies and library staff unfettered discretion to suppress speech before it has been received by library patrons."[60]

A three-judge panel in the federal district court in Philadelphia concluded that CIPA unconstitutionally restricted speech and that it was facially invalid under the First Amendment.[61] The panel determined that strict scrutiny should be applied and that while the government has a compelling interest in protecting children, the regulation as written was not narrowly tailored and did not use the least restrictive means available.[62]

However, in November of 2002, the U.S. Supreme Court disagreed and in a 6–3 decision overturned the lower court ruling and found in favor of CIPA.[63] In a plurality opinion, Chief Justice Rehnquist relied on previous case law concerning the spending clause doctrine, the public forum doctrine, and the unconstitutional conditions doctrine.[64] He rejected the idea that Internet access in public libraries qualifies as a traditional (or even a limited) public forum.[65] As a result, government restrictions of funding are not bound by strict scrutiny. Furthermore, CIPA does not require all libraries to have filtering software, only those libraries that accept government funding.

Finally in 2002, the U.S. Supreme Court ruled on the Child Pornography Prevention Act (CPPA) that was passed by Congress in 1996.[66] This act defined child pornography as any depiction that "is or appears to be a minor engaged in sexual conduct."[67] As a result, even computer-generated images that did not involve actual children in the production of the pornography also were in violation of the CPPA. Congress used social scientific data concerning pedophiles' behaviors to support the position that virtual child pornography has the secondary effect of causing actual sexual child abuse.[68] The Court in *Ashcroft v. Free Speech Coalition* rejected the secondary effects argument, finding that the CPPA

violated the First Amendment.[69] The Court stated: "These images do not involve, let alone harm, any children in the production process."[70] Instead, the
Court found that the statute language "appears to be" or "conveys the impression
of" an unconstitutional restriction on the speech of adults.[71]

Congress continues to be concerned about the possible power of the Internet
to spread hate, fear, and in some cases physical abuse against members of disempowered groups. Throughout all of this legislation, the U.S. Supreme Court
has maintained its unflappable position of its conception of free speech, a conception wrapped up in more than two hundred years of case law developed
around more traditional, conventional forms of communication. As I have already established in previous chapters, many of these legal doctrines, such as
content neutrality and true threats, are problematic even in those traditional
forms of communication. These problems become magnified when the technology of the Internet is brought into the mix. So, before dealing with the errors in
current Internet rulings, the shortcomings in the traditional legal application in
First Amendment law need to be addressed. If, for example, many types of
pornography were found to be unconstitutional forms of speech in general, then
the issue of pornography on the Internet would become easier to regulate.

To illustrate specifically how altering the approach to free speech in general
will relieve many of the problems on the Internet, I explore the issue of pornography, both laws relating to pornography in general and more specifically
pornography on the Internet. Just as hate speech on the Internet must first be
dealt with as hate speech in general, so pornography on the Internet must first
be addressed as pornography in general. Using the alternative framework developed here, I review the ruling in *American Booksellers Association v. Hudnut*, a case that in effect made it impossible to restrict certain forms of pornography, specifically hardcore pornography.[72] I then apply my alternative
framework to show how the MacKinnon/Dworkin anti-pornography ordinance
would have been considered differently by the court had it applied more than
the two-dimensional content-neutrality test. I establish how this new approach
to reviewing speech in relation to disempowered groups would allow for some
level of restriction on pornography. I then review *Ashcroft v. ACLU II* to show
that the Court could have avoided a lot of convoluted case law concerning Internet pornography. Before beginning analysis on the *Hudnut* case, it is important to first understand the theoretical debates concerning pornography.

THEORY-BASED ANTI-PORNOGRAPHY ARGUMENTS

The argument that pornography should be more regulated is not a new one.
Constitutional law scholar Catharine MacKinnon and activist Andrea

Dworkin, both major proponents of restricting pornography, have written extensively on the subject for more than two decades.[73] MacKinnon and Dworkin have written on the topic of pornography both together and separately and both have focused on the role of pornography in the lived experiences of women. In 1995, Dworkin wrote that pornography is "a discrete, identifiable system of sexual exploitation that hurts women as a class by creating inequality and abuse."[74] One way this exploitation occurs is through the use of women in the production of pornography. As MacKinnon explains in *Only Words*:

> What pornography does, it does in the real world, not only in the mind. As an initial matter, it should be observed that it is the pornography industry, not the ideas in the material, that forces, threatens, blackmails, pressures, tricks and cajoles women into sex for pictures. In pornography, women are gang raped so they can be filmed. They are not ganged raped by the idea of a gang rape. It is for pornography, and not by the ideas in it, that women are hurt and penetrated, tied and gagged, undressed and genitally spread and sprayed with lacquer and water so sex pictures can be made.[75]

This focus on the lived experiences of women working in the pornography industry permeates MacKinnon and Dworkin's anti-pornography scholarship. However, those working in the sex industry are not the only ones affected. According to MacKinnon and Dworkin, the problem is much more insidious and widespread: "Pornography is a practice of discrimination on the basis of sex, on one level because of its role in creating and maintaining sex as a basis for discrimination. It harms many women one at a time and helps keep all women in an inferior status by defining our subordination as sexuality and equating that with our gender."[76] In other words, pornography is not just a representation of sex; it is the embodiment, and enforcer, of sexual inequality in society.

MacKinnon's theoretical supposition about the overall role of pornography in the subordination of women transformed itself into a legal reality in 1983 when, along with the assistance of Dworkin, an anti-pornography ordinance was crafted and subsequently passed.[77] The Indianapolis ordinance did not in itself make the production of pornography a criminal act, but instead offered a civil redress for women who were victims of certain types of pornography.[78] This ordinance eventually would be found unconstitutional in the *Hudnut* case, the specifics of which I will discuss later in this chapter.

Despite the fact that the *Hudnut* ruling, which defined pornography as an "idea" or "speech" protected by the First Amendment, seemed to essentially close the door on any anti-pornography legislation, other feminist scholars have offered responses to the First Amendment treatment of pornography.

Following in the footsteps of MacKinnon and Dworkin, several scholars have interrogated pornography as a form of subordination of women. For example, in 1985 Annette Kuhn, relying on psychoanalytic film theory, argued that pornography dehumanizes women in a way that marks them as different from men and thus less than men.[79] According to Kuhn, pornographic images of women are created to "speak to a masculine subject, constructing women as object, femininity as other."[80] A decade later, scholars continued to echo this idea of pornography as constructing an inauthentic vision of women.[81] Complicating the issue, scholars have focused on the intersection of race and gender and have in several circumstances attempted to prove the subordinating power of pornography through quantitative methods.[82]

These critiques of pornography continue today, as do attempts to make a plausible legal argument that could support a legally viable restriction of pornography. For example, Joan Mason-Grant takes the legal system to task for ignoring the effects of pornography on women.[83] She states: "Through a series of decisions and appeals, the courts conceded that pornography fosters aggression and produces contempt and bigotry but argued that this simply demonstrates its power as speech."[84] Mason-Grant agrees with MacKinnon and Dworkin in relation to the theoretical suppositions about the harms of pornography in society. However, she contends that their ideas were found unacceptable because of the strength of the speech paradigm in dictating the conversation about restricting pornography.[85] She defines the speech paradigm as the way in which the liberal conception of speech and freedom has constructed pornography as primarily a form of speech. Inside of the paradigm, if pornography is speech, then restricting it becomes an infringement on First Amendment rights and the anti-pornography movement becomes an anti-freedom movement instead of a movement toward analyzing pornography as a systematic form of subordination. She explains: "As a way of thinking about pornography, speech has become entrenched in public discourse about pornography largely because of the preoccupation with the legal question: Should pornography be restricted by public policy or not?"[86] Relying on this paradigm, Mason-Grant develops an alternative approach to the presentation of the theory that builds off MacKinnon's and Dworkin's earlier work and creates a new legal alternative. She calls this new theoretical approach the "practice paradigm." In this approach, she considers not only actions that create pornography, but the subordinating role of pornography in defining sexual relations in our culture—its role in creating and maintaining the "subordinating forms of sexual know-how."[87] Her legal solution ultimately avoids a direct confrontation with the legal system.[88] Instead, she calls for public policy that would establish countereducation to alter the preponderance of sexual know-how currently taught by pornography.[89]

Another example of current attempts at the legal restriction of pornography comes from Catharine MacKinnon herself. In a talk delivered in March of 2005 at a conference titled "Pornography: Driving the Demand in International Sex Trafficking," MacKinnon builds on her earlier work by focusing on the women used to produce pornography.[90] She explains:

> In material reality, pornography is one way women and children are trafficked for sex. To make visual pornography, the bulk of the industry's products, real women and children, and some men, are rented out for use in commercial sex acts. In the resulting material, these people are then conveyed and sold for a buyer's sexual use. Obscenity laws, the traditional legal approach to the problem, do not care about these realities at all.[91]

MacKinnon discusses various international human rights laws that attempt to deal with sex trafficking and, as a byproduct, pornography. She argues that "the pornography industry, in production, creates demand for prostitution, hence for trafficking, because it is itself a form of prostitution and trafficking."[92] If one sees this connection in the way MacKinnon does, then various laws against trafficking would apply to pornography as well. These laws include the 1949 Convention for the Suppression of the Traffic in Persons and of the Exploitation of Prostitution of Others; the U.S. Protection Act 2000; the U.N.'s Recommended Principles and Guidelines on Human Rights and Human Trafficking; and the Convention on the Elimination of All Forms of Discrimination Against Women.

She points to one particular document as offering "one of the most insightful developments in the international system on the subject of pornography."[93] The Human Rights Committee's General Comment 28 on the Equality of Rights Between Men and Women under the International Covenant on Civil and Political Rights (ICCPR) was ratified by the United States, albeit with reservations concerning freedom of speech.[94] According to MacKinnon, the ICCPR serves an "invitation" to consider pornography as an act that silences speech, rather than as a "barrier" to free speech.[95] Specifically, the committee urged all states to consider various factors that impede women's ability to exercise their legal rights:

> As the publication and dissemination of obscene and pornographic material which portrays women and girls as objects of violence or degrading or inhuman treatment is likely to promote these kinds of treatment of women and girls, States Parties should provide information about legal measures to restrict the publication or dissemination of such material.[96]

MacKinnon believes that this language supports the legality of anti-pornography legislation that does not run afoul of the First Amendment, although she notes that the United States has not interpreted the language in the same way.[97] Mac-Kinnon's argument here is that if the United States viewed pornography as a form of commerce, instead of focusing entirely on the speech aspect, then her anti-pornography ordinance could be constitutionally viable and the United States would come closer to international laws regarding pornography. As a result, MacKinnon sees an opening for the passage of an anti-pornography act similar to the one she developed in the early 1980s.

If MacKinnon's initial anti-pornography ordinance became law, then many of the concerns about Internet pornography could be addressed. However, in order for the ordinance to pass constitutional muster under the First Amendment, the Court must redefine the way in which First Amendment principles get applied to certain free speech questions. The alternative three-prong analytical framework would allow the Court to consider a different conclusion to the *Hudnut* case and, in turn, a new reading of Internet pornography restrictions.

THE *HUDNUT* CASE

The Background

In 1983 MacKinnon and Dworkin were hired by the city of Minneapolis to draft an ordinance that would address the civil wrongs perceived to be caused by the production, distribution, and use of certain types of pornography. In addition, they were asked to hold hearings, which would create a record establishing the need for such a law. These hearings would focus predominantly on the testimony of women who had been victims of pornography.[98] The hearings were held by the Minneapolis City Council on December 12 and 13, 1983.

MacKinnon and Dworkin drafted the ordinance in a way that would allow victims of pornography to file civil charges against the producer, distributor, or user of the pornography. The way in which they defined pornography would later become a key issue. Their definition included several specific parts that defined pornography as:

Pornography shall mean the graphic sexually explicit subordination of women, whether in pictures or in words, that also includes one or more of the following: (1) Women are presented as sexual objects who enjoy pain or humiliation; or (2) Women are presented as sexual objects who experience sexual pleasure in being raped; or (3) Women are presented as sexual objects tied up or cut up or mutilated or bruised or physically hurt, or as dismembered or truncated or fragmented or severed into body parts; or (4) Women are presented as being penetrated by objects or animals; or (5) Women are presented in scenarios of degradation, injury, abasement, torture, shown as filthy or inferior, bleeding, bruised, or hurt in a context that makes these conditions sexual; and (6) Women are presented as sexual objects for domination, conquest, violation, exploitation, possession, or use, or through postures or positions of servility or submission or display.[99]

The ordinance clearly established what practices would constitute unlawful discrimination, including trafficking in pornography, coercion into performing in pornography, forcing pornography on a person, and assault or physical attack due to pornography.[100]

Two different city councils in Minneapolis passed the law in 1983 and 1984. However, the ordinance was vetoed both times by the mayor of Minneapolis. Finally, in April of 1984, the Indianapolis–Marion County City-County Council passed the ordinance. In May, Indianapolis Mayor William H. Hudnut III signed it into law. On June 22, 1984, a motion for summary judgment was filed with the district court, claiming that the ordinance was unconstitutional. Multiple groups, including the American Booksellers Association, the Association of American Publishers, Inc., and the Council for Periodical Distributors Association, joined the motion.[101] The ordinance would ultimately lead to a district court ruling, an appellate court ruling, and a U.S. Supreme Court judgment.

The District Court Ruling

The U.S. District Court found the anti-pornography ordinance to be unconstitutional under the First Amendment because it proscribed speech that was not limited to the areas of permissibly proscribable speech. Judge Baker found: "The City-County Council, in defining and outlining 'pornography' as the graphically depicted submission of women, which it then characterizes as sex discrimination, has sought to regulate expression, that is to suppress speech."[102] Specifically, the court determined the ordinance to restrict protected speech, not the action of sex discrimination.

The court began by acknowledging that the issue of restricting pornography brought with it heated public and private debate and that the court could not "quarrel either with the Council's underlying concern (that pornography and sex discrimination are harmful, offensive and inimical to and inconsistent with enlightened approaches to equality)."[103] However, the court then stressed that it is not its place to get involved with public debate. Instead, the court had a narrow assignment—determine whether the law meets constitutional standards. The court needed to review multiple issues, including whether the ordinance restricts speech or behavior and if it restricts speech, does it restrict speech traditionally protected by the First Amendment.[104]

First, the court stated that despite a "certain sleight of hand" on the part of the city, the ordinance does in fact restrict speech, not action.[105] Subsequently, the court looked at whether or not the speech that was restricted fell into the category of unprotected speech. So, just as with the hate speech cases, the court in this case turned to the content-neutrality principle and the categorical approach to speech restriction. The court found that the ordinance did not fall into the proscribable areas of fighting words, libel, or obscenity. While the defendants argued that the speech they were regulating fell under the fighting words doctrine, the court chose instead to apply the *Miller* test for obscenity to determine whether or not speech falls into the proscribable category of obscenity.[106] The court then distinguished this case from *New York v. Ferber*,[107] *Federal Communications Commission v. Pacifica*,[108] and *Young v. American Mini Theatres, Inc.*, all cases dealing with the restriction of adult content.[109]

Judge Baker, in concluding his application of First Amendment doctrine to the anti-pornography ordinance, reverted to traditional dicta regarding the slippery slope theory of the First Amendment. He wrote: "It ought to be remembered by defendants and all others who would support such a legislative initiative that, in terms of altering sociological patterns, much as alteration may be necessary and desirable, free speech, rather than being the enemy, is a long-tested and worthy ally."[110] This statement is steeped in that heavily entrenched conception in liberal thought of the government as the only possible enemy to civil rights and liberties.

On appeal in the seventh circuit, Judge Easterbrook, writing for the majority, reiterated Judge Baker's concern about the far-reaching possibilities for speech restriction under the anti-pornography ordinance. He stated: "It is unclear how Indianapolis would treat works from James Joyce's *Ulysses* to Homer's *Iliad*; both depict women as submissive objects for conquest and domination."[111] He explained that the anti-pornography ordinance was an attempt to control people's beliefs, comparing the protection of pornography to the protection of hate speech, of criticism of the president, and of other unpopular social perspectives.[112] According to Easterbrook, the ordinance was nothing more than an attempt to "establish an 'approved' view of women, of how they may react to sexual encounters, of how the sexes may relate to one another."[113]

He contended that the defendants were correct in their claim that pornography perpetuates subordination of women, but argued that this only "demonstrates the power of pornography as speech."[114] He offered several examples, such as racial bigotry, anti-Semitism, and violence on television, as other types of speech that shape socialization. However, he stated: "If the fact that speech plays a role in a process of conditioning were enough to permit governmental regulation, that would be the end of free speech."[115] In other words, without the content-neutrality principle, democracy as we know it would cease to exist.

In addition to Judge Easterbrook's lengthy dicta about the role of the First Amendment in a democratic society, he also reviewed *Miller, Pacifica,* and *Ferber,* and reached almost exactly the same conclusion as Judge Baker—the ordinance in question fell outside of the boundaries of proscribable speech established in those cases. One area of difference in their opinions involved Judge Easterbrook's discussion of whether or not the ordinance could be salvageable with some rewriting. While he stated that it was not the court's role to perform that function, he explained ways in which an anti-pornography ordinance might be constitutional.[116] This type of ordinance, he noted, could focus on restricting "fraud, trickery, or other use of force to induce people to perform—in pornographic films or any other films."[117] This language, according to Easterbrook, removes the viewpoint element present in the Minneapolis ordinance, because it would not matter what the content or viewpoint of the film was, only the production would be in question. He added that if the film was produced under illegal circumstances, then distribution would be forbidden.[118] The coercion rule also would apply to all types of coercion, not simply pornographic coercion: "We suppose that if someone forced a prominent political figure, at gunpoint, to endorse a political candidate for office, a state could forbid the commercial sale of the film containing the endorsement."[119] In other words, in order to be constitutional, the ordinance could not cross the boundary between restricting illegal action and prohibiting protected speech.

In terms of the ordinance's language concerning the forcing of pornographic material on others, Easterbrook found it impossible to be rewritten to pass scrutiny under the First Amendment.[120] As to the ordinance's remedies for injuries and assaults caused by the pornography, Easterbrook used the example of libel to show that "the First Amendment does not prohibit redress of all injuries caused by speech."[121] In other words, if the ordinance were written in a manner keeping with the Constitution, then the remedies recommended in the ordinance would be acceptable. In the end, Easterbrook was certain that the ordinance as it stood was an unconstitutional violation of the First Amendment. Indianapolis never attempted to rewrite the ordinance and the U.S. Supreme Court denied a petition for rehearing.[122] As a result, Easterbrook's ruling stands and anti-pornography legislation remains unconstitutional.

Analyzing *Hudnut*

Several similarities exist between the rulings in *Hudnut* and those in *R.A.V. v. City of St. Paul, Minnesota*; specifically, the ways in which both rely on the concept of content neutrality. As a result of the current application of the content-neutrality principle, both Scalia and Easterbrook considered the government as the only possible censor of speech. In *R.A.V.*, Scalia noted that even though the First Amendment recognized certain categories of speech, such as fighting words and obscenity, as unprotected, these categories cannot be used as a way for the government to restrict ideas it does not like. He offered the examples of libel and obscenity in general versus restricting libel and obscenity only targeted at the government.[123] Easterbrook raised a similar concern about overzealous government restriction of speech, exclaiming that "[a]bove all else, the First Amendment means that the government has no power to restrict expression because of its message [or] its ideas."[124]

Both Easterbrook and Scalia invoked the slippery slope argument to illustrate how each of the ordinances would allow the possibility of too much government control over speech and, as a result, over thought. Scalia argued that restricting hate speech against certain groups could (and would) lead to restricting hate speech against other groups, such as "political affiliation, union membership, or homosexuality."[125] Easterbrook pointedly called MacKinnon and Dworkin's anti-pornography ordinance a form of "thought control" and added that while "much speech is dangerous" the remedy, unless narrowly applied, could be even more dangerous.[126]

A significant difference in these cases is that while the Bias-Motivated Crime Ordinance at issue in *R.A.V.* generated three different rulings from three different courts, as well as a split Supreme Court decision, the anti-pornography ordinance in *Hudnut* generated only two opinions that were essentially in complete agreement with each other. One reason for this difference, perhaps the main difference, has to do with different histories developed over time in case law concerning fighting words and those restricting obscenity.

The category of fighting words, first developed in *Chaplinsky v. New Hampshire*,[127] has, from the time of that initial case, been both enormous and empty. Virtually any type of speech might fit into the category and, perhaps as a result of that openness, none has.[128] On the other hand, obscenity has, for the most part, existed as a well-defined category. This is not to say that obscenity law has been a clearly defined area, but only to note that in comparison to hate speech, the Court has remained fairly consistent in its treatment of anti-obscenity ordinances. For example, through the long line of obscenity cases discussed herein, it becomes clear that the courts are only going to uphold those restrictive ordinances if the state can prove a substantial interest in protecting children. Pornography per se then has never been considered a category to be restricted for adult use. In fact, court dicta in many cases, including *Hudnut* and all of the Internet pornography cases discussed in this chapter, speak in terms of an adult's First Amendment right to consume such material. As a result of this uniformity in case law, *Hudnut* jurists naturally had to be in agreement. The anti-pornography ordinance at issue in *Hudnut* did not involve the protection of children and, by its very language, even the somewhat vague standards in the *Miller* test could not be used as support.

Another significant difference between the ruling in *R.A.V.* and the *Hudnut* ruling revolved around the way in which the majority opinions in each case framed the limits of their decisions. While Scalia attempted to shut the door completely on restricting hate speech, Easterbrook spent a substantial part of his ruling discussing the possibility of creating an anti-pornography ordinance that might pass constitutional scrutiny. However, Easterbrook's hypothetical ordinance bypassed the very issue raised by the MacKinnon/Dworkin ordinance. By attempting to fit the ordinance into preexisting legal standards, his option would not permit the ordinance to restrict much of the speech suggested in the original ordinance. Easterbrook appears to have missed the overall point of the MacKinnon/Dworkin anti-pornography ordinance by recasting the question of harm in traditional legal terms. He proposed that one might maintain certain portions of the anti-pornography ordinance, albeit with some rewording, if the focus were to shift from pornography (protected speech) to fraud or trickery (illegal actions). This new reading of the ordinance is comparable to the language in *R.A.V.* discussing banning cross burning through burning ordinances instead of because of the hateful nature of the speech. Both approaches sidestep key issues of power in contemporary society and the role of the First Amendment in maintaining the status quo power relations.

The alternative three-prong framework offers the possibility of acknowledging concern of government abuse of power, while also considering the damage inflicted on women as a result of the production and dissemination of pornography. Ultimately, through this application, it becomes clear that with only minor alterations, the MacKinnon/Dworkin approach to pornography restriction could be constitutionally viable.

Applying the first criterion—the character of the speech being restricted, the nature of the restriction, and the scope of the restriction—complicates the two dimensional content-neutrality principle and allows for a more complex review of the anti-pornography ordinance. In considering the character of the speech being restricted by means of the ordinance, it is easy to categorize this speech as low value.[129] Low-value speech still retains some First Amendment protection, but that protection is significantly less than for other types of speech, such as political speech. Obscenity, like libel and fighting words, has no value. But both Easterbrook in his ruling and MacKinnon/Dworkin in their construction of the ordinance find that pornography has value. The ordinance itself focuses on the role—the power—that pornography has in instilling certain ideological messages about women's role in society.

At the same time, defenders of the ordinance pointedly argue that this speech is low-value speech that is similar enough to obscenity to warrant restriction.[130] As such, the ordinance acknowledges that pornography both preys on the "prurient" interest and also contains very definite ideas. Easterbrook calls the attempt to restrict this form of subordination of women a type of "thought control."[131] And he finds that if pornography has the effect on people's minds that the ordinance claims, then that fact "simply demonstrates its power as speech."[132] He also contends that pornography is not low-value speech in the construct of the ordinance. He explains that low-value speech is based on categorical considerations and not on the viewpoint of the speech.[133] Looking at the more recent ruling in *Virginia v. Black*, Easterbrook's argument is inadequate. Just because speech has power (for example, the power of a burning cross to threaten), that does not necessarily mean that the speech should be protected automatically. Under this reasoning, threatening to overthrow the government forcibly would be protected as well. So, when looking at the speech in question here through my framework, as well as under the guidance of more contemporary Supreme Court case law, the speech in question is low value.

Looking at the criteria of the character of the restriction in light of the argument offered by Easterbrook, one could easily reach the conclusion that the speech is not low value enough to meet the current standard. However, his argument is comparable to that made in *R.A.V.* where the majority found hate speech to be more akin to political speech because they read the category of fighting words as not applying. If, though, we consider that the ordinance in question in *Hudnut* was not restricting all subordinating messages about women but just the way in which those ideas were conveyed, then the ordinance is restricting a "low-value" mode of expression, not the expression itself.[134] Pornography, as defined in the ordinance, does qualify as low-value speech and as such should be open to a certain level of restriction, not outright censorship.

In considering the nature of the speech restriction, First Amendment doctrine clearly establishes that content-based restrictions are acceptable in some circumstances while viewpoint-based restrictions are never allowed. Easterbrook unequivocally found the anti-pornography ordinance to be viewpoint-based, while the defenders of the ordinance argued that it is content-based, regulating the ways in which women are sexually subordinate, not the viewpoint that women should be sexually subordinated.[135] The ultimate question then is: Will the ordinance "drive certain viewpoints from the marketplace of ideas"?[136] In reviewing the language of the anti-pornography ordinance, the answer in most cases is no. Most of the ordinance deals with specific types of imagery, such as women enjoying being raped or being penetrated by animals or objects. Most is content-based. However, part 6 of the ordinance does raise considerable concerns, possibly crossing the line into viewpoint restrictions.

Part 6 defines proscribable pornography as material in which "women are presented as sexual objects for domination, conquest, violation, exploitation, possession, or use, or through postures or positions of servility or submissions of display."[137] Easterbrook raised the concern that the ordinance sweeps past actual pornography and into the realm of popular media and literature.[138] While this "slippery slope" argument frequently is invoked in First Amendment opinions, Easterbrook's focus on the ordinance's specific language in part 6 supports his fears. So, despite MacKinnon's defense that the ordinance restricts pornographic speech only after it has resulted in conduct, part 6 is still too broad. It would encompass everything from advertisements to music videos. Although one may argue that subordinating images in advertising or sexualized images in music videos add to the ideology of patriarchy and so also cause societal problems for women, the ordinance did not claim to attempt to restrict those messages. As a result, part 6 of the ordinance illustrates a solid example of viewpoint discrimination, falling firmly outside of the category of content-based proscribable speech.

In regard to the scope of the ordinance, again all but part 6 should pass constitutional muster. Parts 1–5 of the ordinance do not ban all speech but only that speech that causes specific secondary effects. Again, however, part 6 remains problematic because the language is not narrowly tailored to only ban the speech in the category of pornography. What solidifies the ordinance as being narrowly tailored is the fact that it is constructed as a matter of civil law and, thus, requires proof of harm. Pornography itself is not entirely banned, only that pornography which contains certain elements and that causes physical repercussions.

The above criteria show that an anti-pornography ordinance could be constructed to pass constitutional muster, but that part 6 of the MacKinnon/ Dworkin ordinance fails to meet the nature and scope requirements. Taking into consideration the character, nature, and scope, the remaining sections of the ordinance are content-based and apply primarily to low-value speech. Without adding further context, however, the courts could still weigh in on the side of banning the restriction or, on the flip side, could approve a restriction that impeded too much speech. The other two criteria in the framework, historical disempowerment and relational power, add that needed context. Considering these two additional elements leads to a finding that the anti-pornography ordinance, sans part 6, is constitutional.

The anti-pornography ordinance does not directly discuss history, however, unlike the breadth of the Bias-Motivated Crime Ordinance's undefined "race, color, creed,"[139] this ordinance applies predominantly to women. The ordinance reads:

> What pornography does goes beyond its content: It eroticizes hierarchy, it sexualizes inequality. . . . It institutionalizes the sexuality of male supremacy, fusing the eroticization of dominance and submission with the social construction of male and female. . . . Men treat women as they see women as being. Pornography constructs who that is. Men's power over women means that the way men see women defines who women can be.[140]

Implied in that language is that women, as a category, have been socially and historically dominated sexually. In terms of the relationship between sexual domination and women's diminished position in society, even Easterbrook acknowledges: "Depictions of subordination tend to perpetuate subordination. The subordinate status of women in turn leads to affront and lower pay at work, insult and injury at home, battery and rape on the streets."[141] The courts in other areas of law have accepted this as well. For example, the basis of sexual harassment law is built upon this idea and the courts have allowed certain gendered defenses, such as battered women's syndrome. Taking these points into consideration, both women's historical disempowerment and the role of the sexualization of women in perpetuating that disempowerment are apparent in U.S. history.

Application of the third prong of the framework also supports the constitutionality of the anti-pornography ordinance. This prong, which focuses on the relational nature of power between speakers, requires a consideration of the power dynamic of the specific speech situation occurring. In the ordinance in *R.A.V.*, there was no definition of power involved in the speech moment, only a discussion of hate speech raising "alarm" in the person or persons being spoken to. Not defining power made that ordinance problematic because it failed to address the extent of the harm caused by the speech. On the other hand, the anti-pornography ordinance not only considers the possible harm but also goes so far as to make the harm a prerequisite to punishing the speech. Specifically, the ordinance called for a specific type of speech moment, one in which "anyone injured by someone who has seen or read pornography has a right of action against the maker or seller."[142] If a person consumes pornography alone and does not commit injury against another, then the speech is protected. If a producer of pornography produces the material without violating the specific parts of the ordinance, then the speech is permitted, even if that speech still serves to subordinate women in a different manner. As noted previously, the only problematic aspect of the ordinance is part 6 and it would need to be removed before the ordinance could be constitutional under the First Amendment.

In the end, the anti-pornography ordinance, sans part 6, would offer a legally viable approach to placing certain types of pornography into the category of low-value speech that is proscribable in First Amendment terms. Through application of this alternative framework, the Court could change the way it views certain types of pornography in a general sense and, as a result, could change the way in which it treats Internet pornography. In doing so, it would rectify certain problematic issues in the line of Internet pornography cases, including resolving the question of adults' right to consume all types of pornography, determining what type of forum the Internet should be treated as, and the inability of the courts to apply the community standards element of the *Miller* test to a medium that lacks an easily definable community base. A brief review of *Ashcroft v. ACLU II* will illustrate that acceptance of an ordinance similar to the one proposed in Indianapolis would clear up much of the current confusion in Internet pornography cases and would serve to better protect both women and children.

ASHCROFT V. ACLU II: CONGRESS AND THE SUPREME COURT

In 1996 Congress enacted the Communications Decency Act, which included a provision to protect minors from harmful material on the Internet. Congress defined "harmful to minors" as matter that was indecent or patently offensive. By 1997, the U.S. Supreme Court had found the provision unconstitutional under the First Amendment. Immediately, Congress passed the Child Online Protection Act (COPA) in an attempt to address the Supreme Court's concerns about the language "indecent" and "patently offensive" and to narrow the scope so as to avoid issues of overbreadth. To correct the language issue, Congress crafted a definition of material harmful to minors based closely on the *Miller* test for obscenity. Specifically, the reworking of the *Miller* test read:

> Any communication, picture, image, graphic file, article, recording, writing, or other matter of any kind that is obscene or that (A) the average person, applying contemporary community standards, would find, taking the material as a whole and with respect to minors, is designed to appeal to, or is designated to pander to, the prurient interest, (B) depicts, describes, or represents, in a manner patently offensive with respect to minors, an actual or simulated sexual contact, an actual or simulated normal or perverted sexual act, or a lewd exhibition of the genitals or post-pubescent female breast; and (C) taken as whole, lacks serious literary, artistic, political, or scientific value for minors.[143]

By defining "harmful to minors" in this way, Congress directly answered the 1997 Supreme Court ruling by adding in "prurient interest" and "taken as a whole."[144] The other change in COPA narrowed the scope of the statute by having it apply only to the World Wide Web, not the Internet (which includes communications such as email and newsgroups) and by dropping the age of the minor from eighteen years old to seventeen. COPA further restricted the scope by limiting its reach to only those "communications made for commercial purposes."[145]

Just as quickly as Congress amended the CDA by creating COPA, the ACLU filed suit, claiming the new statute also violated the First Amendment. The case again would be appealed all the way to the U.S. Supreme Court. In this case, *Ashcroft v. ACLU*, the Court did not address the entirety of the constitutionality of COPA, but instead only reviewed the Court of Appeals' ruling concerning the inability of constitutionally applying the community standards criteria to the Internet.[146] As Justice Thomas noted in the plurality: "The scope of our decision today is quite limited. We hold only that COPA's reliance on community standards to identify material that is harmful to minors does not by itself render the statute substantially overbroad for purposes of the First Amendment."[147]

The Court's only role then was to determine whether using community standards in regard to material on the Internet made the statute substantially overbroad, as the Court of Appeals had argued.[148] Specifically, would the application of the community standards criteria "require web publishers to shield vast amounts of material"?[149] The Court looked at two issues in connection with this question. First, the plurality dismissed the appeals court's concerns that a hypothetical jury instruction under COPA would be based on unfair community standards.[150] Justice Thomas acknowledged that when reviewing CDA, the Supreme Court was concerned about this particular overbreadth issue; however, COPA did not suffer from the same lack of definition because of the additional standards from the *Miller* test that had been added.[151]

Secondly, the Court explained that community standards can be defined in various ways and two earlier cases dealing with national, inter-community speech support this analysis. The Court applied the rulings in *Hamling v. United States*[152] and *Sable Communications of Cal., Inc. v. Federal Communications Commission.*[153] *Hamling* dealt with the mailing of obscene material and concluded that "requiring a speaker disseminating material to a national audience to observe varying community standards does not violate the First Amendment."[154] *Sable* dealt with a statutory provision prohibiting obscene or indecent communications for commercial purposes by telephone.[155] In both cases, petitioners were concerned that community standards in the receiving community would be placed on content producers distributing from another location (community). Justice Thomas quoted *Sable* in support of his decision in *Ashcroft v. ACLU*: "If *Sable*'s audience is comprised of different communities with different local standards, *Sable* ultimately bears the burden of complying with the prohibition on obscene messages."[156] In conclusion, the plurality said that if publishers are concerned about the material they are distributing, then they should distribute that material through other mediums that they can control.[157] According to the plurality, to rule any other way would mean that other federal obscenity statutes would have to be found unconstitutional as well.[158]

Despite Justice Thomas's forceful opinion, the Court remained split on the issue of community standards. Justices O'Connor and Breyer each wrote separately to argue for the creation of a national standard for obscenity that would apply directly to the Internet.[159] Justice Kennedy, joined by Justices Souter and Ginsburg, argued that the community standard requirement could not be judged with the information available because determining the overbreadth of the standard means considering elements that the Court of Appeals ignored.[160]

COPA would once more find itself on the U.S. Supreme Court docket, this time in 2004.[161] The Court of Appeals, concurring with the district court's judgment, found that the statute in question in COPA failed the test of strict scrutiny. The lower courts found that COPA failed under both strict scrutiny requirements. In yet another severely divided decision, the U.S. Supreme Court affirmed the lower court rulings upholding the injunction and remanded the case to the district where both parties could present newer information.[162]

Justice Kennedy, writing for the majority, rested the entire decision on the application of strict scrutiny, focusing almost exclusively on the least restrictive means language.[163] He wrote: "Blocking and filtering software is an alternative that is less restrictive than COPA, and, in addition, likely more effective as a means of restricting children's access to materials harmful to them."[164] He acknowledged that filtering software is not a perfect solution, but held that it is just as effective as COPA at meeting Congress's goal of protecting children, but more effective at protecting adult speech rights.[165]

Justices Stevens and Ginsburg concurred in the ruling, agreeing that COPA was not the least restrictive means, but adding that they had a problem with the criminal prosecution element of the statute.[166] Justices Scalia, Breyer, and O'Connor, along with Chief Justice Rehnquist, dissented, each having a difficulty with the application of the strict scrutiny analysis. Scalia, writing his dissent independently, questioned the plurality's decision to apply strict scrutiny to this particular statute.[167] Scalia wrote: "Nothing in the First Amendment entitles the type of material covered by COPA to that exacting standard of review."[168] According to Scalia, if the business itself could be banned in its entirety, then "COPA's lesser restrictions raise no constitutional concern."[169]

Justice Breyer, joined by O'Connor and Rehnquist, agreed with the plurality's decision to apply strict scrutiny analysis, but disagreed with the way in which it was applied. According to the dissent:

> Nonetheless, my examination of (1) the burdens the Act imposes on protected expression, (2) the Act's ability to further a compelling interest, and (3) the proposed "less restrictive alternatives" convinces me that the Court is wrong. I cannot accept its conclusion that Congress could have accomplished its statutory objective—protecting children from commercial pornography on the Internet—in other, less restrictive ways.[170]

Breyer argued that COPA restricts no protected speech, but instead found that it restricts some speech outside of the legally defined category of obscenity. However, the amount of extra speech restricted, according to Breyer, would restrict "very little more."[171]

THE ANALYSIS

As it stands currently, pornography remains protected speech on the Internet. Obscenity is technically restricted; however, due to the Court's inability to assess community standards in light of the national nature of the Internet, defining what constitutes obscene in relation to the Internet has become a difficult process. In short, the Court has yet to reach some agreement as to how to adequately apply *Miller*'s community standards criteria. In terms of the CDA and COPA, the U.S. Supreme Court has established two primary guidelines. First, the Internet is more akin to print medium than broadcast and so any speech restrictions pertaining to the Internet must meet strict scrutiny requirements. According to Justice Kennedy's analysis of COPA, because adults have the right to consume indecent material, restrictions of indecent material on the Internet will not pass strict scrutiny. However, because pornography is considered non-proscribable speech, the Court has been compelled to apply obscenity standards. The question then becomes: If the Court could consider pornography as a proscribable area separate from indecency or obscenity, then would an ordinance such as the one established in *Hudnut* be constitutionally applicable to the Internet?

Secondly, the Court established that the test devised in *Miller* is applicable to the Internet. Both Justice Thomas in the CDA ruling and Justice Kennedy in the COPA ruling relied on the *Miller* test as a determining factor. Justice

Thomas, although finding that the CDA might be constitutional under *Miller* due to earlier rulings in *Sable* and *Hamling*, still held fast to the ability of *Miller*'s community standards to be applied to the Internet. He was primarily concerned with the fact that abandoning *Miller* in regard to the Internet would make all federal obscenity statutes unconstitutional. Justice Kennedy, while not directly addressing the community standards question, implicitly applied it by bringing into play the strict scrutiny test.

The alternative framework here would allow the Court to move past the outdated *Miller* standard. *Miller* was ruled on in 1973, more than two decades before the Court would hear its first Internet indecency case. In addition, switching the focus from indecency and/or obscenity to pornography will circumvent the discussion concerning adults' rights to consume certain material and ultimately better protect both children and women, the two groups most negatively affected by pornography.

Under the new framework, the Court would first need to determine the character of the speech, as well as the nature and scope of the restriction. In terms of the character of the speech in question, whether it is obscenity, indecency, or pornography, all fall into the category of low-value speech with obscenity currently being the least valued. While obscenity and pornography are currently treated differently under First Amendment analysis (one is proscribable and one is not), if pornography in general were reexamined in light of the modified MacKinnon/Dworkin ordinance suggested here, then the character question would definitely be dealt with as the lowest valued speech. Regardless of whether one reads COPA on its own merits or in relation to the *Hudnut* ordinance, the speech still fits into the low-value category.

Clearly under COPA, if one moved away from the ineffectual *Miller* standard, then the restriction would be considered a content-neutral one. It would, as suggested by proponents of the anti-pornography ordinance in *Hudnut*, only regulate one of the ways in which women are sexually subordinated, not the idea in general of women as subordinate. Again, as with the character of the speech, even without accepting the modified anti-pornography ordinance, the restriction still could be read as content-neutral given that COPA does not attempt to restrict all indecent speech available to adults via the Internet.

As it currently is written, COPA would fail under the scope requirement. It would not, under the *Miller* community standard criteria, be viable because (1) it does not address local community standards, and (2) it limits a considerable amount of non-proscribable speech for adults. However, because the ordinance in question in *Hudnut* was not constructed to protect children alone, the question of adults' rights to consume pornographic and/or indecent material would no longer be part of the equation. For now though, given COPA's current incarnation, coupled with traditional levels of protection for pornographic and/or indecent speech, COPA would undoubtedly not hold up under the first prong of the framework. Thus, the analysis shows that there will be no way to limit Internet pornography without first dealing with the general issue of pornography. On the other hand, if the modified version of the MacKinnon/Dworkin ordinance were considered constitutionally viable, then COPA could withstand Supreme Court review.

In terms of historical relationships, COPA does supply support for the disempowered nature of children, but because it is not concerned about adult women, there is no discussion of the relationship between pornography and women's further disempowerment. If that relationship could be considered, then the Court would be required to switch the conversation away from adults' rights to receive the content toward an assessment of the harms caused by pornography.

Perhaps the most important element in Internet speech case analysis comes through application of the third prong—the relational nature of power between speakers. What the CDA cases illustrate is the need for the Court to stop thinking in terms of print or broadcast. The Internet offers an entirely new type of communication that incorporates all previous media types, mixing them in combinations never before seen. The Court's reluctance to develop a new standard for this new technology has led it to determine that the Internet is not as invasive as broadcast media. By doing so, the Court was able to justify applying strict scrutiny analysis to COPA, allowing for virtually no speech restrictions on the Internet. However, this position by the Court is an erroneous one. Not only does the Internet serve as a conduit for video and audio broadcasts, but it also does so frequently in the most invasive space possible—the home. In addition, by its very nature, the relationship between Internet content and the user is especially personal. Interaction on the Internet is one to one, meaning that the technology is seldom viewed by a group sitting together around the computer. It is also immediate in that one can interact in real time with people all over the world.

As I have noted in this chapter, pornography, as well hate speech, continues to proliferate exponentially on the Internet, making it an extremely powerful tool for the further subordination of members of disempowered groups. One can raise the argument that the Internet also serves as a space for counterarguments, for anti-pornography or anti-hate speech campaigns. However, that option does not negate the fact that actual violence has been committed as a result of a hate site targeting abortion doctors or that real women continue to be used for the production of and abused as the result of pornography. Given the simplistic way in which the Court in the CDA cases has dealt with the communicative ability of the Internet, COPA would not stand up under this third prong. If, however, an anti-pornography ordinance such as the one proposed by MacKinnon and Dworkin were in place, then the medium issue would become less crucial.

Applying the three-prong framework to the COPA ruling illuminates multiple problematic areas in the treatment of Internet speech regulation. In particular the Court has become snagged on issues such as how to determine community standards and how to consider the Internet as a communication medium. As a result, pornography (as well as hate speech) continues to multiply. The only possible solution, then, is for the Court to revisit the way in which it treats pornography in general in First Amendment analysis. The ordinance in question in *Hudnut* did not rely on a community standards analysis; proscribable pornography was defined by the content of the speech not by the mores of the person receiving the images. As a result, the *Miller* test would not be applicable. The medium question would also become a mute one, as MacKinnon/Dworkin's ordinance did not specify print or broadcast. Finally, because the ordinance was not constructed to protect children alone, the question of adults' rights to consume pornographic material would no longer be part of the debate. In summary, a general anti-pornography law, such as the one ruled on in *Hudnut*, would be applicable to the Internet in the same manner as it would be to other media.

CONCLUSION

Internet pornography continues to be a contentious issue in both social and legal arenas. Many types of pornography rely on degrading and violent images of women as the basis for sexual pleasure. Traditional theoretical suppositions about the First Amendment do not allow for a consideration of the restriction of any type of pornography, no matter how degrading or violent the images. Under those legal frameworks, speech rights are individual-based and speech cannot be restricted based on the harm it causes. This reliance on content neutrality has led to an exorbitant amount of Internet pornography and has even forced the Court to uphold virtual child pornography because no real children were exploited in the process.

Contemporary understandings of the ways in which modern power operates dictate that assumptions about free speech need to be reconsidered, ultimately altering First Amendment case analysis. In the instance of pornography specifically, this alternative conception of power requires the Court to think about the role of culture in constructing the individual and how pornography works to establish and reinforce men's ideas about women and women's ideas about themselves.

The Court's severely split rulings in the long line of Internet pornography cases exemplify the problems inherent in current judicial definitions of obscenity and pornography. In this chapter, a multifaceted framework was applied in place of traditional obscenity standards. The alternative framework requires the courts to consider three factors: (1) the character, nature, and scope of the restriction; (2) the historical context of the groups involved; and (3) the relational nature of the individual speech moment. Under this alternative framework, an anti-pornography ordinance could be drafted that would restrict certain types of pornography, but not unfairly privilege one view of sexuality or drive certain viewpoints from the marketplace of ideas. The framework does not purport to remove all power imbalances from the legal system. In fact, this framework maintains subjective interpretation on the part of the courts in determining free speech cases. However, what this framework does in the process is to unmask the power to interpret already practiced when applying traditional "content-neutral" principles. This framework, by requiring courts to consider the discursive, historical, and relational nature of power in contemporary society, would bring about new First Amendment jurisprudence complex enough to balance societal and governmental issues of power in relation to individual members of disempowered groups.

NOTES

1. For discussions of the beginning of personal use of the Internet/World Wide Web, *see* som.csudh.edu/fac/lpress/comm.htm (explaining that while there were a handful of commercial activities on the web in the 1980s, the business potential did not take off until the early 1990s). For additional statistical historical user information *see,* Don Heider and Dustin Harp, *New Hope or Old Power: Democracy, Pornography and the Internet,* 13 HOW. J. COMM. 285, 286 (2002); Martha McCarthy, *The Continuing Saga of Internet Censorship: The Child Online Protection Act,* 2005 BYU EDUC. & L.J. 83, 84; D. J. Gunkel and A. H. Gunkel, *Virtual Geographies: The New Worlds of Cyberspace,* 14 CRIT. STUD. MASS COMM. 123 (1997); SUSAN J. DRUCKER AND GARY GUMPERT, REAL LAW @ VIRTUAL SPACE: REGULATION IN CYBERSPACE 66 (2005).

2. World Internet Usage Statistics News and Population Stats, www.internetworldstats.com/stats.htm (accessed October 2006).

3. *ACLU v. Reno,* 929 F. Supp. 824, at 844, n.4 (E.D. Pa. 1996).

4. *See* Douglas Kellner, *New Media and Internet Activism: From the "Battle of Seattle" to Blogging,* 6 NEW MEDIA & SOC'Y 87, 88 (2004) (discussing how the Internet has furthered oppositional politics); HOWARD RHEINGOLD, THE VIRTUAL COMMUNITY: HOMESTEADING ON THE ELECTRONIC FRONTIER (1993) (discussing the development of community through the Internet); JOHN V. PAVLIK, NEW

MEDIA TECHNOLOGY: CULTURAL AND COMMERCIAL PERSPECTIVES 1 (1998) (proclaiming that the Internet is approaching Marshall McLuhan's ideal global village); Don Heider and Dustin Harp, *New Hope or Old Power: Democracy, Pornography and the Internet*, 13 HOW. J. COMM. 285, 286 (2002) (discussing various recent studies that have "framed the net as the new hope for democracy").

5. Robert McChesney, *The Internet and U.S. Communication Policy-Making in Historical and Critical Perspective*, 46 J. COMM. 98 (1996). For other critiques, *see* Jeff Chester and Gary O. Larson, *Sharing the Wealth: An Online Commons for the Nonprofit Sector*, in THE FUTURE OF THE MEDIA: RESISTANCE AND RE-FORM IN THE 21ST CENTURY 185 (Robert McChesney, et al. eds., 2005); Don Heider and Dustin Harp, *New Hope or Old Power: Democracy, Pornography and the Internet*, 13 HOW. J. COMM. 285, 286 (2002).

6. Robert McChesney, *The Emerging Struggle for a Free Press*, in THE FUTURE OF THE MEDIA: RESISTANCE AND REFORM IN THE 21ST CENTURY 9, 17 (Robert McChesney, et al. eds., 2005). "The Internet and the digital communication revolution are in fact radically transforming the media landscape, but how they do so will be determined by policies, not magic."

7. *See* Kimberly Mitchell, et al., *The Exposure of Youth to Unwanted Sexual Material On the Internet: A National Survey of Risk, Impact and Prevention*, 34 YOUTH & SOC'Y 330 (2003); Ethel Quayle and Max Taylor, *Child Pornography and the Internet: Perpetuating a Cycle of Abuse*, 23 DEVIANT BEHAV.: INTERDISC. J. 331 (2002); Christopher D. Van Blarcum, *Internet Hate Speech: The European Framework and the Emerging American Haven*, 62 WASH & LEE L. REV. 781 (2005); GABRIEL WEIMANN, TERROR ON THE INTERNET: THE NEW ARENA, THE NEW CHALLENGE (2006).

8. Van Blarcum, *supra* note 7, at 783.

9. 508 U.S. 476 (1993).

10. 538 U.S. 343 (2003).

11. *Watts v. United States* 349 U.S. 705 (1969). For a lengthier discussion of the *Watts* case, *see* chapter 7.

12. 290 F.3d 1058 (9th Cir. 2002) (en banc).

13. Joshua Azriel, *The Internet and Hate Speech: An Examination of the Nuremberg Files Case*, 10 COMM. L. & POL'Y 477, 479–80 (2005). "The Nuremberg Files case began in 1993 with the murders of three doctors who performed abortions. David Gunn, George Patterson, and John Bayard Britton were murdered after their names appeared on the 'Wanted' posters sponsored by the American Coalition of Life Activists. The posters were displayed in the *Life Advocate*, an anti-abortion magazine published by Advocates for Life Ministries."

14. Jarrod F. Reich, *Internet & First Amendment: Hate Speech Online*, at www.firstamendmentcenter.org/Speech/internet/topic.aspx?topic=internet_hate_speech.

15. FACE is the Freedom of Access to Clinic Entrances Act of 1994, 18 U.S.C. § 248 (2005). The law prohibits the use of force, threat of force, or physical obstruction to intentionally injure, intimidate, or interfere with any person because that person has obtained or provided reproductive health services.

16. 395 U.S. 444 (1969).

17. The *Brandenburg* test is used to determine the constitutionality of speech that advocates violence. This test is discussed in detail in chapter 7.

18. According to the Southern Poverty Law Center, the number of hate groups operating in the United States increased to 803 in 2005 from 762 in 2004 (www .splcenter.org/intel/intelreport/article.jsp?aid=627&printable=1). "A growing Internet presence also helped groups' propaganda to flourish; there were 524 hate sites counted in 2005, up 12% from 468 in 2004."

19. Indhu Rajagopal and Nis Bojin, *Digital Representation: Racism on the World Wide Web*, 7 FIRST MONDAY 10 (firstmonday.org/issue/issue7_10/rajagopal). "The Web, as an unregulated medium, fosters the worldwide dissemination of both 'actionable' and 'nonactionable' hate messages."

20. Eric T. Eberwine, *Sound and the Fury Signifying Nothing? Juren Bussow's Battle Against Hate Speech on the Internet*, 49 N.Y.L. SCH. L. REV. 353, 355 (2004/2005).

21. *Id.* (primarily discussing hate speech laws in Germany). Christopher D. Van Blarcum, *Internet Hate Speech: The European Framework and the Emerging American Haven*, 62 WASH. & LEE L. REV. 781 (discussing the conflict between the First Amendment and European and international law).

22. International Convention on the Elimination of All Forms of Racial Discrimination, March 7, 1966, 660 U.N.T.S. 195. Article 4 provides that parties shall: (1) criminalize the dissemination of ideas based on racial superiority or hatred, (2) declare illegal and prohibit organizations that promote and incite racial discrimination and shall recognize participation in such organizations or activities as an offense punishable by law, and (3) prohibit public authorities and public institutions from promoting or inciting racial discrimination. The United States ratified ICERD but noted that it would refuse to take any actions that would violate the First Amendment.

23. Van Blarcum, *supra* note 8, at 789–92. In January 2003, the European Commission Against Racism and Intolerance added protocol allowing law enforcement officials to take action against dissemination of hate speech on the Internet. The United States refused to sign.

24. Eberwine, *supra* note 20, at 375.

25. 413 U.S. 15 (1973).

26. *Roth v. United States*, 354 U.S. 476, 489 (1957). In *Roth*, the Court held that material could be deemed obscene if "the average person, applying contemporary community standards, [would determine that] the dominant theme of the material taken as a whole appeals to prurient interest."

27. 413 U.S. 15, 23 (1973).

28. Indecent speech has been defined as speech "that, in context, depicts or describes, in terms patently offensive as measured by community standards . . . sexual or excretory activities or organs." Industry Guidance on the Comm'n's Case Law Interpreting 18 U.S.C. § 1464 and Enforcement Policies Regarding Broadcast Indecency. Policy Statement, 16 F.C.C.R. 7999, 8002 (2001).

29. Under strict scrutiny analysis, government regulations restricting speech must be narrowly tailored to serve a compelling state interest and must be the least restrictive means available.

30. 438 U.S. 726 (1978).

31. 485 U.S. 747 (1982).

32. *Id.* at 764–65.

33. For discussion of deficiencies in applying existing case law on obscenity to the Internet, *see* Tara Wheatland, *Ashcroft v. ACLU: In Search of Plausible, Less Restrictive Alternatives*, 20 BERKELEY TECH L.J. 371, 382 (2005) (discussing how Internet laws must operate inside of the constraints of pre-Internet legal decisions); Ryan P. Kennedy, *Ashcroft v. Free Speech Coalition: Can We Roast the Pig Without Burning Down the House in Regulating "Virtual" Child Pornography?* 37 AKRON L. REV. 379, 398 (2004) (reviewing the ways in which the Court has defined child pornography based on the physical abuse of children involved in the production); Robin S. Whitehead, *"Carnal Knowledge" is the Key: A Discussion of How Non-Geographic Miller Standards Apply to the Internet*, 10 NEXUS J. OP. 49 (2005) (examining how *Miller*'s community standards might or might not apply to the Internet); Javier Romero, *Unconstitutional Vagueness and Restrictiveness in the Contextual Analysis of the Obscenity Standard: A Critical Reading of the Miller Test Genealogy*, 7 U. PA. J. CONST. L. 1207, 1208 (2005) (arguing that "the inherent lack of context of the Internet threatens to render the *Miller* test overbroad"); Yuval Karniel and Haim Wismosky, *Pornography, Community and the Internet—Freedom of Speech and Obscenity on the Internet*, 30 RUTGERS COMPUTER & TECH. L.J. 105 (2004) (discussing whether the Internet should be treated under a separate set of legal principles than other media).

34. For discussions of increasing amounts of pornography on the Internet, *see* Martha McCarthy, *The Continuing Saga of Internet Censorship: The Child Online Protection Act*, 2005 BYU EDUC. & L.J. 83 (2005) (stating that "Internet sites are doubling annually and include an estimated 100,000 pornographic sites"); Marty Rimm, *Marketing Pornography on the Information Superhighway: A Survey of 917,410 Images, Descriptions, Short Stories, and Animations Downloaded 8.5 Million Times by Consumers in Over 2000 Cities in Forty Countries, Provinces, and Territories*, 83 GEO. L.J. 189 (1995) (discussing a study conducted by Carnegie Mellon University); D. RICE HUGHES, KIDS ONLINE: PROTECTING YOUR CHILDREN IN CYBERSPACE (1998) (claiming the existence of more than one hundred thousand pornographic websites). For studies concerning the societal impact of Internet pornography, *see* Ethel Quayle and Max Taylor, *Child Pornography and the Internet: Perpetuating a Cycle of Abuse*, 23 DEVIANT BEHAV.: INTERDISC. J. 331 (2002); Catharine MacKinnon, *Pornography as Trafficking*, 26 MICH. J. INT'L L. 993 (2005); Jennifer Lynn Gossett and Sarah Byrne, *"Click Here": A Content Analysis of Internet Rape Sites*, 16 GENDER & SOC'Y 689 (2002); Don Heider and Dustin Harp, *New Hope or Old Power: Democracy, Pornography and the Internet*, 13 HOW. J. COMM. 285 (2002). Articles discussing the invasiveness of Internet pornography include Kimberly J. Mitchell, et al., *The Exposure of Youth to Unwanted Sexual Material on the Internet: A National Survey of Risk, Impact and Prevention*, 34 YOUTH & SOC'Y 330 (2003); Jisuk Woo, *The Concept of "Harm" in Computer-Generated Images of Child Pornography*, 22 J. MARSHALL J. COMPUTER & INFO. L. 717, 719 (2004).

35. Brian G. Slocum, *Virtual Child Pornography: Does it Mean the End of the Child Pornography Exception to the First Amendment?* 14 ALB. L.J. SCI. & TECH. 637, 639 (2004).

36. In June 2003, the U.S. Supreme Court ruled 6–3 in *United States v. American Library Association*, 539 U.S. 194 (2003), that Congress could require any library receiving government funding to filter Internet access in order to retain its funding.

37. Karniel and Wismosky, *supra* note 33, at 109.

38. Telecommunications Act of 1996, Pub. LA. No. 104-104, 110 Stat. 56 (1996).

39. 47 USCS 223 (a).

40. 47 USCS 223 (d).

41. 521 U.S. 844 (1997).

42. *Id.* at 861–85.

43. This type of medium historically has been used to determine the level of scrutiny applied to government regulations of speech. Broadcast regulations have a significantly lower level of scrutiny applied to them than do regulations of printed material.

44. 390 U.S. 51 (1968).

45. 438 U.S. 726 (1978).

46. 475 U.S. 41 (1986).

47. 521 U.S. 844, 868–70 (1997).

48. *Id.* at 870.

49. 47 USCS 231.

50. 47 USCS 231 (e)(6).

51. 413 U.S. 15 (1973).

52. David L. Hudson Jr., *Internet and the First Amendment: Indecency Online*, www.firstamendmentcenter.org/Speech/Internet/topic.aspx?topic=indecency_online (2007).

53. The path of litigation started in a Pennsylvania district in 1996 (929 F. Supp. 824) shortly after the passage of the Communications Decency Act. The Supreme Court heard the case in 1997, ruling that the CDA was unconstitutional (521 U.S. 844). Congress rewrote the CDA, leading to multiple cases reviewing the Child Pornography Online Protection Act.

54. 542 U.S. 656 (2004).

55. *Id.* at 666–70.

56. 20 U.S.C. § 9134(f), 47 U.S.C. § 254(h).

57. *Id.*

58. *American Library Association v. United States*, 201 F. Supp. 2d 401 (E.D. Pa., 2002).

59. *Id.* at 407.

60. *Id.*

61. *Id.* at 411.

62. *Id.* at 410. "Because the filtering software mandated by CIPA will block access to substantial amounts of constitutionally protected speech whose suppression serves no legitimate government interest, we are persuaded that a public library's use of software filters is not narrowly tailored to further any of those interests. In addition, less

restrictive alternatives exist that further the government's legitimate interest in preventing the dissemination of obscenity, child pornography, and material harmful to minors."

63. *United States v. American Library Association*, 539 U.S. 194 (2003).

64. *Id.* at 199–200.

65. *Id.* at 225.

66. 18 USCS 2252A.

67. 18 USCS 2256(8)(B).

68. Daniel W. Bower, *Holding Virtual Child Pornography Creators Liable by Judicial Redress: An Alternative Approach to Overcoming the Obstacles Presented in Ashcroft v. Free Speech Coalition*, 19 BYU J. PUB. L. 235, 241 (2004): "Relying on social scientific research, Congress found that pedophiles often use the materials to encourage children to participate in sexual activity. Moreover, Congress cited a number of studies that concluded that virtual child pornography, like actual pornography, would lead to an expansion in the creation and distribution of child pornography in general, resulting in an increase in the sexual abuse and exploitation of actual children" (citing Congressional findings, notes 4, 10(B), following 2251).

69. 535 U.S. 234, 250–52 (2002).

70. *Id.* at 241.

71. *Id.* at 257.

72. 771 F.2d 323 (7th Cir. 1985).

73. Some of the works produced by Catharine MacKinnon include ARE WOMEN HUMAN? AND OTHER INTERNATIONAL DIALOGUES (2006); WOMEN'S LIVES, MEN'S LAWS (2005); ONLY WORDS (1993); FEMINISM UNMODIFIED: DISCOURSES ON LIFE AND LAW (1987); and TOWARD A FEMINIST THEORY OF THE STATE (1989). Works by Andrea Dworkin include LIFE AND DEATH: UNAPOLOGETIC WRITINGS ON THE CONTINUING WAR AGAINST WOMEN (1997); LETTERS FROM A WAR ZONE: 1976–1989 (1989); PORNOGRAPHY: MEN POSSESSING WOMEN (1989); and *Against the Male Flood: Censorship, Pornography and Equality*, 9 HARV. WOMENS L.J. 1 (1985).

74. Andrea Dworkin, *Against the Male Flood: Censorship, Pornography and Equality*, 9 HARV. WOMEN'S L.J. 1, 9 (1985).

75. MACKINNON, ONLY WORDS, *supra* note 73, at 15.

76. MACKINNON, FEMINISM UNMODIFIED, *supra* note 73, at 178.

77. *American Booksellers Association v. Hudnut*, 771 F.2d. 323, 324–25 (7th Cir. 1985).

78. *Id.* at 326.

79. ANNETTE KUHN, THE POWER OF THE IMAGE: ESSAYS ON REPRESENTATION AND SEXUALITY 275 (1985).

80. *Id.* at 273.

81. Carlin Meyer, *Reclaiming Sex from the Pornographers: Cybersexual Possibilities*, 83 GEO L.J. 1969, 2005 (1995) (stating that pornography "presents a world of women who are aggressive yet compliant, experienced but appreciative, unresisting and never rejecting"); DEBORAH L. RHODE, SPEAKING OF SEX: THE DENIAL OF GENDER INEQUALITY 134 (1997) (stating that "most boys first learn about sex

through pornography, and the messages it sends scarcely encourage relationships of mutual respect, caring and intimacy").

82. For examples of some of these quantitative studies, *see* Don Heider and Dustin Harp, *New Hope or Old Power: Democracy, Pornography and the Internet*, 13 HOW. JOURN. COMM. 285, 290 (2002); Jennifer Lynn Gossett and Sarah Byrne, *"Click Here": A Content Analysis of Internet Rape Sites*, 16 GENDER & SOC'Y 689, 691 (2002).

83. JOAN MASON-GRANT, PORNOGRAPHY EMBODIED: FROM FREE SPEECH TO SEXUAL PRACTICE (2004).

84. *Id*. at 4.

85. *Id*. at 6.

86. *Id*. at 149.

87. *Id*. at 122.

88. *Id*. at 151–52. "If subordinating practices of sexuality are culturally pervasive—produced and sustained so powerfully by this vast, diffuse, and normalized network of meanings and practices—and if we are all, to some degree, implicated in this system, it seems unlikely that its transformation could be effected by legal intervention. The law is focused on incidents: it requires clear and precise definition and a localization of responsibility. While legal interventions are effective in dealing with some subordinating sexual practices—such as rape, instances of sexual harassment, and child sexual assault—the forces of normalization, consolidated in practices such as the use of pornography, clearly outstrip the reach and influence of the law."

89. *Id*. at 152.

90. Catharine MacKinnon, *Pornography as Trafficking*, 26 MICH. J. INT'L L. 993 (2005).

91. *Id*.

92. *Id*. at 999.

93. *Id*. at 1009.

94. *Id*. at 1010 (discussing how the United States maintained that, while in agreement with most areas of ICCPR, it would not violate the First Amendment).

95. *Id*.

96. *Id*. citing, Human Rights Commission, 68th Sess., 1834th Mtg., General Comment No. 28, P22, U.N. Doc. (2000).

97. *Id*. at 1011. "Although the Committee's interpretation is permissive, the United States is clearly out of step with its understanding of the meaning of the ICCPR's guarantee of freedom of speech. Accession of the ICCPR could become one of several intervening developments in the reassessment of the constitutionality of the anti-pornography ordinance in the United States. Passage of the ordinance, federally authorized under the Commerce power—pornography being nothing if not commerce, its trafficking taking place in national as well as global markets—would put the United States back in conformity with the direction of international law."

98. DWORKIN, *supra* note 74, at 91. "They spoke on the record before a governmental body in the city where they lived; there they were for family, neighbors, friends, employers, teachers, and strangers to see, to remember. They described in detail sexual abuse through pornography as it had happened to them."

99. *American Booksellers Association v. Hudnut*, 771 F.2d 323, 324 (Ind. 1985).

100. *Id.* at 325–26.

101. *Id.* at 326–27.

102. *American Booksellers v. Hudnut*, 598 F. Supp. 1316, 1342 (S.D. Ind. 1984).

103. *Id.* at 1327.

104. *Id.* at 1330.

105. *Id.* "In summary, therefore, the Ordinance establishes through the legislative findings that pornography causes a tendency to commit these various harmful acts, and outlaws the pornography (that is, the 'depictions'). . . . Thus, though the purpose of the Ordinance is cast in civil rights terminology . . . it is clearly aimed at controlling the content of the speech and ideas which the City-County Council has found harmful and offensive."

106. *Id.* at 1331.

107. 458 U.S. 747 (1982) (upheld a New York statute prohibiting persons from promoting child pornography through distribution).

108. 438 U.S. 726 (1978) (upheld that patently offensive words did not enjoy absolute First Amendment protection).

109. 427 U.S. 50 (1976) (upheld an ordinance restricting the location of adult movie theaters).

110. *Id.* at 1337.

111. *American Booksellers Association v. Hudnut*, 771 F.2d 323, 325 (7th Cir. 1985).

112. *Id.* at 328.

113. *Id.*

114. *Id.* at 329.

115. *Id.* at 330.

116. *Id.* at 332. "The offense of coercion to engage in a pornographic performance, for example, has elements that might be constitutional. Without question a state may prohibit fraud, trickery, or the use of force to induce people to perform—in pornographic or other films. Such a statute may be written without regard to the viewpoint depicted in the work."

117. *Id.*

118. *Id.*

119. *Id.* "The same principle allows the court to enjoin the publication of stolen trade secrets and award damages for the publication of copyrighted matter without permission."

120. *Id.* at 333. "We therefore could not save the offense of 'forcing' by redefining 'pornography' as all sexually-offensive speech or some related category. The statute needs a definition of 'forcing' that removes the government from the role of censor."

121. *Id.*

122. *Hudnut v. American Booksellers Association*, 475 U.S. 1132 (1986).

123. 505 U.S. 377, 385 (1992).

124. 771 F.2d 323, 328 (1985) (citing *Police Department of Chicago v. Mosley*, 408 U.S. 92 (1972)).

125. 505 U.S. 377, 391 (1992).

126. 771 F.2d 323, 328, 333 (1985).

127. 315 U.S. 568 (1942) (establishing that certain statements have no value other than to instigate a fight).

128. *See*, for example, *R.A.V. v. City of St. Paul, Minnesota*, 505 U.S. 377 (1992); *Gooding v. Wilson*, 405 U.S. 518 (1972); *Cohen v. California*, 403 U.S. 15 (1971); *Speiser v. Randall*, 357 U.S. 513 (1958).

129. *Id.* at 331. "We come, finally, to the argument that pornography is 'low value' speech, that it is enough like obscenity that Indianapolis may prohibit it. Some cases hold that speech far removed from politics and other subjects at the core of the Framers' concerns may be subjected to special regulation." Easterbrook decides that "pornography is not low value speech" within that definition.

130. *Id.* at 331.

131. *Id.* at 328.

132. *Id.* at 329. For a counterargument to this position, *see* MACKINNON, ONLY WORDS, *supra* note 73, at 92–93. "This is like saying that the more a libel destroys a reputation, the greater is its power as speech. To say that the more harm speech does, the more protected it is, is legally wrong, even in this country."

133. *Id.* at 331–32. "The Court sometimes balances the value of speech against the costs of its restriction, but it does this by category of speech and not by the content of particular works."

134. MACKINNON, ONLY WORDS, *supra* note 73, at 94. MacKinnon takes issue with the Court's application of the "low-value" standard: "Nothing in *Hudnut* explains why, if pornography is protected speech based on its mental elements, rape and sexual murder, which have mental elements, are not as well."

135. 771 F.2d 323, 328 (7th Cir. 1985).

136. *R.A.V. v. City of St. Paul, Minnesota*, 505 U.S. 377, 387 (1992) (Stevens, J., concurring).

137. 771 F.2d 323, 324 (7th Cir. 1985).

138. *Id.* at 325–30.

139. *R.A.V. v. City of St. Paul, Minnesota*, 505 U.S. 377, 378 (1992).

140. 771 F.2d 323, 324, 328 (7th Cir. 1985).

141. *Id.* at 329.

142. *Id.* at 325. The ordinance states that: "People may not 'traffic' in pornography, 'coerce' others into performing in pornographic works, or 'force' pornography on anyone."

143. 47 U.S.C. 231(e)(6) (2000).

144. *Ashcroft v. ACLU*, 535 U.S. 564, 570 (2002).

145. *Id.*

146. *Id.* at 573. "We granted the Attorney General's petition for certiorari to review the Court of Appeals' determination that COPA likely violates the First Amendment because it relies, in part, on community standards to identify material that is harmful to minors."

147. *Id.* at 585.

148. *Id.* at 572–73. The District Court ruled that the revisions to the CDA still did not stand up to strict scrutiny. However, when the Court of Appeals heard the case, it ignored the lower court's reasoning and instead focused on COPA's use of "contemporary community standards." When the U.S. Supreme Court reviewed the case, it limited itself only to the question raised in the Court of Appeals' ruling.

149. *Id.* at 573.

150. *Id.* at 576.

151. *Id.* at 578. "COPA, by contrast, does not appear to suffer from the same flaw because it applies to significantly less material than did the CDA and defines the harmful-to-minors material restricted by the statute in a manner parallel to the *Miller* definition of obscenity."

152. 418 U.S. 87 (1974).

153. 492 U.S. 115 (1989).

154. 418 U.S. 87, 99 (1974).

155. *See* 47 U.S.C. § 223(b)(1982).

156. 535 U.S. 564, 581 (2002) (quoting *Sable Communications of Cal., Inc. v. Federal Communications Commission*, 492 U.S. 115, 125–26 (1989)).

157. *Id.* at 583. "If a publisher wishes for its material to be judged only by the standards of particular communities, then it need only take the simple step of utilizing a medium that enables it to target the release of its material into those communities."

158. *Id.* at 584. "[I]f we were to hold COPA unconstitutional because of its use of community standards, federal obscenity statutes would likely also be unconstitutional as applied to the Web, a result in substantial tension with our prior suggestion that the application of the CDA to obscene speech was constitutional."

159. *Id.* at 587–91 (O'Connor, J., concurring). O'Connor argued: "If the *Miller* Court believed generalizations about the standards of the people of California were possible, and that jurors would be capable of assessing them, it is difficult to believe that similar generalizations are not also possible for the Nation as a whole. Moreover, the existence of the Internet, and its facilitation of national dialogue, has itself made jurors more aware of the views of adults in other parts of the United States. . . . In my view, a national standard is not only constitutionally permissible, but also reasonable."

160. *Id.* at 602 (Kennedy, J., concurring). "To observe only that community standards vary across the country is to ignore the antecedent question: community standards as to what? Whether the national variation in community standards produces overbreadth requiring invalidation of COPA depends on the breadth of COPA's coverage and on what community standards are being invoked. Only by identifying the universe of speech burdened by COPA is it possible to discern whether national variation of community standards renders the speech restriction overbroad. In short, the ground on which the Court of Appeals relied cannot be separated from those that it overlooked."

161. *Ashcroft v. ACLU II*, 542 U.S. 656 (2004).

162. *Id.* at 673 (Stevens, J., concurring).

163. For a critique of Kennedy's analysis, *see* Mark S. Kende, *Filtering Out Children: The First Amendment and Internet Porn in the U.S. Supreme Court*, 2005

MICH. ST. L. REV. 843, 851 (2005). "Kennedy misunderstands the concept of less restrictive alternative. For such an alternative to exist, there must be some other proposed legislation or regulation that is just as effective, but that burdens less speech. Otherwise the term is devoid of significance."

164. *Ashcroft v. ACLU II*, 542 U.S. 656, 666–67 (2004).

165. *Id.* at 668.

166. *Id.* at 674. "COPA is a content-based restraint on the dissemination of constitutionally protected speech. It enforces its prohibitions by way of the criminal law, threatening noncompliant Web speakers with a fine of as much as $50,000, and a term of imprisonment as long as six months, for each offense. . . . [E]ven full compliance with COPA cannot guarantee freedom from prosecution. Speakers who dutifully place their content behind age screens may nevertheless find themselves in court, forced to prove the lawfulness of their speech on pain of criminal conviction."

167. *Id.* at 676.

168. *Id.*

169. *Id.*

170. *Id.* at 677 (Breyer, J., dissenting).

171. *Id.* at 679. "Both definitions [in COPA and *Miller*] define the relevant material through use of the critical terms 'prurient interest' and 'lacks serious literary, artistic, political or scientific value.' . . . The only significant difference between the present statute and *Miller*'s definition consists of the addition of the words 'with respect to minors' and 'for minors.' But the addition of these words to a definition that would otherwise cover only obscenity expands the statute's scope only slightly."

Chapter Seven

Terrorism and the Culture of Fear

The previous three chapters dealt with the free speech rights of easily recognizable minority groups—African Americans and women. This chapter focuses on one group not as often referred to as disempowered, but just as significant—the political dissident.[1] Free speech, particularly speech critical of the government, has always existed in an uneasy state. Throughout U.S. history, the government has attempted to restrict the speech rights of those who disagree with its leaders and policies. For example, less than a decade after the First Amendment was adopted, Congress passed the Alien and Sedition Acts, making it illegal to say negative things about the government. First Amendment scholars have shown us that historically anti-government political speech comes under attack by government officials more during wartime than times of peace.[2] In other words, the purely negative liberty approach to speech protection cannot withstand government infringement during times of national crisis.

In the current U.S. climate created by the so-called "war on terror," coupled with the physical war in Iraq, the political dissident again has become subject to speech restrictions. These infringements are far-ranging—from issues of academic freedom to restriction of once public information to invasions of privacy. The need to find a balance between protecting national security and protecting freedom of speech in this new climate requires that one think more complexly. One cannot underestimate the real threat of terrorist attacks. As legal scholar Frederick Schauer noted recently:

Behind every suicide bomber is a wily agitator, and behind every suicide bomb (or airplane) is someone who provided instructions for how to make it. Even the briefest look at the Internet will confirm that exhortations to violence and instructions for terrorism are all around us, and it would be hard to label all of

167

them—or, certainly, their cumulative effect—as inconsequential or exaggerated. In light of this, it would be hard to maintain that everyone who worries about the fact that virtually anyone can learn how to make a bomb on the Internet is a paranoid hysterical zealot.[3]

However, while not everyone is a "paranoid hysterical zealot," that does not mean that U.S. citizens should allow their First Amendment rights to disintegrate under the pressure of fear.

The purpose of this chapter is to offer a way to help maintain the balance between acknowledging the very real threats of terrorism (and the connection to speech) with the rights (and the absolute need in a democracy) for protection of the views of the political dissident. Following, I offer a brief review of some of the infringements recently applied to political dissidents, focusing on two examples—"free speech zones"[4] at presidential appearances and the conviction of terrorist leader Ali al-Timimi.[5] I outline the history of speech restrictions during times of war, culminating in an in-depth discussion of the two cases that established the true threats doctrine and the current incitement standard.[6] I then use examples—"free speech zone" cases and the conviction of terrorist leader al-Timimi—to illustrate what is problematic about current legal interpretations of true threats and incitement. Finally, I address those same cases using my alternative three-prong framework to add context to those tests, thus allowing for a more nuanced way to consider the difference between the true threat of terrorist speech and the protected right of dissident speech.

THE POST-9/11 CULTURE

The most recent governmental assault on free speech rights began almost immediately following the 9/11 attacks. On the morning of September 12, 2001, President Bush set the tone for what would and would not be acceptable behavior for Americans: "The deliberate and deadly attacks which were carried out yesterday against our country were more than acts of terror, they were acts of war. This will require our country to unite in steadfast determination and resolve."[7] In that statement, President Bush implied a need for complete agreement on response to the attacks. What Bush implied, Attorney General John Ashcroft made clear in December of 2001: "To those who scare peace-loving people with phantoms of lost liberty, my message is this: Your tactics only aid terrorists, for they erode our national unity and diminish our resolve. They give ammunition to America's enemies."[8]

Government leaders did more than just talk; they took action. Five days after the attack, the U.S. Patriot Act was proposed.[9] President Bush signed the

act into law on October 26 after only six weeks of congressional delibera-
tion.[10] On September 21, 2001, only ten days following the attack, Chief U.S.
Immigration Judge Michael J. Creppy issued a memorandum ordering the
blanket closure of all deportation hearings for "special interest" cases.[11]

POLITICAL SPEECH OR TERRORIST SPEECH?

In 2002 in a statement before Congress, ACLU president Nadine Strossen
urged, "We cannot allow the government to silence the voice of one dissenter
without weakening the core of our democracy."[12] According to studies conducted by the ACLU and the Freedom Forum's First Amendment Center,
Strossen had reason to be concerned.[13] For example, the ACLU produced a
report, "Under Fire: Dissent in Post-9/11 America," that outlined attacks of
free speech across the country by federal, state, and local government members, as well as by non-state actors.[14] Occurrences reported in that document
and other reports outlined a broad array of instances in which a range of different types of political speech was restricted. For example, the ACLU found
that the Denver police department was monitoring the peaceful protests of activists belonging to the Noble Peace Prize–winning organization American
Friends Service Committee.[15] In St. Louis and Baltimore police did more than
monitor protests; they interfered with them.[16]

Silent, individual protests were also grounds for government intervention.
On college campuses, students have been reprimanded by police for hanging
a U.S. flag upside-down[17] and have been visited by the FBI for displaying
anti-American posters.[18] In high schools, officials suspended two teachers
and a guidance counselor for displaying posters with anti-American sentiments[19] and in another incident a student was suspended for wearing a T-shirt
critical of President Bush.[20]

And the media have not been above suspicion or coercion. Just days before
the invasion of Iraq in 2003, the Dixie Chicks' lead singer made a statement
criticizing President Bush, which led to a boycott of their music by country
music radio stations.[21] Other instances included MSNBC's canceling of the
Phil Donahue Show because the network believed the show would be a conduit for the anti-war agenda and the firing of Peter Arnett by NBC because of
one of his broadcasts from Iraq.[22] Since the beginning of the war in Iraq, jour-
nalists around the country have found themselves penalized by their employers for attending anti-war rallies when not on duty.[23] And, in 2003, the Secret
Service visited the *Los Angeles Times* in an attempt to talk with political car-
toonist Michael Ramirez.[24] Their visit corresponded with the publication of a
cartoon by Ramirez critical of the president.[25]

For the purposes of this chapter, I focus on the creation of "free speech zones" and on the trial and subsequent conviction of al-Timimi. These two examples cover the broad spectrum from what in the past would have been considered protected political speech protesting government policies to speech calling for physical action against the U.S. government. These cases serve to illustrate both the shortcomings of the current true threats and incitement tests and the ways in which the alternative framework applied in the previous three chapters could add much-needed context to better protect speech freedoms during times of national crisis. However, prior to reviewing where we are today, we must first review the history of the suppression of political speech in the United States. The history will illustrate that this is not the first time political speech has come under attack from the government. It also will help to distinguish those past experiences from contemporary issues.

A HISTORY OF SUPPRESSION

The Alien and Sedition Acts were established by the Federalists at time when war with France seemed imminent.[26] Thomas Jefferson, a Republican, pardoned all of those convicted when he took office.[27] During the Civil War period, the government again attempted to curtail speech rights. This assault on speech, however, was not an open one. Instead, the Lincoln administration found other ways to suppress speech, primarily through suspension of the writ of habeas corpus.[28] In his recent book *Perilous Times: Free Speech in Wartime From the Sedition Act of 1798 to the War on Terrorism*, Geoffrey Stone reported that more than thirteen thousand people were detained without being charged.[29] In addition to those federal laws, criminal anarchy and criminal syndicalism laws were used to restrict speech at the state level.[30]

The next round of federal speech regulation would come about in the midst of World War I with the passage of the Espionage Acts of 1917 and 1918.[31] These acts would lead to a trilogy of Supreme Court cases in 1919 and the birth of the "clear and present danger" doctrine. Many of the following cases were discussed to some extent in chapter 2 due to their importance in establishing freedom of speech as an important liberty in U.S. society.[32] What wasn't addressed was the way in which they worked together to build the foundation for today's treatment of political dissident speech. As a result, those cases will be discussed here again in relation to their connection to political speech.

Justice Holmes wrote the opinion for a unanimous Court in the first of these cases, *Schenck v. United States*.[33] This case looked at the conviction of Charles Schenck, general secretary of the Socialist Party. Schenck had been convicted in trial court of violating the 1917 Espionage Act by circulating an anti-draft leaflet.[34] Both the Court of Appeals and the U.S. Supreme Court upheld his conviction.[35] Justice Holmes noted that while the leaflets likely would be protected speech in certain time periods, "the character of every act depends upon the circumstances in which it is done."[36] Words that created a "clear and present danger" could be constitutionally proscribed.[37]

One week later, the Court would hear the next two espionage cases. First, the Court heard the case of *Frohwerk v. United States*.[38] Jacob Frohwerk had been found guilty of publishing a newspaper critical of the U.S. government's involvement in the war. The Supreme Court penned a unanimous decision upholding the conviction. On the same day, the Court ruled on *Debs v. United States*.[39] Again the U.S. Supreme Court held that Socialist Party leader Eugene Debs had violated the Espionage Act, this time by delivering an anti-war speech.[40]

Eight months later, Justices Holmes and Brandeis took their clear and present doctrine to fruition, writing dissenting opinions in *Abrams v. United States*.[41] In this case, the Court in a 7–2 decision affirmed the conviction of Russian immigrants who circulated leaflets critical of the U.S. government's intervention in the Russian Revolution.[42] While the conviction was upheld, what is most significant about this case are the dissents. Justice Holmes argued in *Abrams*, and repeated several more times in dissenting opinions throughout the decade that followed, that in most circumstances the answer to threatening speech is more speech, not restriction.[43] However, he found that some speech "so imminently threatens immediate interference with lawful and pressing purposes of the law" that it does not qualify for First Amendment protection.[44] Key to Holmes's conception of the clear and present danger doctrine was this notion of imminence. Holmes and Brandeis would repeat this idea in minority opinions several more times in cases throughout the next decade; however, it would be 1969 before it would become part of the central argument in a majority opinion.[45]

The next sedition law would come in response to fears of the impending World War II. Congress approved the Smith Act more than one year before the war actually started.[46] Not one case based on the Smith Act reached the U.S. Supreme Court during the war, but with the Cold War looming, the act would become significant in the following decade.[47] Almost immediately, a series of events fell into place that ultimately would lead to a communist witch-hunt. The Soviet Union, a former ally in the fight against Nazi Germany, exerted its authority over the nations of Eastern Europe.[48] By 1949, despite financial efforts by the United States, China fell under communist rule.[49] That same year, the USSR exploded its first nuclear bomb.[50] It was in this environment that Eugene Dennis and ten other members of the Central

Committee of the Communist Party were indicted in New York under the Smith Act.[51]

Dennis v. United States is of particular significance given the similarities between the climate of that period and today's climate. Just like today, the focus of the United States was on fighting an ideology more than a war. In *Dennis*, the Supreme Court in a 6–2 decision found the conviction under the Smith Act to be constitutional. Chief Justice Vinson wrote the plurality opinion in which he distinguished the act of studying ideas about advocacy from the actual advocacy itself. Pointing to the language in the act, Vinson deduced: "Congress did not intend to eradicate the free discussion of political theories, to destroy the traditional rights of Americans to discuss and evaluate ideas without fear of government sanction."[52] However, Vinson did not add further context as to where to draw the line between studying about advocacy and pure advocacy except to state that any member of the Communist Party would be advocating violent overthrow based strictly on his membership. The Court found that Dennis and his associates crossed the line into advocating the overthrow of the U.S. government because the very purpose of the Communist Party is overthrow of noncommunist governments.[53]

In the 1957 decision in *Yates v. United States*, however, the Court applied a more detailed definition of the difference between advocating ideas and advocating illegal action.[54] Justice Harlan, in comparing *Dennis* to *Yates*, wrote: "In failing to distinguish between advocacy of forcible overthrow as an abstract doctrine and advocacy of action to that end, the District Court appears to have been led astray by the holding in *Dennis* that advocacy of violent action to be taken at some future time was enough."[55] With that ruling, the Court began to move away from the fear-induced rulings concerning advocacy of communism toward a more defined doctrine of determining the line between ideas and action.[56] Also with the *Yates* ruling, the period of the U.S. Supreme Court allowing the restriction of pro-communist speech ended. As noted previously in this chapter, anti-government speech has again come under attack post-9/11. None of these attempts to restrict speech have made their way to the Supreme Court yet. When they do, those incidents that fall under the auspices of threats (to political leaders or to national security) will be held to the "true threats" definition from *Watts* and the "imminent lawless action" standard from *Brandenburg*.

Watts and *Brandenburg*

During an anti-war demonstration in the late 1960s, an eighteen-year-old made the following statement:

They always holler at us to get an education. And now I have already received my draft classification as I-A and I have got to report for my physical this Monday coming. I am not going. If they ever make me carry a rifle the first man I want to get into my sights is LBJ. They are not going to make me kill my black brothers.[57]

This statement would lead to *Watts v. United States*, the case that added the true threats doctrine to the preexisting "clear and present danger" test.

Robert Watts was arrested and subsequently convicted of violating a 1917 statute that prohibits any person from "knowingly and willfully . . . [making] any threat to take the life of or to inflict bodily harm upon the president of the United States."[58] The per curiam opinion stated that the statute was constitutional on its face but "must be interpreted with the commands of the First Amendment clearly in mind."[59] The Court's opinion focused on the "willfulness" requirement in the statute.[60] It concluded "whatever the 'willfulness' requirement implies, the statute initially requires the Government to prove a true 'threat.'"[61] In order to determine whether the comments made at the rally constituted a true threat, the Court struck a balance between the language in the statute and "the background of a profound national commitment to the principle that debate on public issues should be uninhabited, robust, and wide-open, and that it may well include vehement, caustic, and sometimes unpleasantly sharp attacks on the government and public officials."[62] The Court concluded that Watts's comments did not constitute a true threat, that they were in fact merely a "very crude offensive method of stating a political opposition to the President."[63]

Brandenburg and Imminent Lawless Action

The Supreme Court heard *Brandenburg v. Ohio* in the same term as the *Watts* case. In *Brandenburg*, a Ku Klux Klan leader was convicted under an Ohio syndicalism statute for "advocating . . . the duty, necessity, or property of crime, sabotage, violence, or unlawful methods of terrorism as a means of accomplishing industrial or political reform" and for "voluntarily assembly[ling] with any society, group, or assemblage of persons formed to teach or advocate doctrines of criminal syndicalism."[64] The Klan leader was charged following a rally at which he made statements that included "Send the Jews back to Israel" and "Bury the niggers."[65] In attendance at the rally were twelve hooded men, some of them carrying guns, and one newscaster who had been invited to film the rally.[66]

Brandenburg was convicted in an Ohio state court. He appealed his conviction, arguing that the syndicalism statute violated his First and Fourteenth Amendment rights.[67] The appellate court affirmed his conviction without an opinion. The Supreme Court of Ohio dismissed his appeal "for the reason that no substantial constitutional question" existed.[68] In a per curiam opinion, the U.S. Supreme Court reversed the lower court ruling.[69]

The Court compared the Ohio statute to the California statute that had been applied in *Whitney v. California*,[70] which had, according to the *Brandenburg* Court, "been thoroughly discredited by later decisions."[71] The majority explained: "[T]he constitutional guarantees of free speech and free press do not permit a State to forbid or proscribe advocacy of the use of force or of law violation except where such advocacy is directed to inciting or producing imminent lawless action, and is likely to incite or produce such action."[72] Any statute or law that would restrict speech not producing "imminent lawless action" would "sweep within its condemnation speech which our Constitution has immunized from government control."[73] The Court did not set any additional parameters of what speech would fit into this category.

Understanding the Rulings

While the significance of *Watts* and *Brandenburg* in relationship to protection of political speech should not be underestimated, how much strength do they carry in today's world where fears of terrorist attack are very intense and very real?[74] The combination of a long history of governmental attempts to suppress oppositional political speech, combined with the vagueness of the *Watts* and *Brandenburg* rulings, establishes elected government officials and the lower courts in the position to determine who gets to speak their political views and who doesn't.

Consider the ruling in *Watts*. While the Court did distinguish political hyperbole from an actual true threat, it did not offer a concrete definition of what types of speech might constitute true threats.[75] One legal scholar noted recently: "Despite *Watts*'s speech-protective language, the Supreme Court's failure to articulate a clear standard in that case or subsequent cases for what constitutes a true threat has contributed to the doctrinal confusion that has persisted for more than thirty years."[76] Lower courts have applied the standard inconsistently.[77] This lack of clarity could lead to the prosecution of political speech that under normal circumstances wouldn't occur. As legal scholar Lauren Gilbert noted: "In light of current doctrinal confusion in this area, and without a strong reaffirmance from the Supreme Court, the decisions in *Brandenburg* [and] *Watts* . . . could be the latest victims of the war on terrorism."[78]

Brandenburg's incitement standard is equally problematic in today's social and political climate. Laura Donohue points out that *Brandenburg* might not "prove so robust in the near future."[79] She suggests that even though no justice "would want to be remembered for the modern-day equivalent of *Dennis v. United States*," we should not allow that to "lull us into thinking that political speech is thus protected."[80] Her overall position is that the ruling in *Brandenburg* did not overturn *Schenck*, *Dennis*, or *Yates*, and so leaves open the door to possibly reintroduce the clear and present danger standard inside (or along side) of the imminent lawless action standard.[81]

Robert Tanenbaum addresses similar concerns about the seeming lack of application of the imminent lawless action standard to today's terrorist concerns.[82] He notes that in terms of the imminent lawless action standard "few cases have offered clarification in the last three decades and none of them have addressed the War on Terror."[83] Specifically, Tanenbaum is concerned that the standard has a strict temporal requirement attached to it and, as such, is not particularly well suited for terrorist speech, which might call for a lengthier time between the speech and the action.[84]

He explains that the *Brandenburg* ruling itself did not set a firm imminence standard and offers that subsequent cases have defined the imminence standard as a key component in the consideration of imminent lawless action.[85] For example, in *Hess v. Indiana* in 1973 the Court added clarification to the imminence standard by holding that "advocacy of illegal action at some indefinite time" did not trigger the Brandenburg exception.[86] Later, in *NAACP v. Claiborne Hardware*, the Court explained that advocacy of violence to occur weeks or months later did meet the *Brandenburg* exception.[87] But terrorist cells work differently, frequently planning events of violence well in advance.[88]

THE AL-TIMIMI CASE

Five days following the 9/11 attack, a Muslim spiritual leader in northern Virginia named Ali al-Timimi gathered together at least eight of his followers to discuss the next steps in physically attacking Americans.[89] Al-Timimi held the meeting in secrecy, drawing the blinds and disconnecting the phone. At this meeting, he encouraged those in attendance to go to Pakistan to receive military training from Lashkar-e-Taiba, a group with ties to the al-Qaeda terrorist network. This training would enable al-Timimi's listeners to fight against American troops in Afghanistan.

Four of al-Timimi's followers heeded his advice and headed to Pakistan. Within eleven days of the World Trade Center attacks, the men had obtained travel visas and flown to Karachi. Less than two weeks later, all four were receiving hands-on weapons training. Al-Timimi was indicted by the government and subsequently convicted by a jury trial for encouraging and counseling his followers to commit illegal acts against the United States.

Al-Timimi's case is "the first significant conviction targeting terrorist speech in the post-9/11 era."[90]

The Analysis

While al-Timimi's conviction did not rest overtly on *Brandenburg*, the court did convict him for "encouraging and counseling his followers to commit illegal acts against the United States."[91] This conviction, based on incitement, places al-Timimi's case squarely into the realm of the imminent lawless action standard developed in *Brandenburg*. Al-Timimi offers an intriguing space to consider both sides of the problematic nature of the *Brandenburg* incitement test.

On the one hand, as both Donohue and Martin Redish point out, the imminent lawless action standard did not overturn the clear and present danger rulings in cases such as *Dennis* and *Yates*. As Redish notes in his recent book *The Logic of Persecution: Free Expression and the McCarthy Era*, "Use of the word imminence readily invited reference to Justice Brandeis's highly protective version of clear and present danger in *Whitney*. Yet, puzzlingly, in an accompanied footnote, the Court expressly relied on *Dennis* and *Yates*, rather than the *Whitney* concurrence, as support for its standard for protecting unlawful advocacy."[92] Reading the *Brandenburg* ruling in this way would mean that *Brandenburg* did little more than add texture to the "abstract advocacy" reasoning from the *Dennis* and *Yates* rulings. Redish offers the ruling in *Rice v. Paladin Enterprises, Inc.* as evidence that the Court intended this lower level of speech protection.[93] In *Rice*, the Fourth Circuit Court of Appeals upheld a lower court's award of damages against the publisher of *Hit Man: A Technical Manual for Independent Contractors*.[94] This book offered specific directions for how to commit murders and, subsequently, a person relied on the book to commit several murders for hire. Paladin Enterprises was found civilly liable despite the fact that a lengthy period of time occurred between publication of the book and the murders. Redish explains that this ruling ignores the more "speech-protective version of the *Brandenburg* test" by not taking into account the imminence factor.[95]

Considering al-Timimi's actions through the prism of the *Rice* reading of *Brandenburg*, his conviction makes complete sense. Al-Timimi encouraged his followers to pursue an illegal attack against the United States. His words led to four of his followers flying to Karachi to receive terrorist training. His role in convincing, or inciting, others to take illegal action is comparable to that of Paladin publishing a book educating a murderer on techniques needed to successfully commit that illegal act. In fact, the facts in the al-Timimi case constitute an even closer correlation between speech and action than the facts at hand in *Rice*. Al-Timimi spoke directly to a specific audience and gave detailed directions to them in how to carry out the illegal act, where in comparison, Paladin had no direct connection to the person who would ultimately use the book for illegal acts. What is problematic about construing *Brandenburg* in the least speech-protective manner is that while it allows us to restrict the most outrageous forms of incitement, it opens the door for the restriction of speech that might merely be unpopular. What might happen to the current-day incarnations of *Dennis* and *Yates*? While the Court has yet to address this issue, Donohue maintains that at this time in history in which national security interests are very real, so is the threat of repeating the overzealous prosecution of anti-government speech during the McCarthy era: "The lesson to be learned . . . is that a relaxation of the these standards to address a national security threat ought to give us pause. In the past, speech restrictions ended up being applied to political opponents, not just those engaged in violence. And they had a significant chilling effect on speech."[96]

While Donohue is correct in being concerned that the lesser speech-protective version of *Brandenburg* could lead to prosecution of political dissidents, the alternative possible reading of *Brandenburg* is problematic as well. This more speech-protective version of incitement carries with it imminence as a key determining factor. As discussed earlier, the U.S. Supreme Court has handed down rulings adding further context to the imminence standard. In *Hess*, the Court was firm that advocacy must occur close to the time of the speech, not at an indefinite moment.[97] Later in *NAACP v. Claiborne Hardware*, the Court was more specific about what that time frame might look like, ruling that speech cannot be restricted if weeks or months pass between the speech moment and the action.[98] This temporal distinction would seem to invalidate al-Timimi's conviction. As Tanenbaum notes, al-Timimi's speech easily meets certain aspects of the more speech-protective incitement standard.[99] He met the first prong of the test by expressly advocating illegal activity. His statements were directed to a particular group of people and offered detailed instruction on how to follow through with joining the Taliban and attacking the United States. It is questionable if he met the second and third prongs. The second prong questions the speaker's intention and there can be no doubt about al-Timimi's intentions. He not only gave directions of how to proceed with the illegal act, he did so in secret to a group already promoting global jihad.[100] But did he intend to incite *imminent* lawless action? The ultimate action he calls for would take months to come to fruition.[101] The third prong is problematic if applied through the reasoning used in *Hess* and *NAACP*. Al-Timimi's instructions called for illegal action that would not come to fruition for months, far surpassing the *NAACP*'s time limit of less than several weeks. This speech-protective reading of *Brandenburg* as it was construed in *Hess* and *NAACP*, brings into question whether or not al-Timimi could be punished for his speech under the First Amendment.

I do not mean suggest that al-Timimi's speech should or should not have been protected. What I am showing here is that the overly speech-protective reading might bar the courts from restricting the exact type of inciting speech that could lead to serious lawless action against the people of the United States. I agree with Tanenbaum that the imminence standard as it currently reads lacks the necessary element of context needed for the test to be effective in dealing with terrorist speech which likely will have a longer time frame and a larger geographic playing field. He explains: "If imminence is constrained by strict temporal limits in space and time and the absence of the consideration of context, it is difficult to prove that al-Timimi intended imminent lawless action."[102]

Given the seemingly contradictory rulings in *Rice* and in *Hess* and *NAACP*, the Court needs to consider offering more context to the incitement standard in *Brandenburg*. I suggest that using the framework developed in chapter 3 might add this needed context to better balance the tensions between national security issues and the right of every American to criticize their government.

Consider the first prong of that framework—the character, nature, and scope of the speech proscribable under the *Brandenburg* incitement test. In terms of the character of the speech, the current incitement category raises no legal concerns. Ever since Justice Oliver Wendell Holmes Jr.'s famous statement about not erroneously shouting fire in a crowded theatre, the Court has held fast to the position that speech intended to incite one to illegal action is low-value speech and hence proscribable.[103] In terms of the nature of the speech restriction, the incitement test is on its face neither content- nor viewpoint-based. Application of the standard seems to support this viewpoint-neutral element. For example, as noted previously, the *Rice* case was considerably different from the al-Timimi case in terms of content and viewpoint. So, while al-Timimi's speech was definitely political in nature, the Court also has applied *Brandenburg* to nonpolitical speech such as the directions for murder in *Rice*.

While the character of the speech and nature of the restriction are already encompassed through the language and application of the incitement test, the question of the scope of the restriction, conversely, raises serious concerns. Specifically, these concerns arise from the lack of consensus on how to read the time element. While the *Rice* ruling certainly supports al-Timimi's conviction, *Hess* and *NAACP* don't. In looking only at character, nature, and scope of the incitement test, previous Supreme Court application illustrates that without considering additional factors, the imminence requirement leaves the Court with too much discretion. In what ways then could this imminence element be constructed to allow for consistency? Perhaps, as with other areas of law, the openness of the imminence standard is not the key concern. I propose that considering additional factors—history and relational power—would offer one way in which depth could be added to the *Brandenburg* test without completely removing the possible speech-protective element of imminence.

Neither the *Brandenburg* incitement test nor the imminence element specifically rely in any way on historical context. But history, both the history of the group itself and its historical relation to inciting violence, must be taken into consideration. As Tanenbaum correctly points out: "Unlike the Communist Party-U.S.A in the 1940s, the goal of Islamist terrorists is not to gather popular support to overthrow the U.S. government. Rather, Islamic terrorists succeed in achieving their goal by maintaining a subversive, amorphous network."[104] His statement speaks directly to the issue of history. In one case, that of the Communist Party in the United States, historically the group has functioned through advocacy of its agenda. It has sought not to incite violent, illegal action, but instead to overthrow the government through a collective ideological metamorphosis. Terrorist groups, on the other hand, are by their very nature violent. They do not speak to garner support for a cause, but instead speak to rally already-existing believers to take violent and/or illegal action in the name of the cause. Acknowledging these historical behaviors brings one more element of consideration to the table.

The third area to consider is the relational nature of power between the speaker and the spoken to, or, in other words, establishing what sort of power dynamics are at play in the specific speech moment. This distinction was drawn in *Virginia v. Black* when the Court identified that burning a cross in the presence of African Americans can be intimidating enough to constitute true threats, while burning a cross at a KKK rally is being done purely to express a particular viewpoint.[105] The same distinction was illustrated in the example of an anti-pornography ordinance that is based on some action occurring.[106] A private viewing of pornography, in that instance, would be treated differently than, say, forcing or coercing another person to interact with it. The private consumption would be a form of protected speech; the other instance would not.

How would this criteria work in conjunction with the incitement test? Again, a comparison can be made between communist speech in the 1940s and al-Timimi's speech. Take, for example, the facts in *Dennis*. In that situation, *Dennis*, along with ten other leaders in the Communist Party in the United States, were arrested for advocating the overthrow of the government. However, their advocacy never led to violence. The speech moment was not only public, it was intended for public consumption. It was, in effect, pure political speech. Al-Timimi offers a different type of speech moment. In that case, al-Timimi was alone with a discreet group of followers. Not only was he not in a public space, he went out of his way to ensure even further privacy by closing the blinds. In addition, he did not seek to advocate ideas; his followers were already primed for the call to violent action that he was imploring. Certainly, the court considered these elements; however, there is nothing currently in the law to consider them in every case. As a result, at some point, the Supreme Court could determine that the individual speech moment is not pertinent and only apply the incitement standard as it currently exists. On the flip side, adding the criteria of the speech moment, along with the historical question, could provide an extra layer of context to help ensure that advocacy is treated differently than incitement.

FREE SPEECH ZONES

Free speech zones are areas set aside in public places, primarily during political events, in which protestors are removed to a secured, cordoned-off space.[107] These zones are supposedly designed to allow protestors a place to express their views free of interference from law enforcement officials. While free speech zones at political events have a history starting in the late 1980s, use of the zones has grown considerably following the 9/11 attacks.[108] Specifically, the U.S. Secret Service now routinely forces protestors who are critical of President Bush into free speech zones during presidential appearances.[109] According to critics of these zones, protestors are removed to remote locations where those opposed to the president are quarantined away from both the view of the president and of the media.[110] Political activists and groups supporting the president are permitted to remain closer to the event and thus to media coverage.[111] Secret Service members and local enforcement officials have arrested protestors refusing to adhere to the free speech zone restrictions.[112]

Three of those arrests have resulted in court rulings in the past three years. In the first instance, sixty-five-year-old retired steel worker Bill Neel was arrested at a presidential appearance during a 2002 Labor Day picnic in Pittsburgh.[113] Supporters of Bush were permitted to stay along the route of the motorcade, while protestors were removed to a free speech zone five hundred feet away from the site of the president's speech.[114] Neel, one of the protestors, refused to go to the free speech zone and instead stood with the Bush supporters. Neel held a sign that read: "The Bush Family Must Surely Love the Poor, They Made so Many of Us."[115] Neel was charged with disorderly conduct for refusing to move to the free speech zone.[116] At Neel's trial in 2002, a Pittsburgh detective testified that local police were directed by the Secret Service to confine people "that were making a statement pretty much against the President and his views."[117] District Court Justice Shirley Trkula threw out the charges against Neel, stating: "I believe this is America. Whatever happened to 'I do not agree with you, but I'll defend to the death your right to say it.'"[118]

Two later cases did not end as favorably for free speech rights. On July 24, 2003, President Bush appeared in front of the Treasury Financial Facility in Philadelphia.[119] ACORN, the Association of Community Organizations for Reform Now, attended the event to picket the president's visit in an attempt to draw attention to what they felt were discriminatory tax benefit laws.[120] When they arrived, they were informed by Secret Service members that "no one except police personnel would be allowed directly in front of the [Treasury Financial Facility]."[121] ACORN agreed to move their protest across the street; however, they soon discovered that citizens supporting the president were permitted to remain directly in front of the building. ACORN's legal counsel to the Secret Service, according to some reports, were retaliated against further by having "several large police vans directly in front of [the protestors]," in effect blocking them from the president's (and the media's) view.[122]

The ACLU filed suit, claiming that ACORN's First Amendment rights had been violated.[123] In addition, the ACLU sought a permanent injunction against the Secret Service to enjoin them from ever establishing free speech zones at presidential appearances.[124] The ACLU raised three issues in its lawsuit: (1) that free speech zones prohibit protestors from gathering in places where other members of the public are permitted to gather; (2) that free speech zones keep the president from viewing or listening to protestors; and (3) that, as result of the first two issues, free speech zones give the impression that there is less political dissent than actually exists.[125]

The U.S. District Court for the Eastern District of Pennsylvania rejected the ACLU's claims, stating that they were "too amorphous to be justicable at [that] point in time."[126] The court did add, however, that "the defendants may indeed have violated plaintiff's First Amendment rights."[127] Thus, the court simply declined to rule on the overall constitutionality of free speech zones.

The third court case grew out of a presidential appearance at an airport in Columbia, South Carolina, on October 4, 2002.[128] On the day of the rally, law enforcement officers were assigned to patrol the perimeter of an unmarked restricted area.[129] Vehicles and people were allowed to travel through the restricted area until shortly before the president arrived. The only pedestrians allowed to stay in the area were those waiting in line with tickets to enter the hangar for the rally.[130] Brett Bursey, the director for the Progressive Network, went to the rally with the intent of protesting the war in Iraq.[131] Bursey proceeded to go into the restricted area with signs and a megaphone. Law enforcement offices requested Bursey leave the restricted area. He did move his location, but stayed inside of the area.[132] After a twenty-five-minute confrontation between Bursey and the officers, he was arrested for trespassing, a charge that was later dropped.[133]

More than four months following his initial arrest, Bursey was charged by the U.S. Attorney with violating Title 18, Section 1752(a)(1)(ii).[134] Following a two-day bench trial in November of 2003, Bursey was convicted and sentenced to a $500 fine and a $10 special assessment.[135] Bursey appealed but his sentence was subsequently upheld by the Court of Appeals for the Fourth Circuit.[136] Bursey argued in court that he was not aware that he was in a federally cordoned-off area. He stated that the law enforcement officers never told him such and that the free speech zone was not clearly demarcated.[137] The Fourth Circuit disagreed, finding that "Bursey thus took a calculated risk when he defied the orders of the officers to leave the restricted area, thereby intending to act unlawfully."[138] Bursey appealed to the U.S. Supreme Court but on January 17, 2006, the justices declined to hear the case, thus leaving the constitutionality of free speech zones still in question.

The Analysis

While none of the above free speech zone cases directly called into question the true threats doctrine, the reasoning employed by the Secret Service and other police officials relies on the belief that these zones are needed to protect the president. Considering the severity of the speech restriction, one would think that a more rigorous proof of threat would need to occur before placing a prior restraint on particular viewpoints concerning political views.[139] If the Supreme Court ever were to rule on the constitutionality of free zones, the government would have a high burden to bear. And, given that testimony from law enforcement officials speaks to concerns of violence against the president, then true threats would be the obvious legal doctrine applied.

How would the lower court free speech zone cases look through the lens of the true threats doctrine? Would the government be forced to stop removing political dissidents from the center stage? Would the *Watts* case, which itself dealt with statements critical of the president, lead to a decision that the free speech zones as they are currently enforced are a viewpoint-based form of discrimination not permitted under the First Amendment? Because the courts have yet to deal with the constitutionality issue, these questions remain speculative, but it is based on this speculation that I will address the possibility of the true threats application to free speech zone cases.

The *Watts* true threat standard raises similar problems as the *Brandenburg* incitement test in terms of lack of clarity. As previously mentioned, the *Watts* case itself only made it clear that political hyperbole could not be considered a true threat. In 2003, the Court in *Virginia v. Black* added to the definition of true threats.[140] Justice O'Connor, writing for the majority, said that true threats "encompass those statements where the speaker means to communicate a serious expression of an intent to commit an act of unlawful violence to a particular individual or group of individuals. The speaker need not actually intend to carry out the threat."[141] As mentioned earlier in this chapter, *Watts*'s speech-protective language is constrained by "the Supreme Court's failure to articulate a clear standard."[142] In addition to this lack of specificity on the part of the Supreme Court, the lower courts have added to the lack of clarity, producing contradictory rulings in some cases.[143] Two recent Ninth Circuit Court of Appeals cases illustrate the significance of the confusion.

In 2002 in *Planned Parenthood of Columbia/Willamette, Inc. v. American Coalition of Life Activists*, the Ninth Circuit ruled that anti-abortion websites featuring abortion doctors' faces in wanted-poster style format constituted a true threat proscribable under the First Amendment.[144] Three years later in *United States v. Cassel*, the court upheld the constitutionality of a federal law that prohibited "intimidation to hinder, prevent, or attempt to hinder people from buying or attempting to buy federal land."[145] What is most problematic about the rulings in these cases is that the court applied different standards in each case. In *Planned Parenthood*, the court applied an objective standard for intent under the true threats test. Specifically, the court defined a true threat as a statement made when a "reasonable person would foresee that the statement would be interpreted by those to whom the maker communicates the statement as a serious expression of intent to harm."[146] In other words, true threats are defined by whether or not a reasonable person would find them threatening.[147] Jennifer Elrod explains:

> As proscribable acts, true threats have a number of detrimental impacts on society in general and on targeted individuals in particular. Chief among these are the fear and apprehension that threats engender, the disruption prompted by such fear, and the cost of protecting against, reducing, preventing, or eliminating the threatened violence.[148]

True threats as defined through the application of the objective standard are about whether or not the words could be construed as threatening, not whether or not the speaker intended to carry out the threat. In *Cassel*, the Ninth Circuit applied a subjective standard. The appeals court determined that "speech may be deemed unprotected by the First Amendment as a 'true threat' only upon proof that the speaker subjectively intended the speech as a threat."[149] In other words, the subjective test relies on attempting to determine the speaker's motive. Does he intend to or can he reasonably carry out the threat? Whether or not a reasonable person would find the words threatening is not significant.

Planned Parenthood and *Cassel* exemplify the confusion that lower courts across the country have been experiencing. Both the subjective and objective approaches as currently conceived are problematic. The subjective standard completely ignores the issue that speech can be threatening to the target even if the speaker did not actually intend physical harm. This criteria seems counter to the language in *Black* that "the speaker need not actually intend to carry out the threat."[150] It also can be considered problematic if one agrees with Elrod that the reason for proscribing threats is largely because of "the fear and apprehension that threats engender,"[151] a position that seems reasonable in light of the ruling in *Black*. The objective standard offers significantly more context to the true threats doctrine. For example, in *Watts* the Court considered questions of both content and context. The Court took into account how the audience reacted to Watts's statements, the location he was in, and who was in the audience he was speaking to. In *Black*, the Court made this distinction even more pointedly, assessing that cross burnings could be used either to intimidate or as a form of ideological solidarity. As a result, the Court had to consider the location of the speaker and the make up of the audience. However, due to the fact that the Ninth Circuit ruled on *Cassel* after the *Black* decision, the true threats doctrine, even with the added discussion in *Black*, still lacks the clarity needed to distinguish critical political discourse from true threats. In other words, the question of the constitutionality of free speech zones is still open.

In chapter 5, I applied my alternative framework to the ruling in *Black*. While that analysis focused on how the framework could assist in hate speech cases, applying it to the broader implications of *Black* also could offer clarification to the content and context elements encompassed in true threats doctrine.

As was the case in the *Brandenburg* incitement test, the true threats test on its face takes the character, nature, and scope of the speech into consideration. However, reviewing the details behind the ultimate arrests of Neel and Bursey, the application of true threats is not always content, nor viewpoint, neutral. In both of those cases, as well as the ACORN example, only protestors of the president were restricted to the free speech zones. Supporters were welcome to appear closer to the president and to the media. Equally problematic in the free speech zone cases is the nature of the speech being restricted. True threats doctrine applies specifically to low-value speech. However, the free speech zones specifically target political speech, the most valued speech under First Amendment protection. Given the climate of the post-9/11 United States, fear of attack against the president is certainly valid. Those people expressing disagreement with the president may well intend to carry out a true threat.

However, without more context in the application of true threats doctrine, the ease of abuse toward those who merely are vocalizing their disagreement with governmental policy can, and in the cases mentioned above, has led to prosecution of people based solely on their criticism, not on any actual proof of intent to threaten the president. This problem could be remedied in one of two ways. Either all attendees at presidential appearances, no matter their political position, could be cordoned off into free speech zones, or the two additional elements concerning history and the individual speech moment could be brought into consideration, thus allowing for the citizenry to continue participating at the level prior to 9/11.

As was discussed in chapter 5, the majority opinion in *Virginia v. Black* focused at great length on the history of cross burning in the United States. It is in the context of this history that Justice O'Connor drew a distinction between cross burnings used to intimidate and those used to reinforce ideological solidarity. The former constituted an unprotected threat and the latter a protected form of political speech. Applying this in regard to political protestors at presidential appearances would force the courts, and in turn law enforcement agencies, to take into account the nature of the political protest in question.

The history of the political dissident in U.S. culture is extensive. Protestors routinely show up at political events, particularly those where the president is on hand. This tradition goes to the root of the town hall meeting concept in our representative government in which the people have a right to redress and hold accountable elected government officials. Given this history, the arrests of Bursey and Neel would have to be considered unconstitutional forms of prior restraint. In both of those cases, the protestors were silenced before their messages could be heard. Conversely, history could be used as a way to determine that some speakers pose a significantly higher threat than others. If, for example, protesters uttering or displaying threatening messages had a record of committing violent acts, their history of violence could be used as a factor in limiting access to the president.

Application of the third prong of the framework—consideration of the relational nature of the power between speakers—not only adds context to the true threats doctrine but also offers a balance between the current conflicting objective and subjective standards. This prong analyzes the power dynamic occurring between the speaker and spoken to, not the objective interpretation of the reasonable person, nor, conversely, the subjective determination of the speaker's intent. Again, the Court in *Black* considers this relationship, albeit not directly. In

Black, the majority drew a distinction between the speech moment occurring when a cross is burned in the yard of an African American and when a cross is burned at a KKK rally in a discreet location. The physical act of burning the cross is the same but the location and audience are the defining factors.

In regard to protestors at presidential appearances, the act of political dissent is the same. The individual ways in which that dissent is manifested and its location and audience makeup change. For example, one person carrying a sign at a presidential appearance saying "Overthrow the Government" might be a significantly different moment from two hundred people carrying those signs. In addition, a sign that reads "The Bush Family Must Surely Love the Poor, They Made so Many of Us" is a different speech moment than a one that reads "Overthrow the Government, Now." Given the multitude of permutations that could occur, free speech zones need to be structured either more concretely or more loosely. In other words, free speech zones could avoid the current viewpoint censorship by restricting all attendees into such zones. Or the free speech zones could be applied much in the same way that the Court in *Black* applied the Virginia statute. This reading would provide for a case-by-case determination based on individual speech moments and not simply on favor or disfavor of the president.

The three-prong analysis shows that as currently constructed, the free speech zones are a form of viewpoint-based prior restraint. By law enforcement's very testimony, only those who disagree with the president are removed from the location of his appearance, leaving only one side of the political spectrum allowed to participate and be visible. However, by adding the elements of history and speech moment, the free speech zones could be constructed and applied in a more neutral fashion that promotes political participation while simultaneously protecting the safety of the president.

CONCLUSION

During times of national crisis, civil rights historically have been proven to lose out in the name of national security. The negative liberty read into First Amendment protection cannot withstand the climate of fear created by concerns of external threats to the country. By reviewing current standards of incitement, it becomes clear that the test has not been applied consistently. As a result, the post-9/11 climate coupled with the lack of clarity leaves open the door for the censoring of dissident political speech. One way to assure that political speech remains protected speech during times of national crisis is to add further context to the *Brandenburg* incitement standard. Through a review of the al-Timimi case and the free speech zone cases, I have shown that by applying the three-prong analytical framework developed in this book, the Court could assure that both the country and free speech rights remain protected at the highest level possible.

Review of the facts in the al-Timimi case served to illustrate that *Brandenburg*'s imminent lawless action standard is simply not viable today without more context. While *Brandenburg* did set a time requirement for defining what imminence should mean, two later U.S. Supreme Court cases and one Fourth Circuit case show that this lack of context has led to contradictory rulings. In both *Hess* and *Claiborne*, the Court expressed that speech could not be restricted if weeks or months elapsed between the speech moment and the actual lawless action. However in *Rice*, the court found just the opposite. An extended period of time had passed between the publication of the book and the murders committed, yet the publisher was still held civilly liable for the deaths. These inconsistent rulings are especially problematic given today's political climate. First, the Court's more protective interpretation in *Hess* and *Claiborne* does little to combat the threat of terrorism given that terrorist cells are prone to extended advanced planning. Second, because of the current fear-heightened U.S. culture, the more speech restrictive application in *Rice* opens the door for a rebirth of the speech restrictive legal reasoning applied in the sedition cases. In considering this dilemma, I concluded that application of the imminent lawless action standard requires exactly the type of context offered through my alternative framework in order to ensure the utmost protection of national security with the least chance of overzealous governmental persecution.

Studying the use of free speech zones at presidential appearances offered yet another example of how lack of context in current speech doctrine pertaining to true threats can have grave consequences—this time in the restriction of protected political speech. The free speech zones in and of themselves are problematic. When political dissidents are cordoned off away from the president, the public, and the press, it creates the illusion that there is no dissent, silencing the dissenters and the leaving the general public ignorant of alternative political opinions. This restriction, particularly if reified through a U.S. Supreme Court ruling, can have long-term ramifications similar to those occurring during the communist scare. For almost forty years, the U.S. government passed legislation restricting the expression of anti-government ideology, and the Supreme Court continued to uphold these restrictions through cases such as *Abrams* and *Dennis*. In other words, political dissidents today run the risk of being labeled as terrorists in the same way that political dissidents of the past were accused and prosecuted for being communists.

What I have established in this chapter is that the possibility of unfair government persecution could be lessened considerably by using my framework to add context to the true threats doctrine. While *Virginia v. Black* appeared to further define the scope of this doctrine, subsequent Ninth Circuit Court of Appeals' rulings demonstrate that this is not the case. Application of my framework would add the necessary context, requiring the Court to move past the issue of content neutrality by broadening the analysis to include a consideration of history and of the particular speech moment occurring.

NOTES

1. For the purposes of this chapter, political dissident is defined as one who disagrees with the U.S. government and is verbal in that disagreement.

2. For a recent book focused on speech restrictions during six war or war-related time periods, *see* GEOFFREY STONE, PERILOUS TIMES: FREE SPEECH IN WARTIME FROM THE SEDITION ACT OF 1798 TO THE WAR ON TERRORISM (2004). For other writings on free speech during times of war, *see* HARRY KALVEN JR., A WORTHY TRADITION: FREE SPEECH IN AMERICA (1988) and LEONARD LEVY, FREEDOM OF SPEECH AND PRESS IN EARLY AMERICAN HISTORY: A LEGACY OF SUPPRESSION (1963).

3. Frederick Schauer, *The Wily Agitator and the American Speech Tradition: Perilous Times: Free Speech in Wartime: From the Sedition Act of 1798 to the War on Terrorism*, 57 STAN. L. REV. 2157, 2167–68 (2005).

4. For a definition of free speech zones, *see* Michael J. Hampson, *Protesting the President: Free Speech Zones and the First Amendment*, 58 RUTGERS L. REV. 245, 245–46 (2005). "One example of how the government has redacted civil liberties since September 11, 2001, is the United States Secret Service's practice of placing political protesters into 'free speech zones' at presidential appearances. The Secret Service has adopted a procedure of removing political protesters from the site where the President is making a public appearance, and instead confining the protesters in enclosed areas that are out-of-sight of the President and the news media."

5. James B. Comey, *Deputy Attorney General, United States Department of Justice, Statement Before the Committee on the Judiciary, United States House of Representatives*, June 8, 2005, reporting that Ali al-Timimi was convicted of promoting terrorism after he verbally urged a group of individuals to go to Pakistan to receive military training.

6. *Watts v. United States*, 394 U.S. 705 (1969) (established the "true threats" doctrine) and *Brandenburg v. Ohio*, 395 U.S. 444 (1969) (established "imminent lawless action" standard).

7. Robert M. Entman, *Cascading Activation: Contesting the White House's Frame After 9/11*, 20 POLITICAL COMM. 415 (2003) (citing President Bush's address to the nation on September 12, 2001).

8. *Department of Justice Oversight: Preserving Our Freedoms While Defending Against Terrorism: Hearing Before the Senate Comm. On the Judiciary*, 107th Cong. 313 (December 6, 2001).

9. The Patriot Act, a 342-page long document, was created to "deter and punish terrorist acts in the United States and around the world, to enhance law enforcement investigatory tools and for other purposes," Congressional Record, USA Patriot Act of 2001, 107th Cong., 1st sess., H.R. 3162, 147 no. 144: S10990 (2001). In 2005, Attorney General Alberto Gonzales commended the Patriot Act for enabling law enforcement officials to "identify terrorist operatives, dismantle terrorist cells, disrupt terrorist plots and capture terrorists before they have been able to strike." *Attorney General Alberto R. Gonzales Highlights Success in War on Terror at the Council on Foreign Relations*, Department of Justice, December 1, 2005.

10. *Id.*, Department of Justice.

11. *See* memorandum from Michael J. Creppy, Chief Immigration Judge of the United States, to Immigration Judges and Court Administrators (September 21, 2001), available at fl1.findlaw.com/news.findlaw.com/hdocs/docs/aclu/creppy092101memo .pdf (last visited May 7, 2007). For a review of the subsequent implications of this memo, *see* Dale L. Edwards, *If it Walks, Talks and Squawks Like a Trial, Should it be Covered Like One? The Right of the Press to Cover INS Deportation Hearings*, 10 COMM L. & POL'Y 217–39 (2005).

12. Nadine Strossen, Forum on National Security and the Constitution (January, 24, 2002), available at www.aclu.org/congress/1012402a.html.

13. For more detailed discussions concerning First Amendment infringement, *see ACLU, Freedom Under Fire: Dissent in Post-9/11 America* (2003) and www .firstamendmentcenter.org.

14. *Id.* For a government response to one of the ACLU allegations, *see* James B. Comey, *Deputy Attorney General, United States Department of Justice, Statement Before the Committee on the Judiciary, United States House of Representatives*, 13 (June 8, 2005).

15. *American Friends Service Committee et al. v. City and County of Denver* (Col. District Court, March 28, 2002), complaint available online at www.aclu-co.org/ news/complaints/complaint_spyfiles.htm.

16. *Supra* note 13, at 8–10. In St. Louis, police injured dozens of protestors at an anti-war rally. In Baltimore, police stopped eight people from holding a silent vigil protesting the war because they did not have a permit.

17. *Id.* at 5. Two students at Grinnell College in Iowa hung an American flag upside-down in their dorm room window. The students were accused of violating an Iowa state law concerning "flag etiquette." The students filed suit in federal district and subsequently were cleared after authorities conceded that the students' actions constituted protected speech under the First Amendment.

18. *Id.* at 5. A. J. Brown, a freshman at Durham Technical College in Raleigh, North Carolina, was visited by the U.S. Secret Service after someone called in an anonymous tip that Brown had an anti-American poster on her wall. The poster was an anti–death penalty poster that featured George W. Bush holding a rope and numerous hanging victims in the background. Brown was questioned by the Secret Service about whether she had information on Afghanistan or the Taliban. She was asked to sign a form; no other action was taken.

19. *Id.* at 14. In Albuquerque, New Mexico, a guidance counselor and two teachers were suspended without pay for displaying posters critical of the War in Iraq.

20. *Id.* at 15. In Dearborn, Michigan, a sixteen-year-old was suspended for wearing a T-shirt to school that showed a picture of President Bush with the words "International Terrorist" underneath. School officials claimed that they thought the T-shirt would cause disturbances at the school.

21. *Dixie Chicks Pulled from Air after Bashing Bush*, March 14, 2003. Retrieved from cnn.entertainment.com on April 15, 2007. Lead singer Natalie Maines was performing at a concert in London when she said she was "ashamed the president of United States is from Texas."

22. Chris Demaske, *The Market Place of Ideas? Global Implications of Market-Driven U.S. Media*, 1 INT'L J. OF MEDIA AND CULTURAL POL. 131 (2005).

23. *Id.* at 131–32.

24. Lauren Gilbert, *Mocking George: Political Satire as "True Threat" in the Age of Global Terrorism*, 58 U. MIAMI L. REV. 843, 849–50 (2004).

25. *Id.* Editors at the *Times* refused to let the Secret Service agents meet with Ramirez. They did meet, however, with a lawyer from the *Times*.

26. Laura K. Donohue, *Terrorist Speech and the Future of Free Expression*, 27 CARDOZO L. REV. 233, 240–41 (2005).

27. *Id.*

28. *Id.* at 241.

29. STONE, *supra* note 2, at 124.

30. Prior to 1925, the First Amendment only applied to federal laws. At the state level, criminal anarchy laws and criminal syndicalism laws, which in many circumstances were used to restrict speech, were immune from First Amendment requirements. This changed in 1925, however, in the case of *Gitlow v. New York*, 268 U.S. 652. The U.S. Supreme Court delivered a landmark ruling in *Gitlow*, deciding that state laws affecting freedom of speech would be held to First Amendment standards.

31. Espionage Act of 1917, Pub. L. No. 65-24, 40 Stat. 217 (1917). The Espionage Act of 1917 focused primarily on acts of sabotage and the protection of military secrets; however, it also made it illegal to encourage insubordination in the military or to promote resistance of the draft.

32. For a discussion of how these cases addressed the idea of the liberty of freedom of speech, *see* 31–35.

33. 249 U.S. 47 (1919).

34. *Id.*

35. *Id.*

36. *Id.* at 52.

37. *Id.*

38. 249 U.S. 204 (1919).

39. 249 U.S. 211 (1919).

40. *Id.*

41. 250 U.S. 616 (1919).

42. *Id.*

43. *Id.* at 630.

44. *Id.*
45. *See, Gilbert v. Minnesota*, 254 U.S. 325 (1920); *Schaefer v. United States*, 251 U.S. 616 (1920); and *Gitlow v. New York*, 268 U.S. 652 (1925).
46. THOMAS L. TEDFORD, FREEDOM OF SPEECH IN THE UNITED STATES 61 (1997).
47. *Id.*
48. *Id.*
49. Hampson, *supra* note 4.
50. *Id.*
51. *Dennis v. United States*, 341 U.S. 494 (1951).
52. *Id.* at 502.
53. *Id.* at 499. "Congress was concerned with those who advocate and organize for the overthrow of government. Certainly those who recruit and combine for the purpose of advocating overthrow intend to bring about that overthrow."
54. 354 U.S. 298 (1957).
55. *Id.* at 320.
56. Robert S. Tanenbaum, *Preaching Terror: Free Speech or Wartime Incitement?* 55 AM. U.L. REV. 789, 802–3 (2006). "The *Dennis* and *Yates* decisions illustrate the Court's approach to free speech in a time of another variable struggle that, like the War on Terror, seemed to advance with no foreseeable end in sight. However, hindsight reveals the flaws of *Dennis* and the significance of *Yates*. In both cases, to the extent that criminals sowed a conspiracy, those actors could have been punished. But, the *Dennis* defendants merely advocated their party's doctrine."
57. *Watts v. United States*, 394 U.S. 705 (1969).
58. *Id.*, per curiam opinion, quoting 18 U.S.C. § 871(a).
59. *Id.* at 707. "What is a threat must be distinguished from what is constitutionally protected speech."
60. *Id.* at 707–8. The statute reads: "Whoever knowingly and willfully deposits for conveyance in the mail or for delivery from any post office or by any letter carrier any letter, paper, writing, print, missive or document containing any threat to take the life of or to inflict bodily harm upon the President of the United States, the President-elect, the Vice President or other officer next in the order of succession to the office of President of the United States, or the Vice President-elect, or knowingly and willfully otherwise makes any such threat against the President, President-elect, Vice President or other officers next in the order of succession to the office of President, or Vice President-elect, shall be fined not more than $1,000 or imprisoned not more than five years, or both."
61. *Id.* at 708.
62. *Id.*, quoting *New York Times v. Sullivan*, 376 U.S. 254, 270 (1964).
63. *Id.*
64. *Id.*
65. *Id.* at 446.
66. *Id.* at 445.
67. *Id.* at 444.
68. *Id.*

69. *Id.*

70. 274 U.S. 357 (1927).

71. 395 U.S. 444, 447 (1969).

72. *Id.*

73. *Id.* at 448.

74. Legal scholar Laura Donohue raises a similar concern about *Brandenburg* in her article, *Terrorist Speech and the Future of Free Expression*, 27 CARDOZO L. REV. 233 (2005). She states: "The importance of the *Brandenburg* test in protecting persuasive political speech ought not to be underestimated. But its strength in the face of modern terrorism remains less clear. The persistence of *Schenck v. United States*, *Dennis v. United States*, *Yates v. United States* and the clear and present danger test suggest a rockier base than one otherwise might expect. Confronted by possible terrorist acquisition of biological weapons, courts may well lower the bar."

75. *See* Jennifer Elrod, *Expressive Activity, True Threats and the First Amendment*, 36 CONN. L. REV. 541, 561 (2004). "To date, the delineation of the true threats doctrine and the relevant test of factors has been the role of the lower federal courts."

76. Gilbert, *supra* note 24, at 868.

77. For an in-depth discussion of lower court application of the true threats doctrine, *see id.* at 869–71. Also, Robert Blakey and Brian J. Murray, *Threats, Free Speech, and the Jurisprudence of Federal Criminal Law*, 2002 BYU L. REV. 829 (2002).

78. Gilbert, *supra* note 24, at 857.

79. Donohue, *supra* note 26, at 237.

80. *Id.*

81. *Id.* at 249. "The court's refusal to overturn these earlier cases . . . may have something to do with deference to legislature in times of need. As Frankfurter wrote, 'Free-speech cases are not an exception to the principle that we are not legislators, that direct policy-making is not our province.' He continued, 'How best to reconcile competing interests is the business of legislatures, and the balance they strike is a judgment not to be displaced by ours, but to be respected unless outside the pale of fair judgment.'"

82. Tanenbaum, *supra* note 56.

83. *Id.* at 804–5.

84. *Id.*

85. *Id.* at 805–6.

86. *Id.* at 805, quoting 414 U.S. 105 (1973), at 108.

87. *Id.*

88. *Id.* at 788–90, contrasting the differences between communists in the 1940s and Islamic terrorists today.

89. For a discussion of the charges against al-Timimi, *see* Indictment of Defendant at 4, 5, *United States v. al-Timimi* (E.D. Va. 2004). For outcome of the case against him, *see* Comey, *supra* note 5.

90. Tanenbaum, *supra* note 56, at 787–88.

91. Comey, *supra* note 5.

92. MARTIN REDISH, THE LOGIC OF PERSECUTION: FREE EXPRESSION AND THE MCCARTHY ERA 104 (2005).

93. *Id.* at 105, discussing *Rice v. Paladin Enterprises, Inc.*, 128 F.3d 233 (4th Cir. 1997).

94. *Id.*

95. *Id.* at 106. "The *Rice* court thus quite obviously chose to adopt the far less protective reading of the *Brandenburg* imminence test, where lack of imminence is somehow equated not with the lack of an immediate temporal connection between advocacy and harm (as both the commonsense use of the word and its historical use by Justice Brandeis in his *Whitney* concurrence necessarily suggests), but rather with purely abstract advocacy, in the sense cryptically described in *Yates*."

96. Donohue, *supra* note 26, at 250.

97. 414 U.S. 105 (1973).

98. 458 U.S. 886 (1982).

99. Tanenbaum, *supra* note 56, at 806–7. "Unlike the defendant in *Hess* whose statements was not directed at a particular person, al-Timimi directed his statements to a specific group of listeners. In these statements, al-Timimi explicitly promoted violation of the law by advocating training at L.E.T., joining the Taliban, and fighting American forces."

100. *Id.* at 807.

101. *Id.*

102. *Id.*

103. *Schenck v. United States*, 249 U.S. 47 (1919), at 52 ("The most stringent protection of free speech would not protect a man in falsely shouting fire in a theater and causing a panic.").

104. Tanenbaum, *supra* note 56, at 789–90.

105. *See* chapter 5 for an in-depth review of how the *Black* ruling distinguished between intimidating and nonintimidating cross burnings.

106. *See* chapter 6 for a discussion of this anti-pornography ordinance.

107. In addition to political events, free speech zones also are associated with contentious areas such as abortion clinics. These zones also can be defined as spaces on college campuses reserved for free speech activities. While arguments can be made (and are being made) that the campus free speech zones are unconstitutional, for my purposes I will focus on those zones connected to presidential appearances.

108. For discussions of free speech zones prior to 9/11, *see* Andrew Blake, *Atlanta's Steamy Heat Cools Protests: More than 25 Groups Rally in Demonstration Area*, BOSTON GLOBE, July 20, 1988. Retrieved from Proquest; Nicholas Riccardi, *Convention Planners Wary of New Style of Protest*, LOS ANGELES TIMES, June 23, 2000. Retrieved from Lexus/Nexus; and Heidi Boghosian, *The Assault on Free Speech, Public Assembly and Dissent—A National Lawyers Guild Report on Government Violations of First Amendment Rights in the United States*, THE NATIONAL LAWYER'S GUILD, 2004. Retrieved from www.nlg.org.

109. For elaborate discussion of this process, *see* Hampson, *supra* note 4. Also *see* Jim Hightower, *Bush Zones Go National*, THE NATION, August 16, 2004; *South Carolina Progressive Network, Free Speech Zone*. Retrieved from www.scpronet .com/freespeech.php.

110. Hampson, *supra* note 4, at 256. Protestors in these zones often find themselves enclosed "behind fences or other barriers," quoting Eunice Moscoso, *Secret Service Quashing Dissent, ACLU Lawsuit Says,* DAYTON DAILY NEWS, September 24, 2003, at A4.

111. *Id.*

112. *Id.*, at 257–58, discussing specific incidents of harassment and arrests.

113. *Judge clears Bush Opponent,* PITTSBURGH POST-GAZETTE, November 1, 2002, www.post-gazette.com/localnews/20021101protester3.asp, retrieved May 8, 2007.

114. *Id.*

115. *Id.*

116. *Id.*

117. *Id.*

118. *Id.*

119. *ACORN v. City of Philadelphia*, civil action No. 03-4312 (E.D. Penn.) (2003).

120. *Id.*

121. *Id.*

122. Hampson, *supra* note 4.

123. *ACORN, supra* note 119.

124. *Id.*

125. *Id.*

126. *Id.*

127. *Id.*

128. *United States v. Bursey*, 416 F.3d 301 (2005).

129. *Id.* at 304.

130. *Id.*

131. *Id.*

132. *Id.* at 304–5.

133. *Id.* at 305.

134. *Id.* at 305. Title 18, Section 1752(a)(1)(ii) states that it shall be unlawful for any person or group of persons to willfully and knowingly enter or remain in any posted, cordoned off, or otherwise restricted area of a building or grounds where the president or other person protected by the Secret Service is or will be temporarily visiting.

135. *Id.*

136. *Id.*

137. Bursey's attorney, Jeff Fogel contended that "the Secret Service has been discriminately enforcing the law in favor of those who support the President and keeping those who oppose the President away from the President and the media." *South Carolina Progressive Network, Free Speech Zone.* Last retrieved on May 8, 2007, from www.scpronet.com/freespeech.html#Other5.

138. *United States v. Bursey*, 416 F.3d 301, 309 (2005).

139. For additional information concerning free speech zones, *see* Jason Borenstein, *Meaningful Speech*, 2005 2 WEB JCLI, last retrieved May 8, 2007. "We should be diligent in our efforts to avoid invoking the doctrine of 'prior restraint' too fre-

quently because doing so weakens the tenets of free speech by victimizing the majority of protesters who would demonstrate peacefully. The proffered motive for creating free speech zones has been dubiously labeled as being for 'security reasons.' Yet, it is unclear why individuals or groups who pose an actual threat to the President would flagrantly display their dislike for him since they would be hoarded away from the area into a speech zone."

140. For an extensive discussion of the ruling in *Virginia v. Black*, 538 U.S. 343 (2003), *see* chapter 5.

141. *Id.* at 359.

142. Gilbert, *supra* note 24, at 868.

143. Elrod, *supra* note 75, at 541, and Paul T. Crane, *"True Threats" and the Issue of Intent*, 92 VIRGINIA L. REV. 1225 (2006).

144. 20 F.3d 1074, 1088 (2002). For additional information about this case, *see* chapter 6.

145. 408 F.3d 622 (9th Cir. 2005).

146. See *Planned Parenthood*, 290 F.3d 1074, 1088 (2002).

147. Crane, *supra* note 143, at 1235–36 (explaining that courts read true threats either through an objective test that focuses on the reasonable listener or the subjective test that focuses on the actual intent of the speaker).

148. Elrod, *supra* note 75, at 547–48.

149. 408 F.3d 622 (9th Cir. 2005).

150. 538 U.S. 343, 360 (2003).

151. Elrod, *supra* note 75, at 547–48.

Conclusion

A New First Amendment Emerges

There is no doubt that the First Amendment to the U.S. constitution is a powerful and necessary tool in the United States. For more than two hundred years, the courts have struggled to identify just exactly how to apply it to ensure the greatest amount of speech protection. From the moment that the U.S. Supreme Court determined that "Congress shall make no law" did not mean absolutely no laws, it has worked to ascertain which speech restrictions still will allow the First Amendment to function in our democratic society. Scholars and jurists alike continue to debate where the parameters should be set and why they should be set there. This book enters into the ongoing debate, arguing that as it is currently conceived of and applied the First Amendment does not function in a way that adequately protects members of disempowered groups.

To correct this oversight, I have proposed an alternative framework for case analysis, one that if applied by the courts would establish a stronger commitment to equal speech rights. What I am suggesting here is at once both simple and radical. Simple because the critique is in keeping with the core value that free speech is a determining factor in democratic societies. Simple also in that the solution offered builds off of existing doctrine, modifying and complicating doctrinal principles such as content neutrality. The proposed framework is radical in that it raises serious questions about several fundamental assumptions embedded in First Amendment discourse and doctrine. Specifically, I challenge the assumptions that the First Amendment should operate only as a negative liberty, that the autonomous individual constructed through the courts exists, and that the content-neutrality principle is able to address the complexities of power in contemporary society.

As expressed in chapter 1 and elaborated on in following chapters, this book had two goals—one normative and one analytic—both connected to the relationship between the First Amendment, free speech, and disempowered groups. The normative goal was to reformulate the liberty of free speech in terms of equality. The analytic goal was to develop an alternative framework for case analysis that protects speech for disempowered groups. The normative goal was facilitated by reconceptualizing individual power in terms of partial agency instead of liberal autonomy. That reconceptualization led to an analytical framework that requires the courts to consider three elements: (1) the character of the speech, the nature of restriction, and the scope of the ban on the speech; (2) historical disenfranchisement; and (3) the interstices of power between speakers.

LIBERTY AND EQUALITY

In addressing the issue of liberty, I relied on two prominent scholars, Michael Kammen and Isaiah Berlin. Kammen, in reviewing the U.S. court system, discerned that there were three separate, yet overlapping, "spheres of liberty." These spheres could be defined by the pairing of liberty with some other concept, specifically liberty and authority, liberty and property, and liberty and justice. For Kammen, the concept of liberty is both fluid and historically determined.[1] It is also best defined in relationship to some other quality. I maintained that liberty and equality are the best combination for ensuring free speech rights. Freedom of speech without some consideration of equality can only maintain the status quo. Freedom of speech without equality among individuals will maintain a status quo in which certain groups remain privileged at the expense of other groups. Focusing on equality acknowledges that freedom is less effective as a liberty if citizens are not equally able to participate or benefit from that government-protected liberty. However, shifting the focus to equality would also necessitate some move toward what Berlin called positive liberty.

According to Berlin: "The 'positive' sense of the word 'liberty' derives from the wish on the part of the individual to be his own master. I wish my life and decisions to depend on myself, not on external forces of whatever kind."[2] Implicit in the First Amendment is this right for the "individual to be his own master." As currently interpreted by the courts, however, the government is the only "external force" to be concerned about. Through that line of reasoning, so long as the government is restricted from censoring speech, freedom of speech remains intact and the individual remains his or her own master. In other words, negative liberty is enough to maintain open dialogue.

If, however, other external forces in society also are at play, then negative liberty alone fails to protect free speech, requiring at least some level of positive freedom to ensure equality. Key to making this shift from predominantly negative liberty to some level of positive liberty would require the courts to recast the autonomous individual as having partial agency.

AUTONOMY VERSUS AGENCY

In chapter 3, I set out to construct a partial agent to replace the autonomous one. Critiques of individual autonomy are not new in legal scholarship. Feminist scholars in particular have taken issue with the ways in which the construct of the autonomous individual is unacceptable. The role of the autonomous individual in law has been defined by one feminist scholar as a falsely constructed "atomistic individual" whose construction "fails to recognize the inherently social nature of human beings."[3] In chapters 1 and 2, I maintained that despite those critiques, the conception of the autonomous individual continues to be reinforced both through Supreme Court discourse and through traditional liberal legal theory.

While current legal doctrine and traditional theory may leave these issues of private power unanswered, feminist legal scholars have critiqued women's place in the legal system by deconstructing those issues of private power and agency. For example, if external, societal forces determine a person's desires, then "rationality" in the liberal sense does not exist. In recasting autonomy in terms of partial agency, one must be careful not remove all agency from the individual actor. Disempowered group members are not cultural dupes; they exist inside of the culture and as a result "are in active negotiation with it."[4] Recently, feminist legal scholars have paid considerable attention to issues of power and agency. However, their theories were developed and explained outside of the confines of constitutional law, except for those formal areas such sexual harassment. As discussed in chapter 3, two legal scholars, Tracy Higgins and Kathryn Abrams, both reviewed partial agency in terms of certain areas of constitutional law. [5] Higgins focused on the ways in which power and freedom are intricately linked, meaning that freedom is not an automatic state, but must be "defined and defended as a set of social conditions, not as the absence of political or social constraint."[6] To Higgins, the ways in which power and freedom are linked in constitutional law (and society in general) have a direct effect on defining the parameters of individual agency.[7] Abrams noted that relations among various social groups determine agency for groups who are socially and politically disempowered. The partial agent then is affected both by governmental power and societal power.[8]

For this book, I focused primarily on the research conducted by Abrams and how it defined partial agency in terms of the U.S. legal system. Abrams juxtaposed "women's capacity for self-direction and resistance, on the one hand, with often-internalized patriarchal constraint, on the other hand."[9] Her research attempted to reconcile self-direction and societal constraint through legal change. According to Abrams, in order for the legal system to accommodate change for disempowered groups, the system has to acknowledge the role of group identity in determining an individual's level of social agency. If laws are restructured to recognize the role of cultural identity on individual agency, then the legal system can function as an effective conduit for social change.

Abrams's construction of the partial agent and its connection to law opens the door for alternative applications of legal doctrine in relation to members of disempowered groups. However, as I noted in chapter 1 and reinforced in chapter 2, the First Amendment is particularly resistant to this type of overhaul both because of its partial ability to foster speech rights for those members and because of its longstanding construction through the Court as a liberty that protects other liberties. Applying Abrams's theory of partial agency, then, is a difficult proposal to support in the area of free speech because of this complicated relationship between the First Amendment and disempowered groups. In areas such as sexual harassment, the oppressive, discriminatory practice is obvious. Sexual harassment works repressively; it offers no possible benefit for women. On the other hand, the First Amendment does offer the ability for some benefit for disempowered groups. As a result, the oppressive power of the First Amendment is passive and discrete, making it more insidious and at the same time more difficult to combat. To unmask the oppressive elements of the First Amendment, the link between power and free speech needs to be considered discursively, historically, and relationally.

By studying power in this way, I brought to the surface several key points. First, power is not owned by one individual or institution but exists in the interplay between the two. For speech law, this is a critical distinction. The power of speech is not in the words themselves but in the ways in which the speech exercises power relationally with the listener. This relational power is supported through social or discursive actions. Second, social power is not primarily located within the government. It exists in the relations that occur at the capillaries of society. Third, as a result of this dynamic, these power relations are maintained through historical convention.

I concluded that in modern society, discursive power operates by concealing the ways in which power can oppress. In the case of the First Amendment, discursive themes pertaining to open debate among autonomous individuals masks the way in which the First Amendment allows the further disempowerment of already-oppressed groups. For example, this First Amendment discourse does not account for social construction of individuals based on group identity. Nor do these discursive themes consider that restriction or censoring of free speech is not always a governmental act. From this reconceptualization of the power dynamics in individual agency, I created a theoretical framework for analyzing free speech cases. This new framework, applied in chapters 4, 5, 6, and 7, relied on traditional methods for case analysis grounded in poststructural feminist theory. I created a framework that called into question a key doctrinal principle in First Amendment law — the content-neutrality principle.

CONTENT NEUTRALITY AND THE NEW APPROACH

While courts always consider context to some degree, the context being considered here is specifically related to the interstices of power between speakers. Considering that traditional application of free speech laws levels issues of power, this contextual shift is dramatic. It brings into question not only the need for the government in certain circumstances to consider the liberty inherent in the First Amendment as a positive liberty (something not currently possible), it also requires the courts to reassess the ways in which they apply content and viewpoint neutrality.

The content-neutrality principle has existed in Supreme Court case law in varying forms since the 1930s.[10] Basically, the content-neutrality principle states that government restrictions on speech that are based on content must pass a strict scrutiny test. The fear is that through content-based regulations the government will abuse its authority. The development of this doctrinal principle led to the creation of various systems to determine when content restrictions would be constitutional. Included in this group are the categorical approach and public forum analysis. These approaches, however, tend to create a two-dimensional system — restrictions are either content-neutral or content-based — thus making the content-neutrality doctrine inadequate to deal with the complexity of modern power.

To correct this erroneous and problematic way of dealing with power and speech, I developed a three-prong framework for free speech case analysis. This framework does not discount concerns about government abuse of power. However, it does maintain that societal restrictions on speech are equally, if not more, problematic for historically disempowered groups. Currently, as illustrated in the analysis chapters, content restrictions by the government are permitted in certain circumstances. Viewpoint restrictions are not tolerated. The framework I developed allows the courts to continue to *consider* whether or not laws are content-neutral. However, this framework acknowledges that content neutrality, while an admirable goal, is bound to concepts of objectivity and truth and as result continues to reinforce empowerment of some over others. In contending that replacing current case analysis in cases dealing with the speech rights of members of disempowered groups, this framework will support the most equitable application in First Amendment doctrine. In order to accomplish this, the content-neutrality requirement must be altered and applied in conjunction with two other elements. The three prongs of this analytical approach to case review are (1) the character, nature, and scope of the restriction, (2) the historical context of the cultural groups involved in the speech issue and (3) the individual power relations occurring in the particular speech moment.

THE ANALYSIS

I first applied the framework to two significant hate speech cases: *Village of Skokie v. the National Socialist Party of America*[11] and *R.A.V. v. City of St. Paul, Minnesota*.[12] In *Skokie*, the court applied the content-neutrality principle and found that banning the Swastika was an unconstitutional abridgement of the hate group's First Amendment rights. However, by applying the framework developed in this book, the result of the case would be completely different. Using research on possible effects of hate speech on traumatized groups, combined with the historical evidence, would enable the Village of Skokie to constitutionally prohibit the demonstration in their community.

In *R.A.V.*, five different justices relied on the content-neutrality principle as the application standard. The results of their individual analyses were five different applications of the same standard and five different opinions concerning the St. Paul ordinance specifically and hate speech restrictions more generally. I applied the framework and found that the St. Paul ordinance still would be unconstitutional. However, unlike the *R.A.V.* decision, which effectively closes the door on constitutional restriction of hate speech, my framework showed that a hate speech ordinance could be constructed that would withstand First Amendment scrutiny. Preparing an ordinance of this type would require proof of historical disempowerment. In addition to supplying evidence of social oppression, the government also would need to supply some support for how the speech being restricted might affect those groups being targeted by the speech.

Using an analytical framework based in partial agency would have the First Amendment applied in a way that supports both sides of the debate, even those that are distasteful or hate-based. The framework would allow for government restriction on speech only when the hateful speech was targeted to a person or group based on their group identity and only when the speech operated to silence that person or group. As a result, this framework offered a way to balance concerns about biased government censorship by requiring the government to support its compelling interest through historical context and individual power relations.

In chapter 5, I looked once again at hate speech, focusing on the most recent U.S. Supreme Court case: *Virginia v. Black*.[13] This ruling reopened the possibility of restricting certain types of hate speech. The Court in *Black* reviewed the constitutionality of a Virginia statute that made cross burnings illegal. In its opinion, the Court distinguished between cross burnings meant to intimidate and those meant "as potent symbols of shared group identity and ideology."[14] O'Connor explained that while viewpoint restrictions like those in the ordinance in question in *R.A.V.* are unconstitutional, the First Amendment does allow for some content-based restrictions inside of proscribable areas of speech.[15]

While the ruling in this case reopens the possibility of constitutionally acceptable hate speech legislation, the Court's failure to articulate a clear standard for determining the boundary between intimidating speech and merely ideological speech leaves little guidance for lower courts. As discussed in relation to *R.A.V.*, my framework could offer that guidance necessary for lower courts to strike a balance that would protect both the most amount of speech possible, while acknowledging that certain speech impedes the speech of members of disempowered groups

In chapter 6, I revisited the issue of the content-neutrality principle, this time in regard to Internet pornography. Because Internet pornography cannot be addressed until the issue of restricting pornography in general is considered, much of this chapter focused on a significant lower court case: *American Booksellers Association v. Hudnut*.[16] The court in this case found that the ordinance was not viewpoint-neutral, and that it attempted to "establish an 'approved' view of women."[17]

Applying my framework, I found that, much like the ordinance in *R.A.V.*, the anti-pornography ordinance in *Hudnut* did encompass too much speech under its umbrella. However, if the ordinance were rewritten to exclude one section, then under the three-prong alternative framework it could withstand constitutional scrutiny. Following the discussion of *Hudnut*, this chapter focused specifically on the U.S. Supreme Court cases that resulted from the passage of the Communications Decency Act. These cases added an extra layer of difficulty to the issue of pornography because the Supreme Court had not, up to that point, dealt with issues of Internet content in general. Prior to these cases, the Court had not determined if the Internet should be treated more like print or more like broadcast in terms of scrutiny. It also had not considered how a community standards test, such as the one developed in *Miller v. California*, would translate to the Internet community. If certain types of pornography in general, however, were found to be one of those constitutionally restrictable categories of speech similar to the burning cross in *Black*, then the issues raised in the various CDA cases would become moot.

Finally, in chapter 7, I looked at dissident political speech, specifically focusing on the ambiguity of the *Brandenburg* incitement standard. By applying my framework to two recent areas of case law—the al-Timimi case and the free speech zones cases—I illustrated how, by applying a more complex test, those ambiguities could be minimized. Reviewing these cases also offered a stark illustration of the danger of relying solely on the negative liberty concept. Without some level of positive liberty, the most highly protected area of speech—political speech—could be restricted by the government in the name of national security.

Ultimately, I have constructed an approach to free speech that will afford disempowered groups the most speech protection possible while maintaining the highest level of speech protection for the general population. Before the Court could apply this three-prong framework, it would first have to reconsider the way it thinks about how individuals interact in society. Are they autonomous agents or do they operate with only limited or partial agency? In addition, the Court also would need to address how power operates in contemporary culture, reformulating its concerns of censorship to encompass more than just government censorship. Finally, in order for this framework to be considered constitutional, the Court would have to acknowledge some level of positive liberty in regard to the First Amendment.

NOTES

1. MICHAEL KAMMEN, SPHERES OF LIBERTY: CHANGING PERCEPTIONS OF LIBERTY IN AMERICAN CULTURE (1986).
2. ISAIAH BERLIN, FOUR ESSAYS ON LIBERTY 131, 1969.
3. Jennifer Nedelsky, *Reconceiving Autonomy: Sources, Thoughts and Possibilities*, 1 YALE J.L. & FEMINISM 7, 8 (1989).
4. Leti Volpp, *Talking "Culture": Gender, Race, Nation, and the Politics of Multiculturalism*, 96 COLUM. L. REV. 1573, 1585 (1996).
5. Tracy Higgins, *Democracy and Feminism*, 110 HARV. L. REV. 1957 (1997), Kathryn Abrams, *Sex Wars Redux: Agency and Coercion in Feminist Legal Theory*, 95 COLO. L. REV. 304 (1995), and Kathryn Abrams, *From Autonomy to Agency: Feminist Perspectives on Self-Direction*, 40 WM & MARY L. REV. 805 (1999).
6. Higgins, *supra* note 5, at 1697.

7. *Id.*
8. Abrams, *supra* note 5 at 346.
9. *Id.* at 346 (1995).
10. *Schneider v. New Jersey*, 308 U.S. 147 (1939).
11. 373 N.E.2d 21 (Ill. 1978).
12. 505 U.S. 432 (1992).
13. 583 U.S. 343 (2003).
14. *Id.* at 356.
15. *Id.* at 553.
16. 771 F. 2d 323 (7th Cir. 1985).
17. *Id.* at 328.

Appendix

CASES

Abrams v. United States, 250 U.S. 616 (1919)

ACLU v. Reno, 929 F. Supp. 824 (E.D. Pa. 1996)

ACORN v. City of Philadelphia, civil action No. 03-4312 (E.D. Pa.) (2003)

American Booksellers Association v. Hudnut, 771 F.2d 323 (Ind. 1985)

American Booksellers Association v. Hudnut, 598 F. Supp. 1316 (S.D. Ind. 1984)

American Friends Service Committee et al. v. City and County of Denver (Col. District Court, March 28, 2002)

American Library Association v. United States, 201 F. Supp. 2d 401 (E.D. Pa., 2002)

Ashcroft v. ACLU, 535 U.S. 564 (2002)

Ashcroft v. ACLU II, 542 U.S. 656 (2004)

Ashcroft v. Free Speech Coalition, 535 U.S. 234 (2002)

Associated Press v. United States, 362 U.S. 1 (1945)

Brandenburg v. Ohio, 395 U.S. 444 (1969)

Branzburg v. Hayes, 408 U.S. 665 (1972)

Brown v. Board of Education of Topeka, 347 U.S. 483 (1954)

Chaplinsky v. New Hampshire, 315 U.S. 568 (1942)

Cohen v. California, 403 U.S. 15 (1971)

Craig v. Boren, 429 U.S. 190 (1976)

Curtis Publishing v. Butts, 388 U.S. 130 (1967)

Debs v. United States, 249 U.S. 211 (1919)

Dennis v. United States, 341 U.S. 494 (1951)

Dred Scott v. Sandford, 60 U.S. 393 (1857)

Doe v. University of Michigan, 721 F. Supp. 852 (E.D. Mich. 1989)

Federal Communications Commission v. Pacifica, 438 U.S. 726 (1978)

Frohwerk v. United States, 249 U.S. 204 (1919)

Gertz v. Welch, 418 U.S. 323 (1974)

Gilbert v. Minnesota, 254 U.S. 325 (1920)

Ginsberg v. New York, 390 U.S. 629 (1968)

Gitlow v. New York, 268 U.S. 652 (1925)

Globe Newspaper Co. v. Beacon Hill Architectural Commission, 100 F.3d 175 (Mass. 1996)

Gold Coast Publications, Inc. v. Corrigan, 42 F.3d 1336 (Fla. 1995)

Gooding v. Wilson, 405 U.S. 518 (1972)

Green v. Bock Laundry Mach. Co., 490 U.S. 504 (1989)

Griswold v. Connecticut, 381 U.S. 479 (1965)

Hamling v. United States, 418 U.S. 87 (1974)

Hess v. Indiana, 414 U.S. 105 (1973)

Hudnut v. American Booksellers Association, 475 U.S. 1132 (1986)

In re *R.A.V.*, 464 N.W.2d 507 (Minn. Sup. Ct. 1991)

Keyishian v. Board of Regents of the University of the State of New York, 385 U.S. 588 (1967)

Lochner v. New York, 198 U.S. 45 (1905)

Marbury v. Madison, 5 U.S. 137 (1803)

Miami Herald v. Tornillo, 418 U.S. 241 (1974)

Miller v. California, 413 U.S. 15 (1973)

Miller v. City of Laramie, 880 P.2d 594 (1994)

Multimedia Publishing Co. of South Carolina, Inc. v. Greenville-Spartanburg Airport District, 991 F.2d 154 (1993)

NAACP v. Button, 371 U.S. 415 (1963)

NAACP v. Claiborne Hardware, 458 U.S. 886 (1982)

Near v. Minnesota, 283 U.S. 697 (1931)

New York v. Ferber, 458 U.S. 747 (1982)

New York Times v. Sullivan, 376 U.S. 254 (1964)

New York Times v. United States, 403 U.S. 712 (1971)

Niemotko v. Maryland, 340 U.S. 268 (1951)

Planned Parenthood of Columbia/Willamette, Inc. v. American Coalition of Life Activists, 290 F.3d 1058 (9th Cir. 2002)

Police Department of Chicago v. Mosley, 408 U.S. 92 (1972)

R.A.V. v. City of St. Paul, Minnesota, 505 U.S. 377 (1992)

Red Lion Broadcasting Co. v. Federal Communications Commission, 395 U.S. 366 (1969)

Reed v. Reed, 404 U.S. 71 (1971)

Reno v. ACLU, 520 U.S. 1113 (1997)

Renton v. Playtime Theatres, 475 U.S. 41 (1986)

Rice v. Paladin Enterprises, Inc., 128 F.3d 233 (4th Cir. 1997)

Roe v. Wade, 410 U.S. 113 (1973)

Rosenblatt v. Baer, 383 U.S. 75 (1966)

Rosenbloom v. Metromedia, Inc., 403 U.S. 29 (1971)

Roth v. United States, 354 U.S. 476 (1957)

Sable Communications of Cal., Inc. v. Federal Communications Commission, 492 U.S. 115 (1989)

Schaefer v. United States, 251 U.S. 616 (1920)

Schenck v. United States, 249 U.S. 47 (1919)

Schneider v. New Jersey, 308 U.S. 147 (1939)

Speiser v. Randall, 357 U.S. 513 (1958)

State v. Ramsey, 430 S.E.2d 511 (S.C. 1993)

State v. Sheldon, 629 A.2d 753 (Md. 1993)

State v. T.B.D., 683 So.2d 165 (Fla. 1994)

State v. Talley, 858 P.2d 217 (Wash. 1993)

State v. Vawter, 642 A.2d 349 (N.J. 1994)

Texas v. Johnson, 491 U.S. 997 (1989)

Time, Inc. v. Hill, 385 U.S. 374 (1967)

United States v. American Library Association, 539 U.S. 194 (2003)

United States v. al-Timimi, No. 1:04cr385 (E.D. Va. 2004)

United States v. Bursey, 416 F.3d 301 (2005)

United States v. Cassel, 408 F.3d 622 (9th Cir. 2005)

United States v. Virginia, 116 S.Ct. 2264 (1996)

Village of Skokie v. the National Socialist Party of America, 373 N.E.2d 21 (Ill. 1978)

Virginia v. Black, 538 U.S. 343 (2003)

Watts v. United States, 349 U.S. 705 (1969)

Whitney v. California, 274 U.S. 357 (1927)

Wisconsin v. Mitchell, 508 U.S. 476 (1993)

Yates v. United States, 354 U.S. 298 (1957)

Young v. American Mini Theatre, Inc., 427 U.S. 50 (1976)

Bibliography

Abrams, Kathryn. "Sex Wars Redux: Agency and Coercion in Feminist Legal Theory." 95 *Colorado Law Review* 304, 1995.

———. "From Autonomy to Agency: Feminist Perspectives on Self-Direction." 40 *William & Mary Law Review* 805, 1999.

Ackerman, Bruce. *We the People: Foundations.* Cambridge, Mass.: Harvard University Press, 1991.

ACLU. "Freedom Under Fire: Dissent in Post-9/11 America." Retrieved from www .firstamendmentcenter.org, 2003.

Azriel, Joshua. "The Internet and Hate Speech: An Examination of the Nuremberg Files Case." 10 *Communication Law and Policy* 477, 2005.

Baker, C. Edwin. *Human Liberty and Freedom of Speech.* New York: Oxford University Press, 1989.

Basler, Roy P., ed. *The Collected Works of Abraham Lincoln.* New Jersey: Rutgers University Press, 1953.

Baum, Bruce. *Rereading Power and Freedom in J. S. Mill.* Toronto: University of Toronto Press, 2000.

Bell, Derrick. *And We Are Not Saved: The Elusive Quest for Racial Justice.* New York: Basic Books, 1987.

Bellamy, Richard. "Pluralism, Liberal Constitutionalism and Democracy: A Critique of John Rawls's (Meta)Political Liberalism." In *The Liberal Political Tradition: Contemporary Reappraisals*, edited by James Meadowcroft. Cheltenham, UK: Edward Elgar, 1996.

Berlin, Isaiah. *Four Essays on Liberty.* London: Oxford University Press, 1969.

Black, Charles, Jr. *Structure and Relationship in Constitutional Law.* Woodbridge: Ox Bow Press, reprint 1985 (1969).

Blake, Andrew. "Atlanta's Steamy Heat Cools Protests: More than 25 Groups Rally in Demonstration Area." *Boston Globe*, July 20, 1988.

Blakey, Robert, and Brian J. Murray. "Threats, Free Speech, and the Jurisprudence of Federal Criminal Law." 2002 *Brigham Young University Law Review* 829, 2002.

Blanchard, Margaret. "The Twilight of the First Amendment Age?" 1 *Communication Law and Policy* 329, 1996.

Blasi, Vincent. "The Checking Value of the First Amendment." In *The First Amendment: A Reader*, edited by John Garvey and Frederick Schauer. St. Paul: West Publishing, 1996.

Bobbitt, Philip. *Constitutional Fate: Theory of the Constitution*. New York: Oxford University Press, 1984.

Boghosian, Heidi. "The Assault on Free Speech, Public Assembly and Dissent—A National Lawyers Guild Report on Government Violations of First Amendment Rights in the United States." *The National Lawyer's Guild*, 2004.

Bollinger, Lee. *The Tolerant Society: Freedom of Speech and Extremist Speech in America*. Oxford: Oxford University Press, 1986.

Borenstein, Jason. "Meaningful Speech." 2005 2 *Web JCLI*, last retrieved May 8, 2007.

Bork, Robert. "Neutral Principals and Some First Amendment Problems." In *The First Amendment: A Reader*, edited by John Garvey and Frederick Schauer. St. Paul: West Publishing, 1996.

Bower, Daniel. "Holding Virtual Child Pornography Creators Liable by Judicial Redress: An Alternative Approach to Overcoming the Obstacles Presented in *Ashcroft v. Free Speech Coalition*." 19 *Brigham Young University Journal of Public Law* 235, 2004.

Cain, Patricia. "Feminist Jurisprudence: Grounding in Theories." In *Feminist Legal Theory: Readings in Law and Gender*, edited by Katharine Bartlett and Rosanne Kennedy. San Francisco: Westview Press, 1991.

Chafee, Zechariah. *Freedom of Speech*. Cambridge, Mass.: Harvard University Press, 1920.

———. *Free Speech in the United States*. Cambridge, Mass.: Harvard University Press, 1941.

Chamallas, Martha. *Introduction to Feminist Legal Theory*. Gaithersburg, Md.: Aspen Law & Business, 1999.

Chester, Jeff, and Gary O. Larson. "Sharing the Wealth: An Online Commons for the Nonprofit Sector." In *The Future of the Media: Resistance and Reform in the 21st Century*, edited by Robert McChesney, et al. New York: Seven Stories Press, 2005.

Christman, John, ed. *The Inner Citadel: Essays on Individual Autonomy*. New York: Oxford University Press, 1989.

Comey, James B. "Deputy Attorney General, United States Department of Justice, Statement Before the Committee on the Judiciary, United States House of Representatives." June 8, 2005.

Cowan, Gloria, and Cyndi Hodge. "Judgments of Hate Speech: The Effects of Target Group, Publicness, and Behavioral Responses of the Target." 26 *Journal of Applied Psychology* 355, 1996.

Crane, Paul T. "'True Threats' and the Issue of Intent." 92 *Virginia Law Review* 1225, 2006.

Crenshaw, Kimberlé, and Gary Peller. "The Contradictions of Mainstream Constitutional Theory." 45 *UCLA Law Review* 1683, 1998.

Creppy, Michael J. "Chief Immigration Judge of the United States, to Immigration Judges and Court Administrators, 2001." Retrieved from fl1.findlaw.com/news.findlaw.com/hdocs/docs/aclu/creppy092101memo.pdf.

Delgado, Richard. "Words that Wound: A Tort Action for Racial Insults, Epithets, and Name-Calling." 17 *Harvard Civil Rights–Civil Liberties Law Review* 133, 1982.

Delgado, Richard, and Jean Stefancic. *Must We Defend Nazis? Hate Speech, Pornography, and the New First Amendment.* New York: New York University Press, 1997.

Delgado, Richard, and David H. Yun. "Pressure Valves and Bloodied Chickens: An Analysis of Paternalistic Objections to Hate Speech Regulation." 82 *California Law Review* 871, 1994.

Demaske, Chris. "The Market Place of Ideas? Global Implications of Market-Driven U.S. Media." 1 *International Journal of Media and Cultural Politics* 131, 2005.

Dewey, John. "The Inclusive Philosophical Idea." In *The Essential Dewey: Volume I: Pragmatism, Education, Democracy.* Edited by Larry A. Hickman and Thomas M. Alexander. Bloomington: Indiana University Press, 1998.

Donohue, Laura K. "Terrorist Speech and the Future of Free Expression." 27 *Cardozo Law Review* 233, 2005.

Downs, Donald A. "Skokie Revisted: Hate Group Speech and the First Amendment." 60 *Notre Dame Law Review* 629, 1985.

Drucker, Susan J., and Gary Gumpert. *Real Law @ Virtual Space: Regulation in Cyberspace.* Cresskill, N.J.: Hampton Press, 2005.

Dworkin, Andrea. "Against the Male Flood: Censorship, Pornography and Equality." 9 *Harvard Women's Law Journal* 1, 1985.

———. *Letters From a War Zone: 1976–1989.* New York: E.P. Dutton, 1989.

———. *Life and Death: Unapologetic Writings on the Continuing War Against Women.* New York: Free Press, 1997.

———. *Pornography: Men Possessing Women.* New York: E.P. Dutton, 1989.

Dworkin, Gerald. "The Concept of Autonomy." In *The Inner Citadel: Essays on Individual Autonomy,* edited by John Christman. New York: Oxford University Press, 1989.

———. *The Theory and Practice of Autonomy.* New York: Cambridge University Press, 1988.

Dworkin, Ronald. *A Matter of Principle.* Cambridge, Mass.: Harvard University Press, 1985.

———. *Taking Rights Seriously.* Cambridge, Mass.: Harvard University Press, 1977.

Eberwine, Eric T. "Sound and the Fury Signifying Nothing? Juren Bussow's Battle Against Hate Speech on the Internet." 49 *New York Law School Law Review* 353, 2004/2005.

Edwards, Dale L. "If it Walks, Talks and Squawks Like a Trial, Should it be Covered Like One? The Right of the Press to Cover INS Deportation Hearings." 10 *Communication Law & Policy* 217, 2005.

Elrod, Jennifer. "Expressive Activity, True Threats and the First Amendment." 36 *Connecticut Law Review* 541, 2004.

Ely, John Hart. *Democracy and Distrust: A Theory of Judicial Review*. Cambridge, Mass.: Harvard University Press, 1980.

Emerson, Thomas. *Toward A General Theory of the First Amendment*. New York: Random House, 1963.

Entman, Robert. "Cascading Activation: Contesting the White House's Frame After 9/11." 20 *Political Communication* 415, 2003.

Feinberg, Joel. "Autonomy." In *The Inner Citadel: Essays on Individual Autonomy*, edited by John Christman. New York: Oxford University Press, 1989.

"Feminist Legal Analysis and Sexual Autonomy: Using Statutory Rape Law as an Illustration." 112 *Harvard Law Review* 1065, 1999.

Finer, Herman. *The Road to Reaction*. Boston: Little, Brown and Company, 1945.

Forell, Caroline, and Donna M. Matthews. *A Law of Her Own: The Reasonable Woman as a Measure of Man*. New York: New York University Press, 2000.

Fraser, Nancy. *Unruly Practices: Power, Discourse, and Gender in Contemporary Social Theory*. Minneapolis: University of Minnesota Press, 1989.

Frazer, Elizabeth. "Feminism and Liberation." In *The Liberal Political Tradition: Contemporary Reappraisals*, edited by James Meadowcroft. Cheltenham, UK: Edward Elgar, 1996.

Frug, Mary Joe. *Postmodern Legal Feminism*. New York: Routledge, 1992.

Gerhardt, Michael J., et al. *Constitutional Theory: Arguments and Perspectives*. New York: Lexis Publishing, 2000.

Gerstenfield, Phyllis B. "Smile When You Call Me That: The Problem with Punishing Hate Motivated Behavior." 10 *Behavioral Sciences and the Law* 259, 1992.

Gilbert, Lauren. "Mocking George: Political Satire as 'True Threat' in the Age of Global Terrorism." 58 *University of Miami Law Review* 843, 2004.

Gilligan, Carol. *In a Different Voice: Psychological Theory and Women's Development*. Cambridge, Mass.: Harvard University Press, 1982.

Gitlin, Todd. "Prime-Time Ideology: The Hegemonic Process in Television Entertainment." 26 *Social Problems* 3, 251–66, 1979.

Gleason, Timothy. "Freedom of the Press in the 1930s: The Supreme Court's Interpretation of Liberty in a Changing Political Climate." Unpublished M.A. thesis, University of Washington, 1983.

——. *The Watchdog Concept: The Press and the Courts in Nineteenth-Century America*. Ames: Iowa State University Press, 1990.

Golding, Martin P., and William A. Edmundson, eds. *The Blackwell Guide to the Philosophy of Law and Legal Theory*. Malden, Mass.: Blackwell Pub., 2005.

Gossett, Jennifer Lynn, and Sarah Byrne. "'Click Here': A Content Analysis of Internet Rape Sites." 16 *Gender & Society* 689, 2002.

Gramsci, Antonio. *Prison Notebooks*. Edited by Joseph A. Buttigieg. New York: Columbia University Press, 1992.

Greenawalt, Kent. *Fighting Words: Individuals, Communities, and Liberties of Speech*. Princeton, N.J.: Princeton University Press, 1995.

Grimshaw, Jean. "Autonomy and Identity in Feminist Thinking." In *Feminist Perspectives in Philosophy*, edited by Morwenna Griffiths and Margaret Whitford. Bloomington: Indiana University Press, 1988.

Gunkel, D. J., and A. H. Gunkel. "Virtual Geographies: The New Worlds of Cyberspace." 14 *Critical Studies in Mass Communication* 123, 1997.

Hampson, Michael J. "Protesting the President: Free Speech Zones and the First Amendment." 58 *Rutgers Law Review* 245, 2005.

Harding, Sandra. *Feminism and Methodology: Social Science Issues.* Bloomington: Indiana University Press, 1987.

Harris, Angela. "Forward: The Jurisprudence of Reconstruction." 82 *California Law Review* 741, 1994.

———. "Race and Essentialism in Feminist Legal Theory." In *Feminist Legal Theory in Law and Gender*, edited by Katharine Bartlett and Rosanne Kennedy. San Francisco: Westview Press, 1991.

Hayek, F. A. *The Constitution of Liberty.* London: Routledge & Kegan Paul, 1960.

Heider, Don, and Dustin Harp. "New Hope or Old Power: Democracy, Pornography and the Internet." 13 *Howard Journal of Communication* 285, 2002.

Hensley, Thomas R., and Christopher Smith. "Membership Change and Voting Change: An Analysis of the Rehnquist Court's 1986–1991 Terms." 48 *Political Researcher Quarterly* 837, 1995.

Heyman, Steven J. "Righting the Balance: An Inquiry Into the Foundations and Limits of Freedom of Expression." 78 *Boston University Law Review* 1275, 1998.

Higgins, Tracy. "Democracy and Feminism." 110 *Harvard Law Review* 1957, 1997.

Higgins, Tracy E., and Laura A. Rosenbury. "Agency, Equality, and Antidiscrimination Law." 85 *Cornell Law Review* 1194, 2000.

Hightower, Jim. "Bush Zones Go National," *The Nation*, August 16, 2004.

Hirschmann, Nancy J. "Difference as an Occasion for Rights: A Feminist Rethinking of Rights, Liberalism, and Difference." In *Feminism, Identity and Difference*, edited by Susan Hekman. London: Frank Cass Publishers, 1999.

Hobbes, Thomas. *Leviathan.* New York: E.P. Dutton & Co., 1914 (1651).

Holmes, Oliver Wendell, Jr. *Collected Legal Papers.* New York: Harcourt, Brace, and Co., 1920.

Horwitz, Morton J. *The Warren Court and the Pursuit of Justice: A Critical Issue.* New York: Hill and Wang, 1998.

Hudson, David L., Jr. "Internet and the First Amendment: Indecency Online." www.firstamendmentcenter.org/Speech/Internet/topic.aspx?topic=indecency_online, 2007.

Hughes, D. Rice. *Kids Online: Protecting Your Children in Cyberspace.* Grand Rapids, Mich.: Fleming H. Revell, 1998.

Johnson, Catherine B. "Stopping Hate Without Stifling Speech: Re-Examining the Merits of Hate Speech Codes on University Campuses." 27 *Fordham Urban Law Journal* 1821, 2000.

"Judge Clears Bush Opponent." *Pittsburgh Post-Gazette*, November 1, 2002.

Kagan, Elena. "The Changing Faces of First Amendment Neutrality: R.A.V. v. City of St. Paul, Minnesota, Rust v. Sullivan, and the Problem of Content-Based Underinclusion." 1992 *Supreme Court Review* 29, 1992.

Kalven, Harry, Jr. *A Worthy Tradition: Freedom of Speech in America.* New York: Harper and Row, 1988.

Kammen, Michael. *Spheres of Liberty: Changing Perceptions of Liberty in American Culture*. Madison: University of Wisconsin Press, 1986.

Kant, Immanual. *Kant's Political Writings*. Edited by Hans Reiss. Translated by H. B. Nisbet. Cambridge, Mass.: University Press, 1970.

Karniel, Yuval, and Haim Wismosky. "Pornography, Community and the Internet— Freedom of Speech and Obscenity on the Internet." 30 *Rutgers Computer & Technology Law Journal* 105, 2004.

Kellner, Douglas. "New Media and Internet Activism: From the 'Battle of Seattle' to Blogging." 6 *New Media and Society* 87, 2004.

Kelman, Mark. *A Guide to Critical Legal Studies*. Cambridge, Mass.: Harvard University Press, 1987.

Kende, Mark S. "Filtering Out Children: The First Amendment and Internet Porn in the U.S. Supreme Court." 2005 *Michigan State Law Review* 843, 2005.

Kennedy, Ryan P. "Ashcroft v. Free Speech Coalition: Can We Roast the Pig Without Burning Down the House in Regulating 'Virtual' Child Pornography?" 37 *Akron Law Review* 379, 2004.

Kernohan, Andrew. *Liberalism, Equality, and Cultural Oppression*. Cambridge: Cambridge University Press, 1998.

Kretzmer, David. "Freedom of Speech and Racism." 8 *Cardozo Law Review* 445, 1987.

Kuhn, Annette. *The Power of the Image: Essays on Representation and Sexuality*. London: Routledge and Kegan Paul, 1985.

Lacey, Nicola. "Feminist Legal Theory and the Rights of Women." In *Gender and Human Rights*, edited by Karen Knop. New York: Oxford University Press, 2004.

Lawrence, Charles. "If He Hollers Let Him Go: Regulating Racist Speech on Campus." 1990 *Duke Law Journal* 431, 1990.

Leets, Laura, and Howard Giles. "Words as Weapons—When Do They Wound? Investigations of Harmful Speech." 24 *Human Communication Research* 260, 1997.

Levit, Nancy. *The Gender Line: Men, Women and the Law*. New York: New York University Press, 1998.

Levy, Leonard. *Freedom of Speech and Press in Early American History: A Legacy of Suppression*. New York: Harper & Row, 1963.

Locke, John. *Two Treatises of Government*. New York: E.P. Dutton & Co., 1924 (1690).

Lowe, Sandra J. "Words Into Stones: Attempting to get Beyond the Regulative Hate Speech Debate." 1992 *Law and Sexuality* 11, 1992.

Mackenzie, Catriona, and Natalie Stoljar, eds. *Relational Autonomy: Feminist Perspectives on Autonomy, Agency, and the Social Self*. New York: Oxford University Press, 2000.

MacKinnon, Catharine. "Feminism, Marxism, Method, and the State: Toward Feminist Jurisprudence." In *Feminist Legal Theory: Readings in Law and Gender*, edited by Katharine T. Bartlett and Rosanne Kennedy. Boulder, Colo.: Westview Press, 1991.

———. *Feminism Unmodified: Discourses on Life and Law*. Cambridge, Mass.: Harvard University Press, 1987.

———. *Only Words*. Cambridge, Mass.: Harvard University Press, 1993.

————. "Pornography as Trafficking." 26 *Michigan Journal of International Law* 993, 2005.

————. *Toward A Feminist Theory of the State.* Cambridge, Mass.: Harvard University Press, 1989.

————. *Are Women Human? And Other International Dialogues.* Cambridge, Mass.: Belknap Press of Harvard University Press, 2006.

————. *Women's Lives, Men's Laws.* Cambridge, Mass.: Belknap Press of Harvard University Press, 2005.

Mahoney, Kathleen E. "Hate Speech: Affirmation or Contradiction of Freedom of Expression?" 1996 *University of Illinois Law Review* 789, 1996.

Mason-Grant, Joan. *Pornography Embodied: From Free Speech to Sexual Practice.* Lanham, Md.: Rowman and Littlefield, 2004.

Matsuda, Mari. "Public Response to Racist Speech: Considering the Victim's Story." 87 *Michigan Law Review* 2320, 1989.

————. *Where is Your Body? and Other Essays on Race, Gender, and the Law.* Boston: Beacon Press, 1996.

McCarthy, Martha. "The Continuing Saga of Internet Censorship: The Child Online Protection Act." 2005 *Brigham Young University Education and Law Journal* 83, 2005.

McChesney, Robert. "The Emerging Struggle for a Free Press." In *The Future of the Media: Resistance and Reform in the 21st Century*, edited by Robert McChesney, et al. New York: Seven Stories Press, 2005.

————. "The Internet and U.S. Communication Policy-Making in Historical and Critical Perspective." 46 *Journal of Communication* 98, 1996.

Meadowcroft, James, ed. *The Liberal Political Tradition: Contemporary Reappraisals.* Cheltenham, UK: Edward Elgar, 1996.

Meiklejohn, Alexander. *Political Freedom: The Constitutional Powers of the People.* Westport, Conn.: Greenwood Press Publishers, 1960.

Meyer, Carlin. "Reclaiming Sex from the Pornographers: Cybersexual Possibilities." 83 *Georgetown Law Journal* 1969, 2005 (1995).

Mill, John Stuart. *On Liberty.* Edited by Emery Neff. New York: The Book League of America, reprint 1926 (1859).

Milton, John. *Areopagitica.* Edited by Sir Richard C. Jebb. Folcroft, Pa.: Folcroft Press, reprint 1969 (1644).

Mises, Ludwig von. *Liberalism: The Classical Tradition*, trans. Ralph Raico. 1996 (1927).

Mitchell, Kimberly J., et al. "The Exposure of Youth to Unwanted Sexual Material on the Internet: A National Survey of Risk, Impact and Prevention." 34 *Youth & Society* 330, 2003.

Moscoso, Eunice. "Secret Service Quashes Dissent, ACLU Lawsuit Says." *Dayton Daily News*, September 24, 2003.

Mouffe, Chantal. *Gramsci and Marxist Theory.* London: Routledge and Kegan, 1979.

Murphey, Mark C. "Natural Law Theory." In *The Blackwell Guide to the Philosophy of Law and Legal Theory*, edited by Martine P. Golding and William A. Edmundson. Malden, Mass.: Blackwell Pub., 2005.

Murray, Brian J. "Threats, Free Speech, and the Jurisprudence of Federal Criminal Law." 2002 *Brigham Young Law Review* 829, 2002.

Neal, Patrick. *Liberalism and Its Discontents*. New York: New York University Press, 1997.

Nedelsky, Jennifer. "Reconceiving Autonomy: Sources, Thoughts and Possibilities." 1 *Yale Journal of Law and Feminism* 7, 1989.

Pavlik, John V. *New Media Technology: Cultural and Commercial Perspectives*. Boston: Allyn and Bacon, 1998.

Peonidis, Filimon. "Freedom of Expression, Autonomy, and Defamation." 17 *Law and Philosophy* 1, 1998.

Pohlman, H. L. *Justice Oliver Wendell Holmes: Free Speech and the Living Constitution*. New York: New York University Press, 1991.

Primus, Richard J. "Canon, Anti-Canon, and Judicial Dissent." 48 *Duke Law Journal* 243, 1998.

Quayle, Ethel, and Max Taylor. "Child Pornography and the Internet: Perpetuating a Cycle of Abuse." 23 *Deviant Behavior: An Interdisciplinary Journal* 331, 2002.

Rabban, David. "Emergence of First Amendment Doctrine," 40 *University of Chicago Law Review* 1259, 1983.

——. *Free Speech in its Forgotten Years*. New York: Cambridge University Press, 1997.

Rajagopal, Indhu, and Nis Bojin. "Digital Representation: Racism on the World Wide Web." *First Monday* website: firstmonday.org/issue7_10/rajagopal.

Rawls, John. *A Theory of Justice*. Cambridge, Mass.: Harvard University Press, 1971.

——. *Political Liberalism*. New York: Columbia University Press, 1993.

Redish, Martin. *Freedom of Expression: A Critical Analysis*. Charlottesville, Va.: The Mitchie Company, 1984.

——. *The Logic of Persecution: Free Expression and the McCarthy Era*. Stanford, Calif.: Stanford University Press, 2005.

——. "The Value of Free Speech." In *The First Amendment: A Reader*, edited by John Garvey and Frederick Schauer. St. Paul: West Publishing, 1996.

Reich, Jarrod F. "Internet and First Amendment: Hate Speech Online." At www.firstamendmentcenter.org/Speech/internet/topic.aspx?topic=internet_hate_speech.

Rheingold, Howard. *The Virtual Community: Homesteading on the Electronic Frontier*. Reading, Mass.: Addison-Wesley Pub. Co., 1993.

Rhode, Deborah L. "Feminist Critical Theories." In *Feminist Legal Theory: Readings in Law and Gender*, edited by Katharine T. Bartlett and Rosanne Kennedy. San Francisco: Westview Press, 1991.

——. *Justice and Gender: Sex Discrimination and the Law*. Cambridge, Mass.: Harvard University Press, 1989.

——. *Speaking of Sex: The Denial of Gender Inequality*. Cambridge, Mass.: Harvard University Press, 1997.

Riccardi, Nicholas. "Convention Planners Wary of News Style of Protests." *Los Angeles Times*, June 23, 2000.

Rimm, Marty. "Marketing Pornography on the Information Superhighway: A Survey of 917,410 Images, Descriptions, Short Stories, and Animations Downloaded 8.5

Million Times by Consumers in Over 2000 Cities in Forty Countries, Provinces, and Territories." 83 *Georgetown Law Journal* 189, 1995.

Romero, Javier. "Unconstitutional Vagueness and Restrictiveness in the Contextual Analysis of the Obscenity Standard: A Critical Reading of the *Miller* Test Genealogy." 7 *University of Pennsylvania Journal of Constitutional Law* 1207, 2005.

Sawicki, Jana. *Disciplining Foucault: Feminism, Power, and the Body*. New York: Routledge, 1991.

Scalia, Antonin. *A Matter of Interpretation: Federal Courts and the Law*. Princeton, N.J.: Princeton University Press, 1997.

Schauer, Frederick. "The Wily Agitator and the American Speech Tradition: Perilous Times: Free Speech in Wartime: From the Sedition Act of 1798 to the War on Terrorism." 57 *Stanford Law Review* 2157, 2005.

Schweber, Howard. *Speech, Conduct, and the First Amendment*. New York: P. Lang, 2003.

Shiffrin, Steven. *The First Amendment, Democracy and Romance*. Cambridge, Mass.: Harvard University Press, 1990.

——. *Dissent, Injustice and the Meanings of America*. Princeton, N.J.: Princeton University Press, 1999.

Slocum, Brian G. "Virtual Child Pornography: Does it Mean the End of the Child Pornography Exception to the First Amendment?" 14 *Albany Law Journal of Science and Technology* 637, 2004.

Smolla, Rodney. *Free Speech in an Open Society*. New York: Knopf, 1992.

Smith, Christopher. "The Malleability of Constitutional Doctrine and its Ironic Impact on Prisoners' Rights." 11 *Boston University Public International Law Journal* 73, 2001.

Smith, Patricia. "Four Themes in Feminist Legal Theory: Difference, Dominance, Domesticity, and Denial." In *The Blackwell Guide to the Philosophy of Law and Legal Theory*, edited by Martin P. Golding and William A. Edmundson. Malden, Mass.: Blackwell Pub., 2005.

South Carolina Progressive Network. "Free Speech Zone." Retrieved from www .scpronet.com/freespeech.php.

Steeves, Leslie H. "Trends in Feminist Scholarship in Journalism and Communication: Finding Common Ground Between Scholars and Activists Globally." Presented at Annual Conference of Association for Educators in Journalism and Mass Communication, Washington, D.C., August 2001.

Stone, Geoffrey. "Content Regulation and the First Amendment." 25 *William & Mary Law Review* 189, 1983.

——. *Perilous Times: Free Speech in Wartime From the Sedition Act of 1798 to the War on Terrorism*. New York: W.W. Norton & Co., 2004.

Strossen, Nadine. *Defending Pornography: Free Speech, Sex, and the Fight for Women's Rights*. New York: Scribner, 1995.

——. "Forum on National Security and the Constitution." Retrieved from www.aclu.org/congress/1012402a.html, 2002.

——. "Liberty, Equality and Democracy: Three Bases for Reversing the Minnesota Supreme Court's Ruling." 18 *Mitchell Law Review* 965, 1992.

———. "Regulating Racist Speech on Campus: A Modest Proposal." 1990 *Duke Law Journal* 484, 1990.

Sunstein, Cass. *The Partial Constitution.* Cambridge, Mass.: Harvard University Press, 1993.

Tanenbaum, Robert. *Preaching Terror: Free Speech or Wartime Incitement?* 55 *American University Law Review* 789, 2006.

Taruschio, Anna M. "The First Amendment, the Right not to Speak, and the Problem of Government Access Statutes." 27 *Fordham Urban Law Journal* 1001, 2000.

Tedford, Thomas. *Freedom of Speech in the United States.* Carbondale: Southern Illinois University Press, 1985.

Trager, Robert, and Donna L. Dickerson. *Freedom of Expression in the 21st Century.* Thousand Oaks, Calif.: Pine Forge Press, 1999.

Tsesis, Alexander. "The Empirical Shortcomings of First Amendment Jurisprudence: A Historical Perspective on the Power of Hate Speech." 40 *Santa Clara Law Review* 729, 2000.

Unger, Roberto. *The Critical Legal Studies Movement.* Cambridge, Mass.: Harvard University Press, 1986.

———. *Democracy Realized: The Progressive Alternative.* London: Verso, 1998.

Van Alstyne, William. *Interpretations of the First Amendment.* Durham, N.C.: Duke University Press, 1984.

Van Blarcum, Christopher D. "Internet Hate Speech: The European Framework and the Emerging American Haven." 62 *Washington and Lee Law Review* 781, 2005.

Van Zoonen, Liesbet. *Feminist Media Studies.* London: Sage, 1994.

Volpp, Leti. "Talking 'Culture': Gender, Race, Nation, and the Politics of Multiculturalism." 96 *Columbia Law Review* 1573, 1996.

Weimann, Gabriel. *Terror on the Internet: The New Arena, the New Challenge.* Washington, D.C.: United States Institute of Peace Press, 2006.

Weinstein, James. "Symposium: Free Speech and Community: A Brief Introduction to Free Speech Doctrine." 29 *Arizona State Law Journal* 461, 1997.

West, Robin. "The Difference in Women's Hedonic Lives: A Phenomenological Critique of Feminist Legal Theory." 3 *Wisconsin Women's Law Journal* 138, 1987.

———. "Jurisprudence and Gender." In *Feminist Legal Theory: Readings in Law and Gender*, edited by Katharine Bartlett and Rosanne Kennedy. San Francisco: Westview Press, 1991.

Wheatland, Tara. "Ashcroft v. ACLU: In Search of Plausible, Less Restrictive Alternatives." 20 *Berkeley Technology Law Journal* 371, 2005.

Whitehead, Robin S. "'Carnal Knowledge' is the Key: A Discussion of How Non-Geographic *Miller* Standards Apply to the Internet." 10 *Nexus: A Journal of Opinion* 49, 2005.

Williams, Susan H. "A Feminist Reassessment of Civil Society." 72 *Indiana Law Journal* 417, 1997.

———. *Truth, Autonomy and Speech: Feminist Theory and the First Amendment.* New York: New York University Press, 2004.

Wing, Adrien Katherine, ed. *Critical Race Feminism: A Reader.* New York: New York University Press, 1997.

Wolfson, Nicholas. *Hate Speech, Sex Speech, Free Speech*. Westport, Conn.: Praeger, 1997.

Woo, Jisuk. "The Concept of 'Harm' in Computer-Generated Images of Child Pornography." 22 *John Marshall Journal of Computer and Information Law* 717, 2004.

Yamamoto, Eric. "Symposium—Civil Rights in a New Decade: Dismantling Civil Rights: Multiracial Resistance and Reconstruction." 31 *Columbia Law Review* 523, 2000.

Young, Robert. *Personal Autonomy: Beyond Negative and Positive Liberty*. London: Croom Helm, 1986.

Index

free speech zones, 168, 170, 187, 204;
analysis of, 182–86; discussion of,
180–82
Frohwerk v. United States, 171

Geduldig v. Aiello, 17
Gertz v. Welsh, 44
Gilbert, Lauren, 174, 175
Gilligan, Carol, 17–18
Ginsburg, Ruth Bader, 16, 65, 124, 151
Ginsberg v. New York, 133
Gitlow v. New York, 34–35, 46–47, 51,
190n30
Gooding v. Wilson, 93
Gramsci, Antonio, 71–72
Greenawalt, Kent, 12, 88

Hamling v. United States, 150, 153
Harlan, John, 37, 39, 172
hate speech, xv, xvii, xviii; critiques of
traditional legal perspectives, xi, xii,
4, 13, 76, 89–91, 129; and hate
crimes, 87, 88; and pornography,
144–45; statistics, 87; traditional
legal perspectives on, 4, 37, 49, 78,
88–89. *See also* Internet; *R.A.V. v.
City of St. Paul, Minnesota*; *Village
of Skokie v. the National Socialist
Party of America*
hegemony theory, 71–72, 75, 74, 77
Hess v. Indiana, 175, 187
Higgins, Tracy, 21, 63–66, 72, 199
Holmes, Oliver Wendell, Jr.: and "clear
and present danger," 33, 47, 170–71;
and the First Amendment, 9–10, 11,
34, 38, 47, 178; and legal realism, 7
Hughes, Charles, 35

imminent lawless action, 131, 171–78,
184–87
incitement, xviii, 47, 79, 168, 170, 174,
176–80, 183, 184, 186, 204
incomplete agency. *See* agency.
indecent speech, 132, 133, 149, 150,
153, 154. *See also* obscenity

Internet, xv, xvi, xviii, 49, 203–4; and
hate speech, 98, 130–32, 136, 154;
history, 129–30; and pornography,
37, 129, 132–36, 140, 144, 149,
150–56, 203; and terrorism,
167–68

Kalven, Harry, 11
Kammen, Michael, 2–5, 29, 37, 198
Kennedy, Anthony, 124, 151, 152–53
*Keyishian v. Board of Regents of the
University of the State of New York*,
48
Kuhn, Annette, 138

Lacey, Nicola, 15
legal realism theory, 7–8, 13
Levit, Nancy, 15, 16
liberty: critique of, xii, xiv, xv, 1, 13,
30, 50–52, 59; defining, 2–4, 37, 59;
and equality, xvi, xvii, 4, 21, 29, 60,
63, 65, 198; and First Amendment,
11, 29, 31–46, 74, 78, 87, 170, 204;
negative and positive, x, 3, 30, 31,
61, 65, 125, 167, 186, 197–99, 201,
204
liberalism, xii, xvi, 4, 13, 16, 29–31,
61–62
libel, 36, 44–45, 47, 92, 142, 144, 145.
See also seditious libel
limited agency. *See* agency
Lochner v. New York, 5, 34, 38–39

MacKinnon, Catharine, xii, xviii, 19,
20, 61, 69, 75, 136–38, 139–40,
145–47, 154–55
marketplace of ideas, 9, 10, 34, 37–42,
45–46, 51, 56n69, 63, 73–74, 146,
156
Marxist theory, 12, 13, 14, 72
Mason-Grant, Joan, 138
Matsuda, Mari, xi, xii, 90
McChesney, Robert, 130
Meiklejohn, Alexander, 10–11
Miami Herald v. Tornillo, 40–41, 48

Breinigsville, PA USA
15 February 2011
255634BV00001B/2/P